Stéphane Grappelli

A BIOGRAPHY BY GEOFFREY SMITH

PAVILION
MICHAEL JOSEPH

This book is dedicated, with
gratitude and happy memories, to
everybody who talked

920B/GRA   CE

C2 108664 99

First published in Great Britain in 1987 by
Pavilion Books Limited
196 Shaftesbury Avenue, London WC2H 8JL
in association with Michael Joseph Limited
27 Wrights Lane, Kensington, London W8 5TZ

Designed by Lawrence Edwards

British Library Cataloguing in Publication Data

Smith, Geoffrey
   Stephane Grappelli.
   1. Grappelli, Stephane   2. Jazz
musicians – France – Biography
   3. Violinists – France – Biography
   I. Title
   787'.1'0924   ML418.G7

ISBN 1-85145-012-2

Back cover picture from the Max Jones Collection
Photoset by Rowland Phototypesetting Limited
Printed in Great Britain by Biddles Limited

Contents

Acknowledgments

No page is as purely pleasureable to write as this one, with the book finished and leisure to recall help received along the way.

Andrew Best, Caroline Belgrave, Charles Rodier and Judith Eagle combined to launch the project, and Andrew saw it through with his inimitable support. Information, materials and access were provided in London by Laurence Aston, Charles Alexander, Chris Clark and the staff of the National Sound Archive, Roy Burchell of *Melody Maker*, Eddie Cook of *Jazz Journal*, David Meeker of the British Film Institute, Norma Jones of the BBC and the audio staffs of the Sutton and Southwark libraries. In Paris, similar assistance came from Corinne Leonet, Mike Zwerin, Marc Albert, Michèle Maurin of the Conservatoire National Supérieur de Musique, and above all from *mon pote*, the indispensable Pascal Anquetil at the Centre d'Information du Jazz.

In America, Charles and Clara Highhill hunted down tapes and records, Earl W. Smith quarried back issues of *Down Beat* and Ginny Archer supplied a necessary book in the nick of time. As guides to the world of French jazz between the wars, I have found the following books particularly useful: Chris Goddard's *Jazz Away From Home*; *Les Grands Orchestres de Music Hall en France* by Jacques Hélian, and *Delaunay's Dilemma* by Charles Delaunay. A London American, Diana Lee Driscoll, offered unfailing aid and comfort, as well as occasional healthy scepticism. At Pavilion Books, Colin Webb weathered crises calmly, while Marilyn Watts nicely combined persuasion and persuadability.

My greatest debt is acknowledged in my dedication, to those who shared with me their experiences of Stéphane. Sometimes the exchanges occurred in passing (Roy McCurdy, Humphrey Lyttelton, Jack Sewing) or by post (Michael Parkinson, Abby Hoffer). For formal interviews, sometimes of several hours' duration, always absorbing and often hilarious, I am grateful to Svend Asmussen, François Billard, Ed Baxter, Patrice Caratini, Michel Chouanard, Alan Clare, Bob Clarke, Charles Delaunay, Diz Disley, John Etheridge, Coleridge Goode, Adelaide Hall, Audrey Harrisson, Marc Hemmeler, Daniel Humair, Max and Betty Jones, Nigel Kennedy, Didier Lockwood, Niels-Henning Ørsted Pedersen, Arthur Smith, Martial Solal, Martin Taylor, Denny Wright. I owe a special debt to Diz Disley who gave unstintingly of his time, his recollections and the material he has collected in his long association with Stéphane. Without him, the book would have been close to impossible.

And finally, thanks to Stéphane himself, for angles and anecdotes and a life very much worth the telling.

Illustrations

Manoir de Mes Rêves

Stéphane made our appointment for three o'clock, but when I ring his flat from a nearby hotel there's no answer. A departing neighbour admits me to the well-kept building, and I trot up the few flights of stairs, declining to use a charming little lift with old-fashioned grill-work. Sitting on the steps outside Stéphane's door, waiting as well, is Michel Chouanard, the violinist's European agent; agent as well to stars like Claude Luter and Jacques Loussier. We have talked before. Courteous, diplomatic, Chouanard seems the kind of representative an artist would trust, and there can't be many men of sixty or so who seem distinguished even in a Nike sweat-shirt and Levis.

We exchange greetings, shake hands. 'Yes, Stéphane told me he was going to meet you. I have to speak with him too. He had to go to some kind of reception this morning and was afraid he might be delayed.' Stéphane has just returned from a very successful tour of Israel; in two days he will be off to Miami to play on a Caribbean cruise. After that, as a holiday, he intends to cruise the Nile. And after *that* he's bound for India for a concert tour and his first visit to the Taj Mahal. His capacity for travel has become almost as much a part of the Grappelli legend as his extraordinary music-making, and both seem to increase with age. His itineraries regularly take him around the world, and he has made scores of records with renowned musicians of every stripe, by far the greater part of them since he was sixty. Chouanard's summary of his career is apt – celebrity before the Second World War as co-leader with Django Reinhardt of the Quintet of the Hot Club of France, then 'a calm period', preceding a growing tide of acclaim in the late sixties and seventies that today has made him the most famous jazz musician in France and one of the most famous in the world.

It is a remarkable life story, the more so because Stéphane by most accounts has changed very little in the course of it. Only in the details: years ago he did not like to fly; now he spends more time in the air than an American Under-Secretary of State, merely complaining occasionally that 'the inside of an airplane is not a museum'. He has enormous resilience and that *joie de vivre* that unfailingly comes through in his playing. As Chouanard says, 'he is never bored'. He has always taken pleasure in life and music, despite circumstances that sometimes would have deflated a less buoyant spirit. Above all he likes to keep moving. Typically, the freshness and immediacy of improvising are what appeal to him most in jazz. So too in his life: he does not like to plan too far ahead, which poses some problems for his agent. Chouanard finds him somewhat 'hard to drive': he wants to know what's happening next, but not very far into the future.' Stéphane craves security and activity, but not constraint. 'I have always worked . . . because I must keep away the miseries that happened to me as a child. Also, when I'm not working two weeks, I'm *mélancolique*. The world stops. And I like different scenery. If I am offered a beautiful contract in the best place for a year I refuse it. I must fold up my blanket and move on.' A survivor, he retains his right of surprise, even of caprice, on stage or on the road. Like jazz itself, the rhythm of his life is structured but flexible, and he relishes novelty. As he summed up his outlook to an interviewer, 'I'm not blasé at all. I prefer to be an *ignorant* and be amazed when I see something that's new to me.'

However, the man who presently appears from the little lift is obviously far from ignorant. Listeners invariably describe Stéphane's music as elegant, and he reflects the same quality in dress and manner. A month from his seventy-eighth birthday he is trim and alert, casually but stylishly attired in a wind-breaker and beige pullover, with a paisley foulard at his throat. You can imagine why he was an object of general admiration among London ladies in the forties and why his British pianist, Alan Clare, recalls him then as the best-dressed man he had ever seen. He apologizes for his tardiness, giving a weary shrug at the way these affairs go on. With age his face has become somewhat rounder than before, but I recognize what guitarist John Etheridge meant when he spoke of 'the two impressions' it gives, depending on the angle of view. 'From the front he looks sort of soft – a nice sort of soft, gentle face. But if you look at him from the side, he's got an incredibly sharp profile, Roman.' And such are the sides of his character – sentiment but acuteness and clarity.

He ushers Chouanard and me inside his flat, which is warm and cozy, comfortably furnished. The décor is not contemporary, despite the television, sound system and video recorder. Oriental rugs cover the floors, a well-stuffed settee stands against one wall, a coffee-table bears an impressive silver coffee-pot. The whole apartment reflects Stéphane's longtime fondness for antiques and his taste and assiduity in collecting. Among the attractive pieces are carved bookcases, a Directoire desk with glassed-in shelves, and a graceful wooden music stand laden with manuscripts. The paintings on the walls, in gilt or wooden frames, are mostly landscapes and flowers and, on the mantelpiece above the upright piano, his love of the exquisite shows itself in a cluster of figurines in *ancien régime* mode – shepherds, shepherdesses, little gentlemen in tricorne hats. All about, the shelves are lined with records and books. Stéphane has said that it is 'impossible to live without reading'. On tour, he claims if there is nothing else in his hotel room, he will even dip into the Bottin commercial directory, but, given a wider choice, he particularly enjoys the *contes* of Maupassant and the lyrics of Verlaine. He also has a passion for dictionaries, which offer him 'a voyage to the land of words'. On the coffee-table in the living room I notice a copy of Pascal's *Pensées*. That too fits what I think of as Stéphane's taste. Like Maupassant and Verlaine, Pascal is a miniaturist with a style shapely, direct and full of implication, who offers considerable scope for meditative voyaging.

On a small table in the living-room stands a silver-framed photograph, in which a handsome couple dressed formally in turn-of-the-century manner pose with a small child. It is a classic family portrait from another age: the young woman pretty and gentle in a full-length dress, the man dark, mustachioed and intense in a black suit. I saw the picture for the first time when Stéphane brandished it in a London hotel room, denouncing a slight against his family which I had unknowingly perpetuated. Early in my research I had come across a small biography that identified Grappelli *père* as a dancer, and I included the information in some notes which reached Stéphane, who was irate. It took me several meetings before I was able to prove my innocence by producing the original book. At the last of these, out came the photo. 'Does he look as if he were a dancer?' he demanded. Out came the guilty volume, inspiring redoubled wrath against its hapless author. It was a vivid example not only of Stéphane's filial loyalty but also of his occasional bursts of Italian temper.

That lively encounter has brought me to Stéphane's flat to straighten out facts and chronology. Much further research had produced a basic picture, but with variations in sequence and detail. Stéphane has given interviewers slightly different versions of his story, not with any intention to mislead, or even in the spirit of playful fibbing demonstrated by Frederico Fellini, who once replied when asked how he had first got into movies, 'I've lied about that so often I can't remember the truth.' On the one hand Stéphane has acknowledged that 'my memory's anything but good'. On the other he is much more interested in the present and future than the past. He does not dwell on what has happened but what will happen next. Only a slur on his reputation – like the notion that Django was the only star of the Hot Club Quintet – will provoke him, or a *canard* against his father.

Sitting in his study, Stéphane is understandably tired, but relaxed and pleased at his success in Israel. He talks about the practical advantage of working with guitar rather than piano. With piano, he says, you're at the mercy of whatever instrument you find on the night, in whatever condition. 'It's always a comedy; it's too much trouble. One guitar, boom boom, the bass, it's finished. No problem.' He then moves on to that other occupational hazard, writers and journalists. 'Once a girl came from a magazine, with a list of questions from her editor. The first was, what *musiciens* have influenced you? I said, "Louis Armstrong." She said, "Who is that?" Incredible! I said, "*Bien*: you go away till you find out who Louis Armstrong is." And now this other man. . . .' He shakes his head. 'It's nothing personal. I can tell you are *bien documenté*. You're always very polite to me. But you can see why I am a bit uneasy. Perhaps one day I will write my own book. My memory's not very good, but after sixty-two years I know some tricks.'

He invites me to have a beer, and goes on amiably. 'You say what you want, only don't say my father was a dancer, because he was not. The real story is that my father was widowed, and I was orphaned from my mother when I was four. Four years and one month. I am born in January; she died in February. One year later it was the war of fourteen–eighteen, and my father was called in the army. It's incredible, but he was called. And he didn't know what to do with me. He had no money; he didn't want to put me in the orphanage for the poor. As he was doing a bit of journalism as well – he was a teacher of philosophy, he was a teacher of Italian, he did some translation of Latin and Greek, he was living like that, where he could get some money – he knew of the existence of Isadora Duncan. He came to her and asked her if she wanted me as a little *sujet* because she needed someone to shine. Of course, when he showed me I was good-looking, slim; I was the type she wanted, who liked music, and she engaged me. After one term the police closed the Isadora Duncan school, because they said it was a nest of Germans. In fact, the man who paid for all that was a man she called Lohengrin, who paid for Isadora Duncan and her house and everybody. He was the head of the Singer – you know, the *machine à coudre*. Singer was very rich, and he was German. And there were a lot of young ladies, and young girls and young boys, all German.

'When they stopped they sent me to a terrible *pension*, with many others. Ah, you know, when I say it was like a Dickens story, it was!' Stéphane shakes his head, makes a face. 'Bad food, no *hygiénique* . . . And I finish up in a school called St Nicolas, near by here. And then my father came back; we stayed together. He used to travel, and I was already on my own when I was twelve. He used to travel in the evening doing any kind of job, so I was on my own and I got used to it. And one day he brought me a violin, a small one he found somewhere. He brought it to me because he liked music very much, and I started like that. But he didn't bring me that to make a profession, because he never asked me what I wanted to do. And I don't think he was thinking of my making a living out of it; he didn't find a teacher.

'Every day he used to go to the Bibliothèque National, you see, and there he would copy some notes, to show me where is the A on the piano, like that. He didn't read music. Then I started to learn piano by playing in the bistros. Because in those days, sixty-five years ago, Paris was not like today. You know, it was like the *belle époque*. All the women got dressed very formal, you know, with a hat. I used to go out in a hat. It was a different way of life, you see. And every bistro had a piano, along with a billiard table. The owner would play, people would play tunes. And I would go in and try things out.

'You know, I have always lived in this *quartier*. It's changed. The houses are the same; inside it's changed. The life has changed. In some ways it was better, but there was misery.

Not everybody had shoes. We used to have one room on the sixth floor – 59 *bis* rue Rochechouart. We had a room on the sixth floor, overlooking the court. And when the *musiciens* went into the court, that gave me the idea to do the same.'

By now Michel Chouanard has joined us, and we're both absorbed in Stéphane's tale. 'So you had to think about earning your living very early,' I interject. 'Ohhh,' says Stéphane, with another shake of the head. 'I did different things different times. I worked in a laundry, I worked for a hatter who made hats just of felt and sent them to shops where they put on the decorations. And I worked at a florist's in the rue Vivienne, making artificial flowers. But I wasn't any good at it, so I stopped. But I began busking from watching the *musiciens* in the court.' Chouanard speaks good English, but it doesn't include 'busking'. 'Qu'est-ce que c'est *busking*?' he asks. 'Faire les cours,' Stéphane translates, and grins: 'I invented busking. And it is from busking that I began at the cinema. One day a woman came down into the court where I was playing. Her husband played the violin in a cinema orchestra, he was ill, and she asked if I would take his place. So I began there.'

I bring up Stéphane's only spell of academic training. 'Were you at the Conservatoire while you were in the cinema?'

'Ah, no. That was before. I was busking to support myself there. I show you.' And he produces a folded card which turns out to be his membership in the musicians' union, recording that he joined in October 1923. 'You see, I was fifteen when I joined and started at the cinema. I went to the Conservatoire to learn to read, so I studied *solfège*. And I got a prize – a second prize. Some people say I got a first prize, but I got a second.' The Grappelli twinkle appears in his eye. "Maybe that's because . . . at the end of the year at the Conservatoire there are examinations for the prizes. My exam was in three parts, first, the harmony, where you must say what is the higher interval of a chord: I get that by adding four plus four. Then there is the *dictée*, where you write down the melody they play you: I get that because my ear is all right. And last is the performance, which, since I am studying *solfège*, is sight-singing for me. And, you know, in those days, there were eight or ten professors there in a row, in their robes, looking very solemn. *Alors*, since I am that age, my voice is changing; it goes up and down, like that. And while I am singing, that happens: it goes up and down, it cracks. It sounds very funny, and I start to laugh while I am singing. But the professors are sitting there, you know – long faces – and they don't like that. So I got a second.'

6

Chouanard and I are chuckling, and Stéphane grins in that absolutely boyish way you sometimes see on stage. 'And, you know, my friend Stéphane Mougin, the pianist, when he took his exam, since he is a pianist, he must play a piece. He played "Tea for Two", and the professors didn't like that either!'

'It's at the cinema I really learned to read. I played second violin, you know, the *ripiane*. I played the accompaniment while the first had the melody. We played every day of the week, three hours in the afternoon, three hours in the evening. On Friday after the last show we rehearsed the music for the next week – that's at eleven, eleven-thirty at night. I keep the job because the other violinist was very old, and he didn't get better from his sickness. They liked me because although I didn't have as much technique as him, I played more in tune and my tone was better.

'I've always been lucky in my associates. The *chef d'orchestre* in the cinema was a very good *musicien*, who cared about music. A lot of them just played rubbish, but he would look at the film before and select something appropriate. You know, if it was a movie about Louis XV he chose some Mozart or Vivaldi. And I learned by watching him and listening and asking questions. I was lucky that way at the Conservatoire, too. I made friends with an old professor, eighty or so, who lived nearby here, in the rue des Martyrs. Every night I walked with him to his house and we talked about music. I asked him questions – "who is Vincent d'Indy?" – and I learned like that.

'I was at the cinema about a year, steady. My father re-married – a woman from Alsace, so he went there with her. We kept a room in Paris, but he didn't come back very often, or send money.'

'So you were really on your own,' I observe. 'When did you start playing the clubs and dances?'

'Ah, after that, things began to snowball . . .'

Stéphane is living now, as he said, where he has always lived. Every day he is at home – which, with his peripatetic mode of life, is not often – he is close to the scenes of his childhood. The *quartier* is very much in the middle of things, close to Pigalle in the west and just below Montmartre, with the Gare du Nord to the east. Its streets still bustle, though the atmosphere is probably less heady than when Stéphane was growing up in the years of the *belle époque* and just after, with their opulence and turbulence, gaiety and poverty. As a boy Stéphane used to play in the Place d'Anvers, a little park behind his present home. When taxis would pull up, he would scurry out and open the door with a bow in hopes of a tip.

From the Place you could get a splendid view of the Sacré-Coeur looming like some kind of white Catholic mosque on the *butte* of Montmartre. After almost forty years of building, it was still being completed at the beginning of the First World War, intended as a symbol of national penitence and unity following the massacres during the suppression of the Commune in 1871, which people alive in Stéphane's early days could still recall. The Dreyfus affair was much fresher in the public mind, and there was still considerable political agitation on the right and left. But the prevailing tone of the time was festive. France was prosperous and Paris the centre of that prosperity. Despite the extremes of rich and poor, everyone shared in the climate of high spirits and display; even political activists showed a love of the bravura gesture. Entertainment seemed everywhere the spirit of the age, and the contrast between want and prodigality only quickened the vital sense of life and pleasure.

A remark of Stéphane's showed he has never forgotten the lessons of those times. 'Nowadays people live as if they were going to live for a thousand years,' he said to me. 'In those days, it was like a month.' The outlook of the *belle époque* was a blend of alertness, celebration and acceptance. The participants ranged from the *haute bourgeoisie* – who arrived at the *Opéra* resplendent in evening dress and fabulous jewels, seeming to the young Jean Renoir 'not creatures of flesh and blood, but figures in a picture' – to the penurious buskers and beggars. Sometimes there was a leap from one rank to the other, as in the case of the renowned La Goulue, who, by way of her charms as a can-can dancer, ascended from humble origins to portraits by Toulouse-Lautrec and private performances for the Grand Duke Alexis, who showered her with money. But, lacking the necessary business sense, her fall was just as dramatic, and she died in rags, fat and alcoholic.

They were 'the banquet years', vivacious and precarious. You could starve at the banquet too, unless you had something to offer. Everyone was invited to dine, but was expected to perform – even down to boys opening cab doors or busking for *sous* in a courtyard. Recalling his days at the Pension St Nicolas and the other orphanages at which he stayed, run by nuns, Stéphane once said, 'It was free, of course. And what is free is rarely good.' To obtain something good you needed a skill to exchange, and if you liked what you did, so much the better. *Joie de vivre* came from a *joie de survivre*, and so, almost from the beginning, Stéphane learned to play for love and money. He has said he has never forgotten his early years – the ebullience and the elegance, the squalor and the hunger.

Undoubtedly Stéphane's *quartier* has changed, but there are echoes of the old time because Paris is Paris. Though there are no statues in the Place d'Anvers now, as there were when Stéphane played here, children still scamper along the paths, between the patches of grass fenced off with low wrought-iron railings. From the Boulevard Rochechouart comes the merry racket of a fun-fair, recalling the three carnivals permanently in operation in the area at the turn of the century. Bistros abound, though the one across from Stéphane's building is a small, tacky establishment, vibrating to Middle Eastern disco music. The Sacré-Coeur is as imposing as ever, though few people connect it with the Commune. The impressionists and their racy subjects have left Montmartre, replaced by hacks who all turn out the same lachrymose pictures of children for tourists in the place du Tertre. Shoppers visit the up-to-the-minute boutiques in the rue des Martyrs. A stone's throw from the rue Rochechouart Stéphane Grappelli makes his home, though it is no longer one room on the sixth floor. Thinking of it, I suddenly identify its distinctive character. With the carpets, the knick-knacks, the antiques, it has the warmth and ease of a fashionable home in the *belle époque* – the kind of place that might have been coveted by a boy of the time who knew that such security and comfort existed, but only dreamed of possessing it.

I Can't Give You Anything But Love, Baby

Stéphane has gone over his early years many times to many journalists, like a Homeric singer of tales relating and reworking an ancient myth. Sometimes the records of events diverge. Just as when he plays he elaborates what strikes him at the moment, different aspects of the distant past – now a lifetime away – prompt different features of recollection. In 1960 the French writer Lucien Malson prefaced an interview with the violinist by observing, 'Stéphane's memories are recalcitrant,' and went on to describe his physical efforts to propitiate them: 'His body sways back and forth, as in a kind of oriental rite.' In fact, I have found that casual encounters with him can produce more fresh information than a formal meeting. Fellow musicians have mentioned the same thing: Stéphane will often come up with bits of remembrance, anecdotes and episodes in the course of a journey or a conversation, responding to the stimulus of the instant. Again, this is the jazz player's psyche, tuned in to now – this gig, this tune, this phrase. Nothing is pre-planned. The material may be familiar, but it is not repeated with a view toward exhausting its possibilities, reducing it to the one complete and final version. It is in comparing various accounts, then, that we can arrive at a more complete picture of Stéphane's earliest years than he would be inclined to give at one time himself. It will not be exhaustive, either, but it will round out and clarify the picture of a certain kind of boy in a certain kind of setting that we have seen so far.

Stéphane was born 26 January 1908, the day before Mozart's anniversary, and almost exactly two years before Django Reinhardt (23 January 1910). He came into the world in Paris on a Sunday, at the Hôpital Lariboisière, 'the hospital for the poor,' as he once said. His mother, Anna Emilie Hanocque, was French, from St Omer in Normandy. He has given the date of her death as 1911 or 1912, his age three or four. Whatever the precise year, the fact of the bereavement remains the same. Stéphane has kept the effects of the loss to himself, but no doubt it is part of the reason he carries the Grappelli family photograph with him. On tour, he once said to John Etheridge, 'When I hear of people being rude to their mother I want to punch their nose, because I lost my mother – I know what it is like.' I have heard him vouch for the truth of a statement by saying, 'I swear it on my mother's grave,' and it did not seem an expression he used lightly.

The event left him alone with his father: 'He was everything to me.' Ernest Grappelli sounds an intriguing and lovable man, but wholly unworldly. He came from his native Italy to Paris when he was nineteen, a political refugee. Times were hard in Italy then, both politically and economically, and conditions promoted an exodus not just to other European countries but further afield to America, for a new start in the land of promise. Crossing the Atlantic at about the same time that Signor Grappelli was crossing the Alps were the families of Giuseppe Venuti (better known as Joe) and Salvatore Massaro (better known as Eddie Lang).

A passion for music was Stéphane's great legacy from his impecunious sire – that, and a necessary self-reliance. He has always paid tribute to his father's very sincere, very Italian feeling for the art: 'My father didn't know anything about music, but he loved it *so* much . . .' As far as the son was concerned, love and taste largely made up for the lack of technical familiarity: 'My father taught me the whole musical story, for he knew everything except how to play.' In fact, his father went even further, actually 'considering theory more exciting than practice'.

That preference for theory was typical of him in most things. 'Original and intelligent' he was, but, as Stéphane came to realize, 'the only intelligence he missed was the intelligence to make money' – which in turn taught his son to be 'very practical'. The older Grappelli's main intellectual joy was translation: 'As soon as he'd earned four sous, he would dash off to the Bibliothèque and for days he translated Virgil or Latin and Greek writers. He claimed his translations were better than the official ones.' His father's commitment to his projects made for a rather precarious life, but father and son were 'very good friends', and their separation shortly after Mme Grappelli's death was difficult. But there was nothing to be done. Ernest Grappelli could not pursue his scattered free-lance chances to make money and leave the small boy alone, so he took him from the family home in the rue Montholon and put him into the care of a strict Catholic orphanage.

Too strict, it soon became evident. Realizing 'that *pension* was not right', Stéphane's father looked around for something more suitable but within his meagre financial capacity. Since he was 'sensitive to all forms of art', and a sometime journalist, he knew of Isadora Duncan, the expatriate American who had revolutionized the world of dance by basing her choreographic principles on the ancient Greeks. Her interpretations were very free (she was a native Californian) and stressed spontaneous grace of movement, which was emphasized by the flowing costumes copied from the images she had seen on Hellenic pottery in the British Museum. The beautiful Isadora was soon amazing artistic hostesses (and their husbands) with her terpsichorean liberties, performed in short robes and bare feet – 'as scantily clad as a woodland nymph', one critic has said.

She was equally radical and controversial in her private life. Finding the ties of marriage as constricting as the routines of traditional ballet, she dismissed them as well. Two liasions produced two children. The avant-garde director and designer Gordon Craig fathered her daughter Dierdre; her son Patrick came from her union with Paris Singer. A devoted Hellenist, she must have been delighted by Singer's first name, but she also admired his dash and generosity, the largesse that his Singer connections permitted. He was indeed heir to the family who had been one of the pioneers of the sewing machine, and he used his vast fortune to support artistic enterprises. To a biographer, Isadora referred to him coyly and mysteriously as 'my Millionaire'. In her autobiography, *My Life*, she uses the name that Stéphane remembered – 'Lohengrin'. The Singer family was American, from upstate New York, and the affectionate nickname indicates not German roots, but rather Isadora's love of Wagner and her gratitude to her knightly protector and benefactor.

A true child of the *belle époque* and the artistic and intellectual ferment it fostered, Isadora saw herself not merely as a dancer, an entertainer, but as an apostle of new forms of creativity. At various times she opened schools in Germany, Russia and America, based on the pedagogical principle of inspiring children to dance freely and naturally by exposing them to great music. Though he did not know her personally, Ernest Grappelli must have perceived Isadora as a kindred spirit, an unworldly votary of art and talent who would accept his son for what he had to offer. In 1913, Isadora had opened a new school in a great private *hôtel* at Bellevue with gardens sloping to the river and 'rooms for a thousand children'. Paris Singer had purchased it for her, as a way of relieving the personal tragedy that had struck them both. In the spring of the year her two children had been drowned with their nurse when their car had rolled into the Seine. With a kind of desperate bravery – for the presence of children must have reinforced the absence of her own – she threw herself into her plan of 'transforming this rather banal *hôtel* to a Temple of the Dance of the Future'.

Great music was essential to the enterprise, and, funded by sewing machine money, musicians came to play Isadora's favourite composers for the children – Beethoven, Debussy, Wagner, Brahms and Franck. It was a golden opportunity. When Grappelli senior approached the dancer hopefully with his request, she responded, 'Bring me the child,' and Stéphane did not disappoint. Lively and graceful, he would have fitted right in with her conceptions. Specifically he recalls that he was asked to 'personify an angel, which, when you're not an angel, is *difficile*'. His idea of freedom was not wholly akin to Isadora's but, given the alternative of another grim orphanage, he was glad he was 'hired'.

His tenure only lasted a few months, but the experience was a revelation. The choreographic curriculum did not much interest him; he realized very quickly, 'I was not born to be a dancer,' and an active six-year-old must have found the Duncan performance garb *de trop*. 'We were dressed in Greek costume, with a wreath of roses and a white peplum.' But the music made all the difference. Isadora herself described how, on Artists' Day, painters and sculptors would come to sketch the students. A gala lunch was prepared. 'As the weather grew finer, it was served in the garden, and after lunch there was music, poetry and dancing.' It was such an occasion that gave the little Stéphane Grappelli one of the great experiences of his life, his 'first impression of live music'.

One afternoon a full symphony orchestra had been engaged, and among the works they performed was Debussy's master-piece, *Prélude à l'Après-midi d'un Faune*. At that time it was

a contemporary classic, only twenty years old, by a living
composer. We can imagine the spell of that rich, evocative score
with its sinuous opening flute solo, especially on a summer day
amid the attic luxuries of Isadora's garden. Almost sixty years
later, the images of that moment were still vivid to Stéphane:
'I was dazzled. It was all there, the music, the setting, the
beautiful blue sky. The music made me *feel* the faun. What's
more, on the lawn there were groves of trees with statues, and
I immediately imagined them as fauns. It was marvellous . . .'

Stéphane's life seems to be one of those in which you can
point to an initial moment of discovery. It may not have
indicated a definitive course at once, but it revealed an
emotional source that would always remain available to him.
And it seems natural that the agent was Debussy, one of the
composers closest to him, and one who is both quintessentially
French and a favourite of many jazz musicians – an important
influence on the impressionist strain in jazz.

Stéphane's taste of this new world was short-lived, cut off
by the events that transformed that world itself. Even during
this halcyon afternoon, war clouds were gathering, presaging
the demise of what had been the *belle époque*. His career
at Isadora's ended because the school closed at the end of
term in the summer of 1914. The ominous international
signs had become sufficiently clear for Isadora to arrange with
her Lohengrin to transfer her students to another of his
palatial residences, in Devonshire. Their ultimate destination was to be America. The Duncan ménage may well have
been affected by the increasing anti-German sentiment of
the time. It would not have been unlikely, given the state of
French feeling ever since the nation's defeat in the Franco-
Prussian war, Isadora's fondness for German music and a
Teutonic representation among her pupils and staff. After the
outbreak of war, however, she soon disarmed any suspicion
by presenting the *hôtel* at Bellevue to the nation for use as a
hospital.

Not all her students made the trip to England: Stéphane
remained behind, and for him the war was a particular disaster.
In some ways he was not deeply sorry to be free from Isadora's
regime. In spite of his initiation into music, he was still a
typical six-year-old: 'I liked doing somersaults better than
exercises.' But the school's closure forced him back to the nuns
and the charity orphanages. And there was an even more
drastic separation from his father: Ernest Grappelli was called
into the Italian army despite being the sole support and relation
of his small son.

Life was bad enough in Paris during the war, with everything geared to support the troops in an interminable war of attrition, and the Germans close enough to shell the capital with their 'Big Bertha' guns. But for Stéphane and other poor orphans, the privation was extreme. These are the years when his life resembled a Dickens novel. To begin with, there was the simple, shocking contrast between the comforts and felicities *chez* Isadora and the starkness of life in an institution. But by any standards the living conditions in the orphanage where Stéphane found himself were disgraceful. 'This place was supposed to be under the eye of the government, but the government looked elsewhere. We slept on the floor, and often we were without food. There were many times when I had to fight for a crust of bread. It was abominable. And music was obviously out of the question.' Sometimes he ran away, preferring to get what he could by living by his wits rather than tolerate such treatment.

It was that way for the duration, with Stéphane, between the ages of six and ten, fighting his own battle to stay alive. He did not emerged unscathed: the years of malnutrition took their toll of his physical resistance. 'Since then,' he told a reporter, 'all my life I have been *lymphatique*. Feeble. Several times I nearly died.' It is true that Stéphane has had a checkered medical history, with several operations, which makes his apparent heartiness and indestructibility in old age the more remarkable. (Once he offered me a characteristically breezy explanation: 'All my life I have had bad health, but now it's good because I have nothing left inside.') The other effect was psychological. Eating regularly was by no means something to be taken for granted, and eating well would always seem a kind of celebration. Because of his experiences, 'I never have a meal without finishing it with dessert.'

By the end of the war, the slender, appealing little boy who had charmed Isadora had became a waif – emaciated, ragged, ill-cared for and alone. He looked like a refugee, which, in a way, he was. The one bright possibility on his horizon was the return of his father, who, impractical or not, was all he had in the world. And only when he did return at last could the boy feel his war was truly over: 'My father found a room and life started again.'

Before, the rue Montholon, now the rue Rochechouart. And for Stéphane, new, official status, as of 28 July 1919. Ernest Grappelli had had enough of Italy: 'When he came back from the war, the first thing my father did was to take me to the Mairie, get two witnesses off the street and make me a certificated Frenchman.' But everything else remained the same. The elder Grappelli was still intense, volatile, devoted to his translating projects, interested in the outpouring of innovation in the arts released by the end of the war. His passion for music had not altered; certainly he had missed it as much as his son during the years of the fighting. The high point of their week was Sunday, when they would go together to the Concerts Colonne. There, from the cheap seats at the top of the hall, they heard performances of the symphonic classics. Stéphane renewed his fondness for Debussy and discovered Ravel, his pleasure and receptiveness increased by his father's enthusiasm. After the years of isolation and insecurity, shared delight was all the more delectable.

But there were plenty of times that were not shared, when Stéphane could be glad of the habits of self-reliance that hard times had taught him. His father's piecemeal free-lancing kept him away a lot, on the trail of jobs translating or teaching or writing journalism. From the age of twelve the pattern was set: 'I was on my own and I got used to it.' Whether he enjoyed getting used to it is hard to say, but the orphanage had no doubt schooled him in finding contentment in his own company. Even now, Stéphane is never at a loss for diversion.

His father's reliability as a provider was as haphazard as his presence. Generally there would be food on the table. But, depending on his preoccupations, he might become 'a bit absent-minded . . . then there often was not enough to support the two of us.' These were the results of the elder Grappelli's preference for the theoretical over the practical. In his various capacities he was respected: Stéphane was very impressed once when a bishop came to consult his father on a translation. But his habit of intellectual absorption did have its drawbacks. Sometimes Stéphane would awake in the morning to find the light still burning, his father having sat up all night with a book. 'I would ask, "What are you doing?" and he would say, "Oh, I have found something very interesting about Virgil." And I would say, "Who *is* this?"' It is understandable how Stéphane, having had to worry about keeping body and soul together at an age when most children are pottering happily in a playground, would find his father's fine intellectual indulgence mysterious and hard to take. Indeed he once mused to me, 'I wonder how intelligent my father really was.' In several interviews he has called him 'the first hippie I ever met', and once said, 'He was not a gypsy, like Django, but he lived like one.' Twice, gypsy talents would stimulate Stéphane, but make demands of him too, forcing him to provide his own stability without expectations. By the time he met Django he would be better prepared, but already he could see that his father was 'a wonderful scholar – but a dreamer. You do not get money that way, so I see what I can do myself.'

What he could do first of all was practise the little expedients necessity had taught him in the orphanage years, such as acting as self-appointed doorman for taxis in the Place d'Anvers. But, though he had not yet made the connection, a more promising trade had already presented itself. The furnishings at 59 bis rue Rochechouart may have been scanty, but they did include a small harmonium. As Stéphane told me, 'I don't know where my father got that, and because a child is not curious I didn't ask. But I liked it because you played it like riding a bicycle – you know, pumping the pedals. And that's how I started the piano. But it's interesting that it was not like the piano, because you must keep the keys pressed down to make the sound.' The need to apply steady pressure to produce the tone meant the harmonium was, in a way, related to the violin, and, however amusing the little organ was, it was with the purchase of a three-quarter-size violin that Stéphane's music-making really began.

It is unclear whether this was the father's idea or the son's – very likely it was mutual, given the inspiration of the Concerts Colonne and, perhaps, M. Grappelli's wish to give his son something to do – 'to distract me and keep me a bit quiet – while he was occupied with his projects. (Stéphane's formal schooling seems to have been as informal as the other elements of his early life, though he was enrolled for a while after the war at a nearby *école communale*.) According to the standard version of the story, the instrument came from a friend, a fellow-Italian shoemaker who dealt in violins as a sideline. One of Stéphane's recollections – 'All the way home I hugged it so hard I almost broke it' – has been repeated often, and it is easy to imagine the thrill of owning something as personal as an instrument to a boy who had owned very little. Interviewed by a French magazine in the fifties, Stéphane referred to taking a few lessons 'with a worthy lady in the rue Pigalle' at first, but the experience was not agreeable: 'I preferred to hear music played than to play it myself.' However, his curiosity and interest soon prompted his own attempts, and he became absorbed in trying 'to make some sound come out of that damn violin . . .' It was not long before he could play tunes, all by ear. Then his father suggested he should learn to read. As Stéphane once observed, '. . . you know, a teacher will always be a teacher,' and his father was a good one, even if he was more committed than commercially successful. He made his son's studies part of his own routine at the Bibliothèque National. There he would copy out musical passages so

Stéphane could see the notes and learn to name them. It was a slow process, but Stéphane progressed steadily. For the actual playing, he was on his own as much as ever: 'I learned good position and posture from sheer luck.' He also watched violinists who played in cafés or in the streets, thereby illustrating what was to become the Grappelli method for learning anything: 'from books and from watching others'.

One of the striking things about Stéphane's career, from its earliest stages, is that he has always seen music as public. It has never simply been a mode of self-communing; the community is always present. Even his lessons took place in the street. It was perfectly natural for him to learn by watching people play for other people, by observing the actual technical and social process. In the same way, he would learn piano in public, dropping into bistros and trying things out quite unselfconsciously. This means that the kind of egotism common to more romantic performers is absent from his artistic make-up. When Stéphane plays, he is doing something which is pleasurable both for him and for his audience. Of course music is enjoyable in itself, but a listener is required to complete the connection.

The tradition of public music – ubiquitous till the advent of sound reproduction – quite naturally gave Stéphane his start as a professional. That came from watching people too – the buskers who would come into the courtyard of his building and play for *sous* dropped from windows. Their example attracted him because he needed to find a way to make some money of his own. From then on, playing, playing for people and playing for money were the same. He went out with his fiddle, and his life as a musician was launched.

His new occupation had its hazards. There was the weather: 'It rained, and not always *sous* either.' When it was *sous*, they were often thrown by the sympathetic poorer residents of a building, who lived, like the Grappellis themselves, on the top floor. Coins dropped from that height, however welcome, became offensive weapons on the way down. Then, having managed to avoid concussion from his wages, Stéphane would 'pick up the coins . . . and run like crazy, chased by the concierge and the pails of water thrown at me by the non-musical tenants.'

His first actual formal 'gig' came not long after he had begun his do-it-yourself studies with his father. After he had learned a few tunes a neighbour who was a violinist – 'or rather a fiddler!' – proposed he replace him at a Christmas-eve party. The boy went, accompanied by his father. 'It was my first professional engagement.'

It is very likely that that first engagement preceded by just a few days the beginning of his period of academic training. Records from the Conservatoire National Supérieur de Musique de Paris show that S. Grappelli enrolled for a three-year course on 31 December 1920. It was a natural progression. The idea of doing what was fun for pay had established itself, and making the most out of his talent, musically and financially, meant being thoroughly trained. His time at the Conservatoire was Stéphane's only experience of formal study. Independent by temperament and necessity, he was never keen on academic routine. Practical and empirical methods suited him much better – watching and talking to people who were actually engaged in music on the spot, feeling the excitement of musical shapes being produced. On the street, he told a French interviewer (making a typical Grappelli *mot* that can only be clumsily translated), "I was more intent on learning airs than breathing air." The Conservatoire was another institution, and music there seemed more abstract. But the course in *solfège*, with ear-training and harmony, would provide a solid grounding in basic musicianship that he could apply anywhere. It would tune him properly, since the musician himself is the essential instrument.

Solfège is the traditional system of learning to read music by singing, using the familiar syllables, do re mi, etc. It has long been the basic method of tuition in European music. By a perfectly predictable coincidence, it was the way that other pioneering jazz violinist, Joe Venuti, began. His academic training was much more extensive than Stéphane's but, as Joe said, it started exactly the same way: 'Solfeggio, of course. That's the Italian system under which you don't bother much about any special instrument until you know all the fundamentals of music. It's the only way to learn music right.'

So Stéphane learned right, helped along by natural abilities – which included perfect pitch – that had already enabled him to make considerable progress by himself. It is this firm technical grounding, plus his own catholicity of taste, that has made him so adaptable. For him, music is music whatever the category, the product of a lingua franca he speaks superbly well.

He personalized the learning just as he would personalize his music, continuing his natural and lifelong practice of seeking people out who knew something that interested him. Striking up an acquaintance with an old professor who lived nearby, and who no doubt would welcome the company of an eager student on his way home, was typical. So were his questions, reflecting his desire to acquire as much knowledge of music as possible, not least of contemporary music, in which so much was going on, accompanied by so much controversy. That kind of keenness kept his Conservatoire experience alive, making it much more than academic. Though Stéphane has not spoken extensively about his three-year stint it seems to have been not just painless but enjoyable. The comic picture of him taking his examination and having to contend, first with his voice cracking as he sang, and then with his own laughter, does not suggest a boy either anxious or awed by his surroundings.

Perhaps the reason was that he already had seen enough not to be intimidated by abstractions. Stéphane's portentous professors cannot have known much of the world in which their pupil's music functioned. All the while he was attending the Conservatoire he was working as a musician, 'doing the courtyards' and the café terraces. By his early teens his father's ways had taught him the ways of the world: 'If I wanted a box of matches I had to go out and earn it.' Yet his recollections do not seem bitter. He simply learned early that a living is something to make and to make it playing music is a bonus.

It was during his last year at the Conservatoire that the event occurred that left him completely on his own. His father had been keeping company with a woman Stéphane did not like, and one day he announced that they were going to be married. There was no necessity that their family be broken up. Their prospects would improve if Stéphane accompanied the new couple to his step-mother's home in Strasbourg. But for Stéphane there was nothing appealing about the proposal. Leaving his father – with whom, whatever his practical shortcomings, he had had the only close relationship he had known – was a blow. But the bond between them had never meant that Stéphane did not have his own life. He had no desire to bring into it a woman whom he both disliked and resented. (Years later he told a journalist, 'It's probably the reason I never got married.')

At length it was arranged. The boy would not go to Alsace, though his father would visit when he could and help with his support. But Stéphane knew better than to expect much from that. In the fifties, he summed up the episode simply: 'Something went wrong with my family and I had to work – somehow.' It meant being totally on his own in Paris, at fifteen, but the experience of course was not altogether new. With the resilience that was second nature by now, he simply busked full-time, and his increased skill and determination soon got him his break. He was playing his first audition (in public, appropriately) without knowing it, when the old violinist from the cinema heard him in the courtyard and asked him to deputize. After that, as Stéphane said sixty-two years later, things just snowballed.

Fascinating Rhythm

Stéphane has described how he was prepared for his cinema job at the Gaumont Theatre by the violinist he was replacing. 'Listen, it's not difficult, what you have to do. We play some waltzes, we play other little music. Would you do it just for one night?' So the fifteen-year-old ex-Conservatoire busker went along, not altogether at ease, to meet the band. 'I found a pianist who was very good. As a matter of fact he was quite an original person himself. He thought he played better than Chopin. Well, I didn't want to contradict him, you see, but in fact for me at my young age he impressed me a lot. We had a very good cello, a very lovely violinist, and I went there a bit nervous. When they saw me arrive in my short pants they asked what I was going to do there. Naturally I did the best I could. Another time that old man couldn't go, he sent me and then they kept me there. I was at the cinema for nearly two years. Every day, six hours a day. Then, I learned to play the violin. I must say without modesty I was getting a bit better, because I read the music, and we were playing some very good music – Schumann, Mozart (even better). But it all depended on what the film was. The programme would last a week, and after three or four days we could play an easy piece from memory.'

21

Once the little band had mastered the show, they would watch the film as they played, dispensing with their parts. The *chef d'orchestre* was M. Meunier, a well-trained musician who really loved music, whose taste and ability Stéphane has praised. Again, he was someone the young second violinist could watch and learn from, catching his tricks. The experience enlarged his knowledge of the repertoire as well as his technique. One aspect of the job, however, offended him, and revealed the pride that has always been part of Stéphane's make-up. As we have seen, playing for people is second nature to him; a musician entertains. But the cinema manager tried to use him as a flunkey. As a friend of his recalled, 'One day he came to me almost crying, saying that they had asked him to take the candy around between the two films. That wasn't Stéphane's style at all.' It never would be.

His colleagues in the band were accomplished old-school musicians, basically adapting the classics, popular airs and dance melodies they had always played to this novel entertainment, the movies. Modernity may have been on the march, with new inventions and mores appearing in the aftermath of the First World War, but standard musical taste was still that of the *belle époque*. Stéphane, already a practical professional despite his short pants, had recognized this very well in his busking: 'In the courtyards I played little classical tunes – the "Berceuse" by Fauré, melodies from *Thaïs* and the 'Serenade' by Toselli, which was a great success . . . if you wanted to make money you had to play that . . .'

But in music, as in everything else, it was a time of transition and upheaval, and the new fashions were coming from the New World. Well before the war, America had begun to export ragtime, a musical style that proclaimed the country's freshness and cultural diversity. Though lacking the later subtleties of jazz, ragtime combined some of the black heritage of rhythmic sophistication with European form. The resulting mixture of bright tunes and snappy syncopation entranced the Old World, and ragtime became a bit of a craze, along with the dance that it accompanied, the cakewalk.

The music was pure middle America, originally a product of several towns in Missouri, particularly St Louis and Sedalia. The latter city boasted Scott Joplin as its leading musical citizen, the composer who (as our time has rediscovered) was the leading creator of artful rags. He began publishing in the mid 1890s, and by 1900 the spirit of St Louis (or Sedalia) had already landed in Paris. The somewhat unlikely medium was the band of John Philip Sousa, the March King. As an American correspondent reported on 10 June 1900, 'The principal topic of conversation all along the boulevards these days seems to be the remarkable success Sousa has met with introducing "Le Temps du Chiffon", commonly known in this country as ragtime. The native bands have taken up this peculiar style of distinctly American music, even going so far as to play the "Marseillaise" in ragtime. It is also reported that many of the most blasé Parisians are practicing the delicate steps of the cakewalk, a feat which to them is extremely difficult, owing to the French habit of wearing boots with heels extraordinarily high.'

French composers incorporated their versions of the sprightly genre into their pieces, probably the most famous example being Debussy's 'Golliwog's Cakewalk from the *Children's Corner* suite of 1908. In 1917, a full-scale orchestral treatment of ragtime appeared in *Parade*, an avant-garde ballet with designs by Picasso, scenario by Cocteau, music by Satie – all produced by Diaghilev. Satie's lucid, lively score included a 'Ragtime du Paquebot' ('Steamship Rag'). The whole undertaking revelled in modernity, employing automobiles, sirens, a pistol, a typewriter and morse code. In a programme note, the poet Apollinaire said it foretold 'a sort of sur-realism . . . [a] New Spirit which promises to modify the arts and the conduct of life from top to bottom in a universal joyousness.'

Brave words in the depths of the First World War, but Apollinaire not only turned out to be right in predicting a new style, but coined a prophetic term in 'sur-realism'. The New Spirit that followed the war would gyrate with still greater abandon to a newer American music that would identify the whole era. 'The Jazz Age', the boisterous Americans would call it, and even if the rubric was not the same in France, the music was equally central.

The advent of jazz in Europe was one positive offshoot of the war, in part the result of the simple presence in France of a large number of American troops, including blacks. Among the latter were the Harlem regiment, the 369th Infantry, with its remarkable brass band, the Hellfighters. The group was lead by Lt James Reese Europe who, before the war, had been the most successful bandleader in New York. As music director for the celebrated dance team of Irene and Vernon Castle, he had had a hand in introducing their much-acclaimed dance step, the fox-trot. In France in 1918 his specially organized band was no less acclaimed in a six-week tour of twenty-five French cities.

What was it like, the music that would transform the features of both French classical and popular music – and influence the repertoire of streetwise buskers and cinema players? It was still closer to ragtime than anything else, though the name 'jazz' was first used in France in 1918, given currency by the reputation of the Original Dixieland Jazz Band, who had captivated New Yorkers and made the first jazz records in 1917. The most immediate features were the insistent rhythm, somewhat march-like, but enlivened by exuberant syncopation, so different from the more deliberate sequences of conventional dance music let alone the serious concert repertoire. As long as the band played, the beat surged on, generating insinuating melodies embellished by bizarre instrumental colours. It almost seemed these colours *were* the melody – brays, growls, squeals and honks that had never seen the inside of a conservatoire, that seemed the pure musical translation of cries of emotion, as much animal as human. The harmonies had an ambiguous, exciting charm, defying academic conceptions of key, sequence, even mode, revelling in the 'blue note' which was neither major nor minor. And the beat went on – nervous, joyous, devil-may-care; shamelessly physical, intoxicatingly free.

Those qualities suited the mood of post-war Paris perfectly. People had had enough of tradition, convention and sentiment. Fresh from his music for *Parade*, Eric Satie wrote, 'Jazz shouts it sorrows at us, and we don't give a damn. That's why it's fine, real.' Jean Wiener, a young classically-trained pianist who had been overwhelmed by a little ragtime piece a friend had brought back from New York before the war, made his living playing American music at a night-club called the Bar Gaya. For him, 'the prestige of jazz' came from its being 'music of the heart, music of the legs, music of the circulation of the blood; based on the logic and made of the elements of life itself . . .' His repertoire shows how plastic the notion of 'jazz' could be: the latest tunes by George Gershwin, Cole Porter and their Broadway colleagues – interspersed occasionally with Bach, in an early instance of the jazz/baroque crossover. His ever-growing clientele included artists, intellectuals and the highest society. Picasso and Duchamp came, as did Artur Rubinstein and the Prince of Wales.

However jazz was defined (and to the confused general public it was almost anything that wasn't a waltz) it was obviously a hit. The Bar Gaya soon moved to larger quarters and opened in December 1921 as Le Boeuf sur le Toit, the first night-club devoted to jazz. It owed its name to a ballet by Darius Milhaud, one of the group of composers which came to be known as Les Six, all of whom were dedicated to injecting new life into French music, for which jazz seemed admirable material. (Milhaud would go on in 1923 to write *La Création du Monde*, a ballet score based on jazz elements. Le Boeuf sur Le Toit would be enshrined not only in musical history but jazz slang. In France, 'faire le boeuf' means 'to have a jam session'.)

The most distinctive feature of a jazz band was the set of drums. Indeed, as pianist Alain Romans put it, 'At that time the jazz in an orchestra was the drummer. The drummer used to be in the front and he had all these different things for making noises – cowbells and so forth – and he used to throw his sticks about and sometimes even stick his tongue out.' Thus, for many people this percussive miscellany with its exotic racket was symbolic. Among the smart set, playing drums became the latest gentlemanly accomplishment. Jean Cocteau occasionally took a tap at a drum set in the Gaya, and even the Prince of Wales was known for sitting in.* Professional jazz drummers, especially black Americans, became extremely chic. Two in particular stood out, both alumni of James Reese Europe's band. Buddy Gilmore made a great reputation as a solo performer and showman, playing at several different clubs a night, doing short flashy stints of acrobatics and pyrotechnics. Louis Mitchell began at the Casino de Paris, where Cocteau described this 'barman of noises under a golden pergola, laden with bells, triangles, boards and motorcycle horns. He mixed cocktails with them, putting in an occasional dash of cymbal, standing up, swaggering and smiling brilliantly.'

Subsequently Mitchell formed his own band, the Jazz Kings, which made some of the first jazz records in France, beginning in December 1921. The set included titles as various as contemporary ideas of jazz itself. There was that anthem of the twenties, 'Ain't We Got Fun', Irving Berlin's 'Everybody Step', a French song, 'C'est Paris'. And there was 'Stumbling', a bouncy tune by Zez Confrey, a novelty pianist who had had a hit with a cute speciality number called 'Kitten on the Keys'. 'Stumbling' is not a great piece, but it served as the means by which young Stéphane Grappelli, still somewhat insulated by the Conservatoire and the conventional requirements of workaday playing, would discover a new world of musical possibility.

It was a question of being at the right place at the right time. Busking had led him to the cinema and the invaluable experience of 'violin-playing six hours a day, six hours making

---

* He always played 'Don't Put All Your Eggs in One Basket' (in retrospect a title with a certain rueful irony). Asked about the Prince's performance, the American drummer Dave Tough replied, 'Well, he might make a good king.'

the fingers go'. As it happened, close by the cinema was a boutique that dealt in all the latest amusements for a nervous, amusing age. 'It was a little shop with all sorts of gadgets. There was one, a machine box – from America, of course – where you could hear some records with something in your ear, for *cinq sous*.' That proto-jukebox gave him his first taste of a black band playing at least proto-jazz, and it was a shock. 'It was "Stumbling" by Mitchell's Jazz Kings. It drove me insane. I was absolutely hypnotized by that kind of music; I used to go every day to listen to the same tune.'

Though he had seen the band advertised on a poster near his home, he was still completely unprepared. 'I knew nothing about this imported music; neither did my father.' Looking back in 1960, he remembered that he even found the record label mystifying: it read 'Jazz Band Mitchell' and Stéphane thought that 'Jazz Band' was the performer's curious first name. In 1980 he paid tribute to that original *coup de foudre* by recording 'Stumbling' with Martial Solal, but is too wise to want to revisit the original experience. 'I would prefer never to hear again that record that charmed me. If a man killed all his illusions, life wouldn't be worth very much any more.'

Yet, given the circumstances of that first hearing, you can understand why 'Stumbling' cast its spell. The Mitchell band were good New York musicians who performed with conviction and panache. As was customary then, they concentrated on ensemble playing rather than solos, and melody rather than improvisation, but they had that novel jazz lift, that distinctive sound that Parisians found so bewitching. 'Stumbling' itself is more rag than jazz. The tune's principal feature is the two-bar syncopated pattern that dominates the melody: *one* and two and three, *four* and one and two, *three* and four and one. It is a very basic kind of cross-rhythm, but for someone with Stéphane's orthodox background the snappy effect must have been captivating – especially when enhanced by the sonority of the 'dirty notes' which he once called 'the very essence of jazz'.

The American machine box gave the young devotee further thrills. He was soon spending a lot of *sous* there, in intervals from the cinema, and the gadget was stocked with all the latest hits. They dazzled him not only by their racy texture and rhythm, but by their harmonies. Unlike the traditional sequences Stéphane was used to, the tunes coming through the primitive headphones seemed to move all over. 'That was the first place I heard "Tea for Two", and that sequence of chords was the first time I heard somebody playing piano with sevenths, minor sevenths and all that. I used to play with

people who did boom boom boom boom – like that. But the
first time I heard that change of chords, even at that time I
was amazed.'

He must have been in a constant high at the cinema, and he
passed his excitement on to his colleagues. His friend the
pianist, who 'was a little illuminated, a little *fou*' and who said
'he had invented a way to play Chopin better than Chopin
himself' was a likely candidate. 'I took him to hear those
records. He was still living in the middle of the nineteenth
century, so the music exploded in his head.' The recognition
of just how new the new century really was must have come
as even more of a shock to the old romantic than to Stéphane,
but they were gay and shocking times, the twenties.

The revelations engineered a revolution in the pit. Now
the band had music that suited the most up-to-the-minute
Hollywood productions. Of course Charlie Chaplin was in his
heyday, and Stéphane was 'dying of love for his films', laughing
so hard he was almost sick. The gadget shop experience
suggested the fitting accompaniment for his genius: 'After that,
whenever Charlie Chaplin came on, we played "Stumbling"
and "Tea for Two".'

Like the new films, new music kept pouring out of America.
Stéphane discovered he responded almost the same way to
George Gershwin as he had to Chaplin. At the boutique he
heard 'Lady Be Good' – 'sung in French, which is *diabolique*.
But never mind, that tune absolutely hypnotized me.' He
had the same reaction to another Gershwin hit from 1924,
'Somebody Loves Me'. But the action was not only on record.
By now Stéphane was aware that this music could be heard
live, and that Pigalle was the centre of it. Prowling about with
his ears open yielded other stunning moments: 'I listened
through a door of a night-club to a pianist, saxophone and
drums playing "Hot Lips", and that drove me mad too. Practically just two notes and the chords changed all the time."

This series of jazz epiphanies was as significant to Stéphane
as exposure to Debussy had been. However, he still had not
had the deepest jazz experience of improvisation, with the
potential of these extraordinary tunes fully, personally ex-
plored. Before 1925 jazz itself was still finding its way, moving
from the rather stilted, if piquant, temper of ragtime to the
suppleness of its maturity. But the rich influence of New
Orleans was having its effect in America, where artists who
would bring further revelations to Stéphane – especially Louis
Armstrong and Bix Beiderbecke – had launched their careers
and were developing a unique expressiveness.

In the meantime, the cinema violinist and busker was avid

27

for as much of this music as he could get, whatever it was. His contact with it – coupled with an awareness that his movie job was not very well paid – started him looking for more interesting and remunerative work. He had formed a busking partnership with an older guitarist, which earned quite well. After his 'one year, steady' at the cinema, he began sending substitutes. In 1925 he left altogether, to play a summer job in the resort town of Wimereux, near Boulogne, with a prototype string group – violin, two guitars and banjo. At the end of the season he returned to Paris, first to busk and then to take another cinema job at the Palais Rochechouart. It would not be long, of course, before the arrival of talkies made cinema orchestras – and Stéphane – redundant. As he once said, it was a development he opposed on principle.

He suffered another setback around this time, when his violin was stolen, a misfortune that led to a temporary withdrawal from the music business in favour of odd jobs as delivery boy and florist. But music was never far away. He once delivered a hat to a prostitute: 'Her boyfriend and a friend of his were there playing banjos, and that woman had a violin around. So the three of us had a wonderful concert that afternoon.' Busking again, with a replacement violin, he noticed from time to time a group of musicians also working the courtyards, with a tall, striking guitarist. It was Django Reinhardt, whose family was well-known in the district but Stéphane and his future partner neither spoke nor played together.

His next break came when he was asked to deputize at a dancing school. For Parisians, inspired by black stars like Josephine Baker, dancing was the important thing, jazz simply the catchy music that accompanied it. Dancing schools flourished, and some, like cinemas of the better sort, provided their pupils with more than just a pianist. As it happened the pianist at the school where Stéphane appeared was a forward-looking young musician named Stéphane Mougin. In meeting him, Stéphane 'made the acquaintance for the first time in my life of a true jazz musician. He was a year younger than me, but he was so developed musically, really very advanced for his age.'

Grappelli was impressed with Mougin's mastery of 'Tea for Two' – which seems to have been to the twenties avant-garde what 'How High the Moon' was to the forties – and delighted with the pianist's story of how, a year or two after Grappelli's somewhat rocky exam at the Conservatoire, he had shocked the pompous panel of professors with that very piece. Mougin was also 'the first person I met who could play around the

melody, which gave me the idea of doing the same with the
violin'. These initial attempts at improvisation were hesitant
because of the lack of models. (They were also risky, with the
dancing teacher threatening to sack them.) For European
musicians, the new music was still largely a matter of repertoire. That was almost all they heard on the available records,
however lively the mood was.

Stéphane the violinist has acknowledged that Stéphane the
pianist 'helped me a lot'. He took the dancing school job
regularly because of the chance to learn, to compare notes with
a player who loved the same music he did. Performing at the
school was a motley experience, a hodgepodge of all the trends
in the contemporary music scene. They played 'tango, waltz,
one-step, some funny Spanish dance. Then we played fox-trots
. . . the first time I played a fox-trot.' No doubt it had its
boring side (and there wasn't a movie to watch) but it only
took three days a week, and meant being able to play Gershwin
tunes like 'Lady Be Good'.

Mougin introduced Grappelli to new people and experiences. Stéphane recalls it was in the pianist's company that he
got drunk for the first time, in a late night binge at Les Halles:
'I left on all fours.' More productively, he became part of the
circle of eager players fascinated with the new music, all of
them in their late teens, like himself. In a short time they
would be the stars of French jazz, including the trumpeter
Philippe Brun, the trombonist Léo Vauchant (who would
ultimately settle in Hollywood) and the altoist André Ekyan.
They were all trying to make headway with what they understood of jazz, meeting to play on Saturday and Sunday nights
at the dances held at l'Association des Etudiants (abbreviated
student-fashion to 'l'A') in the Latin Quarter. The music was
the usual mixed bag, but the band did what they could with
it. Stéphane says, 'We set out to play tangos and ended up
playing jazz. That's where I began to embellish. It was stronger
than I was; I was supposed to play tangos and I improvised
without knowing how.' But generally the playing was virtually
straight: 'Not many people threw themselves into what you
could call a chorus.'

Spirit and flesh were willing, but there were no recordings.
Playing American music required the example of American
players, but they were still developing. However some explos-
ively inspiring models were soon on their way, to extend the
lessons that Gershwin and the Jazz Kings had started.

Anything Goes

Years afterwards, looking back on his discovery of jazz, Stéphane recognized the extraordinary nature of the experience. 'I didn't reflect at that age, all the more because I was an orphan and my childhood had been very hard. . . . In fact, I had to fight to survive, and I'll never be able to explain the joy I felt when I heard that for the first time. I understood immediately what it was.' It was almost mystical: 'There isn't any reason why, hearing that music, I fell in a faint. . . . I believe that I was born with jazz.'

He pursued it purely by instinct. 'I plunged into jazz the way you throw yourself in the water, without knowing where I was going. . . .' But he was sure it was where he belonged. 'As soon as I heard it, I understood that it was truly *my* music. That there wasn't any "great" or "small" music, but one music and musicians. And that jazz seemed to have been invented expressly for me.'

But the idea of real jazz mainly concerned musicians only. The dancers – the habitués of the clubs in Pigalle, Montmartre, Montparnasse – were quite happy with bouncy tunes, tricky noises and lots of drums. For jazz players, the jazz age did not offer a lot of opportunity. Charles Delaunay, who was discovering the music as a listener, has said that 'being a jazz lover in Paris in the twenties was like being an early Christian in Rome' (though no doubt the penalties were milder). 'The name of jazz was popular well before the real jazz came to Europe. The music of the jazz age was dance music. Schmaltz.'

Stéphane agrees that in France until the mid-thirties, 'the public was completely ignorant of jazz: there were only a few jazz lovers, though they were genuine.' For him, while the jazz that was popular in the twenties may not exactly have been schmaltz, it was only 'le jazz mélodique' – which did not do much with that insistent rhythm and those provocative chords. The difference was revealing itself in the records that were gradually coming across from America. By 1926 the great days of recorded jazz had begun, with masterworks by the likes of Armstrong, Beiderbecke, Joe Venuti and Eddie Lang. The latter pair would have wide distribution in Europe, and much has been made of Venuti's influence on Stéphane. He gives full credit to Joe's talent, calling him 'the first, the father' of jazz violin, and acknowledges he was absolutely amazed by his ability and his beautiful sonority'. But there was a difference from the beginning between what the American was doing and what he felt he wanted to do. 'The first time I heard him he was playing jazz tunes, but he wasn't embellishing so much. He was especially a melodic player. . . . I loved Venuti as I loved Heifetz or Menuhin . . . but at that time I wasn't considering his music as real jazz.'

Other qualities peculiar to jazz attracted Stéphane more, and other players. In his various accounts it seems clear that what struck him most in his late teens were the examples of Armstrong and Beiderbecke. They were two more of the musical shocks that overwhelmed him at several points in his life. Hearing Armstrong, he said, 'changed my destiny', precisely because his Hot Five and Seven records indicated a new course for jazz: 'I was inspired by those people who played modern and not so much melodic.' What was astonishing about Armstrong was the way he transmuted tunes and chords into a new musical structure. It was much more than trick effects or colours, more even than simple embellishment. His solos were rounded expressive shapes that began with the melody but transformed it. Of course his technique was stunning – these were the days when goggle-eyed trumpet players were queueing up to hear him climax a stage performance with a string of high Cs capped by an F. But what struck Stéphane most was the feeling with which he invested every sound he made. 'Louis Armstrong with two notes could make you cry. Jazz music is that; technique does not have that much to do with it in my opinion.'

31

Over close to sixty years, Stéphane has remained true to Armstrong's example and those criteria. Talking to me, he made his preferences even clearer by stressing that it was Armstrong the *singer* that mattered to him particularly. Though Satchmo's voice was one of the purest jazz instruments of all time, no one would say he was endowed with technique in the conventional sense. 'But,' Stéphane said, 'when he sings with Ella Fitzgerald, she will sing an introduction with all her wonderful *vocalise*, you know, then he comes in with his two little notes and it's all the difference in the world.'

In 1972, invited to choose eight indispensable records for the BBC radio programme *Desert Island Discs*, Stéphane made his first jazz selection Armstrong's 'I Can't Give You Anything But Love, Baby', from 1929. It is a perfect example of the art that enthralled him, with Louis, supported by anodyne saxophones crooning straight melody, turning schmaltz into ambrosia. Even singing the words he improvises his own melody, bursting with energy and yet tender, passionate but relaxed, inventive and effortless. He pays the barest attention to the banal background, and his inspired commentary includes comments on itself. It is a definitive performance by a unique musical voice.

Such expressiveness in general Stéphane associated with black players. Reviewing his career in 1985 he said, 'What I've wanted to do on my violin all my life is to attempt the sonorities of black musicians.' At the same time he has credited the deep influence of Bix Beiderbecke and Frank Trumbauer, who were important models for the rising generation of French jazzmen. Though white, they too have their expressive sonorities and other distinctions as well. Trumbauer's easy fluency on C-melody sax inspired the lean, elegant genius of Lester Young.* Bix, like Armstrong, offered 'little notes' unmistakably his own, evolving marvellous phrases, and solos like 'Singin' the Blues' and 'I'm Comin' Virginia' that were masterpieces of profound refinement.

Of the two, Bix was the greater influence, as he was the greater musician. But, as with his regard for Armstrong, what Stéphane appreciated in Beiderbecke was not what most aficionados would consider his area of greatest achievement. In the twenties, black and white trumpet players alike copied his peerless cornet solos; fewer listeners paid much attention

---

* It should not be a surprise to find not only a common influence but admiration. Touring France in the fifties with pianist René Urtreger, Lester Young heard a jazz violin on the radio and thought for a moment it might be Stéphane: 'No? Too bad! I'd want to be in Paris and listen to him! Stéphane is my man; I love that music!'

to his work on piano. It was the latter aspect, however, that especially appealed to Stéphane: 'It had a fantastic *pyschologique* effect on me.' There are very few recordings of Bix on piano. Though he was constantly trying things out at the keyboard whenever one was available, he approached the instrument more as a composer than a performer. He had his difficulties with composition because his command of the technical, formal side of music was very rudimentary. Composing meant dictating a piece to a more conventionally accomplished friend, note by note – a labourious process not made any easier by Bix's habit of changing a passage each time he played it.

Still, he did record his most famous piano piece 'In a Mist', which was another of Stéphane's Desert Island choices. It is an episodic, rhythmic work with a decidedly impressionist tinge. Its combination of big chords, with surprising twists, plus a beat, attracted Stéphane, extending the harmonic mobility of the popular tunes he had heard. His ear responded at once to the richer palette that Beiderbecke employed, and there must have been recognition of an influence he and the American shared. For Bix's homegrown impressionism was no accident. He had a passion for the modern French composers and, when Ravel visited New York, introduced himself in a burst of boyish enthusiasm with 'I've loved everything you've done!'

Thus, the elements of Stéphane's musical language had begun to emerge by the time he was twenty. Fundamental to it was the expressive sonority of jazz, the sound of direct feeling that he heard in Armstrong and that he would continue to respond to in musicians like Ben Webster and Billie Holiday. No conservatory could teach it; decades later, reflecting on his celebrated association with Yehudi Menuhin, Stéphane would say, 'He is a very great violinist, but he doesn't have my little blue note.' From Bix came the sense of harmonic scope in expanding sonority into structure, which in turn brought him back to his native roots. Ultimately as he told a journalist, 'It's from Debussy and Ravel that my little music takes its source.'

Violinists did not influence him notably because, apart from Venuti (and little-known players like Shrimp Jones and Juice Wilson), there were none. But Stéphane's musical interest has never been defined simply in terms of an instrument. He played jazz on the violin because he was playing violin when he discovered it. What has always mattered most is making a voice – his voice – out of the musical elements that have moved him. There was no way to study this abstractly or academically, and it is why what he plays has such a personal character. As he once said, 'I'm playing my own style. I bought it myself from my body.'

Indeed, Stéphane's first problem, as he tried to absorb the music coming out of his hand-cranked record player, was the violin. Difficult and treacherous to play at all, it was almost unthinkable as a medium for playing jazz. Dance bands all had violins, but they were there to play sweet melodies and impart an air of legitimacy and sophistication. Bandleaders often were violinists, like Paul Whiteman, or a band's front man, like Joe Venuti with Jean Goldkette. Either way, the fiddle set the right figurative tone, and the bow was effective as a baton, evoking images of gorgeous balls and the great days of the Strauss family.

But *jazz* . . . It was hard enough for any form of real jazz to get a hearing, but the preconceptions attached to the violin made it even more difficult. 'At the beginning,' Stéphane has recalled, 'when I started to play my own way, people thought I was playing out of tune, becauser they were used to the strict melody.' At any rate that was what they thought when they could hear him. The twenties were the dark ages of electronic amplification, and while we may feel a certain yearning at the thought of crooners' voices projected by nothing more aggressive than a megaphone, it had serious drawbacks for a dulcet instrument like the violin, at least outside the genteel attentiveness of the concert hall. Playing for noisy dancers in noisy bands of brass and drums – which the public regarded as properly jazzy – was a fight for aural survival for a fiddler. Stéphane well remembers the hopeless odds of 'a guitar and a violin before five hundred people dancing . . . lost in an orchestra of brass. It was inaudible, one heard nothing.'

It had its compensations. Necessity was the mother of technique: 'Even now I don't have the same technique that I had, being young. Young, I was obliged to attack a lot more to make myself heard, especially at a dance.' But despite that benefit – and once more it is notable how everything in Stéphane's approach to music springs from actual musical situations – the conditions were frustrating. The new sound he had in his head was barely audible to him, let alone anybody else. Fortunately he had another string to his bow, which he had begun to cultivate.

Stéphane has often acknowledged the influence of pianists on his playing. The first of these had already arrived in the records of Bix Beiderbecke. For some years Stéphane himself had been playing piano, starting with the bistros, and he had continued to experiment, filling in at the cinema when the

regular pianist was late, and then at the dancing classes. Given
his frustration with the violin as a jazz instrument, it is not
surprising that he soon came to prefer the piano.

First of all, it made sense musically. Stéphane has said it
was the '*harmonique* aspect' of the keyboard that appealed to
him, which is perfectly understandable in a musician who was
captivated by the movement of multiple lines and chords. The
charm has endured, so that he has called the violin merely his
'gimmick', while the piano is his 'violin d'Ingres', his passion.
As his long-time partner Diz Disley observed, 'When he arrives
at a hall he heads straight for the piano, and you can hardly
get him away from it.'

The keyboard also offered brighter financial prospects. By
working hard at a wide variety of musical jobs, Stéphane was
paying his way, but his situation was usually precarious. He
had moved from his single room to a small flat, but by the
time he was making his jazz attempts, he was sharing lodgings
with a friend and fellow-violinist, Michel Warlop. Immensely
talented, Warlop would ultimately enjoy a following among
French connoisseurs as a jazz player, but in the twenties he
already had a considerable reputation for his classical skill. He
loved jazz but felt inhibited by his extensive conservatoire
training, though it had earned him a string of honours. He
admired and envied Grappelli's ease and naturalness, which
was beyond the conservatoire's power to bestow.

Stéphane, in turn, admired his flatmate's ability to support
himself by playing the violin. 'Warlop was making a living with
his classical concerts, but me, I was not making a living at *all*.'
The piano provided the solution. Enough of weary scraping
against strident horns and the sour looks of dancers. 'I . . .
shut my violin case and *pouf*! – Stéphane Grappelli, pianist.'
He had made his move by 1928, and things looked up very
quickly, with more jobs of all kinds. The Paris bourgeoisie
took every chance to celebrate, and celebrations meant music.
'I played for dancing, in restaurants, things like that . . . we'd
play dance music when a lady wanted to give a party for the
first teeth of her baby!' Solo society functions turned out to be
the most lucrative of all: 'I discovered I could play parties by
myself in the 16th arrondissement for Madame This and
Madame That and make a lot more money. . . .'

Once and for all, he was out of the courtyards and dancing
schools and into the gilded world of the late twenties. Well-to-
do Americans were everywhere, taking advantage of French
culture and inflation. So were American entertainers, taking
advantage of the Parisian love of the *à la mode*; 'tout nouveau,
tout beau,' as Stéphane says. A steady job at the exclusive

club, Les Ambassadeurs, gave him heady exposure to the beautiful people of the day and their transatlantic taste in music, which they still thought of as 'jazz'. 'Voilà! – one thousand dinners every night for five hundred men and five hundred women all covered with diamonds. Two or three maharajas. Clifton Webb singing Cole Porter's 'Looking at You'. Paul Whiteman playing. Bing Crosby, who was one of the Rhythm Boys, asking me at the bar, 'Hey man! Where can I get a *chasseur*?' Fred Waring and twenty girl singers going from table to table. Oscar Levant and George Gershwin playing "Rhapsody in Blue" on one piano with two keyboards. I managed to congratulate Gershwin on his way out, near the kitchen. I grasped his hand and nearly kissed him. He smiled and was very polite to me.'

It was the *belle époque* all over again, plus short skirts, fast cars and the Lost Generation, and now Stéphane was much better placed to enjoy it. The whole experience must have been symbolized by meeting his hero: the composer of 'Somebody Loves Me' and 'Lady Be Good' in the flesh (if in the kitchen). Grappelli the pianist moved in circles Grappelli the violinist only heard about. And it was only the beginning. His next opportunity came from one of his colleagues at the Association dances. The excellent trumpeter Philippe Brun was making his way as well and was featured with the celebrated Grégor and his Grégorians, the French answer to Paul Whiteman. It was the leading band of the day and proposed by Brun, Stéphane became one of its two pianists.

The other, in fact, was the man who had brought Stéphane to the Association in the first place, Stéphane Mougin. Grégor thus became, according to the more recent arrival, 'the only orchestra where they had two Stéphanes on the piano'. It also had, among others, Léo Vauchant on trombone and André Ekyan and Alix Combelle on reeds, which meant that band was not only an Association alumni club, but home to the best French jazz talent of the time. In this too, of course, it resembled Whiteman, who was paying handsomely for the services of Bix Beiderbecke, Frank Trumbauer and Joe Venuti.

Grégor himself – 'the sublime Grégor', as he liked to be called – was one of the great characters of an epoch that cherished eccentricity, and his rise to fame reveals a lot about the era's attitude to music. Born Krikor Kélékian, he fled his native Turkey during the Armenian massacres. A champion boxer, he put his athletic ability to good use by becoming an acrobatic dancer in England and Belgium and, by 1922, his finger firmly on the syncopated public pulse, he was half of a team specializing in American dances. His partner was a

Belgian lady named Loulou, and they were a great success, renowned for their sumptuous costumes, stylish manoeuvres and off-stage fights.

Grégor got into the band business initially with the little group he carried to accompany their (on-stage) performances; it featured the obligatory black drummer whose antics were part of the show. Later he managed bands as a sideline. Grégor was a great creator and taker of opportunities, and his most remarkable chance came in Amsterdam, simply as a result of his showmanly instincts. He had just finished a solo dance number and, carried away by enthusiasm, remained on stage, energetically leading the band. Two guests invited him to their table to say they thought his orchestra was sensational: they wanted to hire it for their summer season. They turned out to be the directors of the Casino de la Forêt at Le Touquet-Paris-Plage, a famous club catering to a rich English clientele.

A lesser man would have confessed that not only was the group not his band, but that he did not possess one. However, what Grégor did possess was an infallible instinct for 'le bluff' and 'le standing'. He perusaded the directors that the band of the moment was simply not good enough for their establishment, but what a band he *could* recruit . . . They were convinced, the deal was struck, and Grégor dashed to Paris and the Tabac Pigalle, the musicians' hangout, where he assembled a motley crew. Notice was very short and the available talent very mediocre, but Grégor's confident flamboyance sold the show.

It was the first grand success of what he came to regard as his true gift: 'to serve people soup and make them believe it's chocolate'. Still, he was not a charlatan; he was simply a showman. His public loved whatever they got. And, very soon, what they got was some of the most forward-looking music French popular musicians could provide. Grégor believed in sharing the wealth and paying for the best. His subsequent bands, sparked by his inimitable moves up front, were staffed by the best French jazzmen of the day, whom he remunerated handsomely. They did the band's excellent arrangements too, which meant their book comprised something as close to real jazz as a French audience would hear, played by real jazz musicians.

Unfortunately, relative authenticity seemed to make little difference to the public, for whom Grégor's airs and gyrations to rhythmic tunes were the whole show. The basic reason for the band's popularity corroborates the other evidence that there was little sensitivity to jazz in France in the twenties, that the music merely gave a modish spice to entertainment, and that spectacle was what really mattered. As Stéphane himself said, 'Although we occasionally played something "hot" for the public, we mostly just clowned around.'

Spectacle Grégor constantly supplied. His motto was 'Innovate and please': he had the instincts of a rock star. On stage, non-stop energy, flashy costumes, music stands bearing his distinctive profile, even a primitive light show. Off stage, the act continued. His clothes were a combination of the elegant and fantastic: a morning coat with striped trousers, polychrome vest, cane, derby and an ever-present monocle (of plain glass); or a turban, in which he sometimes conducted, adorned with a plume. He strolled the boulevards with a perfect pair of Afghan hounds (who were perhaps still not as *distingués* as the single leopard who escorted Josephine Baker).

His arrivals at performances were *coups de théâtre*. Pianist Alain Romans remembered how, at Le Touquet, 'Grégor would drive up each evening in a large open car wearing spats, a top hat and white gloves. He then marched up to the waiting orchestra preceded by a little boy with a trumpet who blew a fanfare and announced, "Grégor! Le Roi du Jazz!"' In Nice, Stéphane was impressed by his arriving every night in a luxurious Renault with *two* black chauffeurs. At other times he favoured a white Rolls which boasted a number plate with his name in gold letters, topped with a crown. It was staffed by just one black chauffeur, who was also responsible for opening the door for Grégor – after unrolling a red carpet.

Grégor was obviously a hard act to follow, and sometimes the band found his conducting hard to follow too. Usually, this didn't matter: orchestra leaders were there for the public, not the musicians. But once, at their début at the Olympia in Paris, Grégor had to cue the band in as the curtain went up. Though this wasn't difficult to do, he managed to confuse himself and his players so thoroughly that the music jerked to a stop almost as soon as it had started, whereupon two hornmen threw themselves valiantly into two different tunes, whereupon the curtain quickly descended. Though Grégor knew nothing about music, he did care about 'jazz', to the extent that he published the first magazine in France devoted to it. *La Revue du Jazz*, dedicated to 'everything concerning dance music and records', appeared in the summer of 1929, but folded after a few issues, principally because its readership consisted largely of its staff.

By the summer of 1929, though, the band was flourishing in its second season at the Casino de la Forêt. Thanks to the intuitive whim of its leader, one of its pianists, S. Grappelli, was in the process of switching instruments. During the group's season in Nice, there had been the usual after-hours socializing, and one evening Grégor and Stéphane were together at a club. The champagne was flowing, Stéphane recalls, 'and we were all a bit gay, and Grégor said "I heard you used to play the violin."' Stéphane tried to duck the question, knowing how out of shape he was, but Grégor (who didn't usually drink and was feeling particularly merry) persisted. 'There was an orchestra there . . . and he said, "Why don't you take his violin and do something?" I said, "I'm sorry," but he obliged me, and I was a little bit not myself, and I started to play "Dinah", very gauche, because when you go for three years without playing the violin you can't use the trick. Piano you can stay on top of without playing, but the violin is an awfully difficult instrument. Then I started to play and, you know, to play an instrument is like swimming: you never really forget. Then Grégor said to me, "I would like you to do something on the violin." We had nothing, no microphone, and he worried me so much about it. Then Warlop gave me one of the violins he got from the conservatoire when he won first prize. So I get back to the violin and finally Grégor decided I would leave the piano and I remained on the violin.'

He was worried at first by the old dilemmas of amplification and public incomprehension. But Grégor always encouraged his musicians, and Stéphane 'was quite curious myself to see if I still could play,' which did not mean just getting by technically. The pleasure was in starting 'to play dance music in the way I feel'. His return to his first instrument did not mean abandoning the piano forever, but it did mean he would not again abandon the violin. The episode had other long-term repercussions: the fiddle he received from Michel Warlop would take on symbolic status in the world of French violinists, and, in a few years, Stéphane would use it on the first record to be released by the Quintet of the Hot Club of France – a much less gauche version of 'Dinah'.

Stéphane owed more to Grégor than his return to the fiddle. One debt, indirectly and unexpectedly, seems to have been a change in the spelling of his surname. Stéphane's student record at the Conservatoire confirms that he and his father spelled the family name as we know it today, with a final 'i'. But for almost forty years, beginning sometime in the late twenties or early thirties, Stéphane signed himself 'Grappelly'. He has said the alteration was a concession to the British he had met, who pronounced 'foreign' names any way they wanted to, so that Grappelli came out 'Grappell-eye'. When he observed that words like 'Betty' and 'Piccadilly' received the

terminal sound he sought, he made the switch, with apologies
to his father.

He was using the 'y' spelling on the earliest Quintet recordings, long before the group's first trip to England, and indeed
in a photo of the Grégorians autographed by the whole band
he is already 'Grappelly'. So it seems likely that the variation
resulted from contact with Grégor's British patrons. By the late
sixties, however, he was more confident of having established
himself, and he restored the paternal version.

Life with the Grégorians could be quite unpredictable, but
it gave him his first taste of travel outside France and a further
taste of the colour and affluence he had begun to experience
at Les Ambassadeurs. In June 1930, with Stéphane leading
a three-man violin section, the Grégorians sailed for South
America. They landed at Buenos Aires, and the subsequent
tour was a revelation to Stéphane. 'It was at that moment,' he
recalled in 1957, 'that I began to know the good things of life.'
For a twenty-two-year-old who had never been anywhere,
whose natural environment had been the courtyards of Paris,
the gaudy excitement of South America must truly have seemed
another world. Never by any means a dour character, Stéphane
had still been wrapped up in the twin realities of music and
survival, concerned for much of his life with simply getting
enough to eat. He must have been hungry for stimulation, too,
and we can imagine him revelling in everything South America
had to offer.

The other Grégorians did not quite know what to make of
it. Looking back on the tour, trombonist Léo Vauchant said
in *Jazz Away From Home*, 'Stéphane Grappelli was with us,
but we never saw him. He wasn't exactly a cagey guy, but he
didn't have any friends in the band that I knew of. Not that
they didn't want to be friends with him . . . We enjoyed going
to a place where there was a piano and jamming, but Grappelli
would never come. He had other things to do, I guess. He was
a dull boy as far as the orchestra was concerned. We had our
jokes – he never did. He was very talented. He played piano
very well for the jazz stuff.'

Not exactly a cagey guy and not a dull boy; but used to
making his own way, relying on himself and his own company.
These instincts have not changed. After many years of touring,
Stéphane has many friends, but he still maintains firm control
over his life and the way he spends his time. For him, every
day there is still so much to see, and the first amazed awareness
of it emerged in South America.

In October the Grégorians arrived back in France and began
once more to tour. But some time afterward the band suddenly

found itself dissolved, when Grégor made a hasty solo return to South America to avoid prosecution in connection with a fatal automobile accident. Still, the legacy of his outlook remained. Stranded in the South of France, Stéphane heard of an opening at a club in St Tropez. He would have no trouble getting the job on piano, but there was a hitch. 'The woman who ran the club asked me if I could play saxophone, and of course I lied and said yes. In those days I would do anything to make money. I got one of the five guys from the Grégorians to show me where to put my fingers.' It was his old pal André Ekyan, and Stéphane worked on the horn for a week. However, since this was the Jazz Age, Grégor's example stood him in better stead than Ekyan's assistance – the costumes and the jokes, the golden rule that you did everything to please the people.

'Now this damn woman asked me for an audition. I remember I played "I Want to be Happy". *Alors*, you know, you don't need a century to learn that tune. But I was unlucky even with that tune, and I played some terrible notes – so I finished up that damn audition by dancing the Charleston! You can do those kind of things when you're twenty. Well, she was terribly happy, and I kept on playing the saxophone, and I got quite good.'

And Grégor would have been delighted.

Djangology

After the 1930 season, Stéphane went back to Paris. During his tenure at St Tropez, he had improved his spontaneous proficiency on the saxophone (and perhaps his Charleston too); he might even have had a few chances to demonstrate a knack for the violin as well. As it happened both skills would stand him in good stead at his next job, at Le Croix du Sud.

Le Croix du Sud was a lively club in Montparnasse whose clientele reflected the character of that famous locale. The Wall Street crash seemed not to have affected the enthusiasm of the artists and the *beau monde* for Paris, and together they were still creating a scene of *outré* sophistication, style and wit, for which jazz was the preferred accompaniment. As usual this did not mean the music got much actual attention. No matter what the band played, as Stéphane said later, 'Most of the habitués were too blasé to notice.'

Indeed jazz was not the only exotic flavour. The tango was as prevalent as ever, and devotees of popular culture regarded them as part of the same potpourri: the magazine that succeeded Grégor's *Revue du Jazz* was called *Jazz Tango Dancing*. Obviously bands had to be able to deliver versions of the latest hits from both North and South America, and it was to help supply the latter that Stéphane had been hired by his fellow old Grégorian and erstwhile tutor, André Ekyan. The violin, he well knew, was the ideal instrument for tangos, and he felt more kindly disposed to them since his trip to Argentina. For the jazz he sometimes played violin, sometimes saxophone, though Ekyan was perfectly capable of playing duets by himself, having mastered the esoteric art of blowing sax and clarinet at once.

It was a successful club and a good job, although, as in all Paris engagements at the time, the hours were long – ten at night to four in the morning. Le Croix du Sud was popular with bohemians and fanciers of bohemian atmosphere. Stéphane remembers that 'painters like de Kooning came in in bare feet and shorts pants and . . . the Prince of Wales sat in on drums with us . . . Paris was marvellous then.' With such company he must have found plenty of opportunities for cultivating his taste for the good things of life. He also felt completely at ease with his musical partners, Ekyan and the pianist Alain Romans, who shared his love of jazz. And the music could become more than an acceptably lively background when visiting musicians sat in. Romans recalled that 'sometimes you had a band of fifteen or sixteen musicians. Jimmy Dorsey used to come and Muggsy Spanier . . . Sometimes there was very good music in those days.'

One night in late 1931, however, Stéphane found himself being stared at by a type distinctly unfamiliar to Le Croix du Sud, certainly neither *beau monde* nor bohemian. The violinist remembered the impact of the encounter clearly. The intruder was 'a young man, strangely dressed. He was staring at me fixedly as if he didn't like my music and wanted, at any moment, to throw himself on me and give me a few good strokes with a club.

'This young man with the very hostile look resembled none of the other guests who came regularly to that place; you would rather have said he was a gangster straight out of an American film. He had skin the colour of *café au lait* and greasy hair, black as coal. His upper lip was topped by a thin black moustache in the shape of a circumflex. He really didn't inspire confidence.

'All at once, he started to move in the direction of the orchestra. I had a bad premonition and instinctively took a step backward – I came within a whisker of falling off the bandstand.

'The young man came toward me and, awkwardly, proceeded to speak to me in strange-sounding French: "Monsieur Drappelli, I believe?" he began, standing before me. It was

43

only later that I realized it was difficult for him to say his G's.

"Yes," I answered, and asked him what I could do for him.

'Then he told me – with his left hand hidden as deep as possible in the pocket of his trousers (which were too large) while his right held a cigarette-butt – that he was a musician too, and was looking for a violinist who played like me.

'I asked him what instruments he played, to which he answered that he could get by pretty well on the banjo and the guitar.

'"And what is your name?" I asked.

'"Django Reinhardt!"

'The name meant nothing at all to me. But I told him that I seemed to have seen him somewhere, though I didn't know where. He answered that he was sometimes in Paris with his brother Joseph, and they played or begged together in restaurants. Then I remembered in fact seeing them in a restaurant, when they asked me for a little money.

"And that's how I made the acquaintance of this extraordinary guitarist, with whom, a few years later, I would know some of the greatest triumphs ever accorded to French musicians.'

Not exactly an epic meeting, but already characteristic of the two soon-to-be partners: Stéphane suave but a little timid, liking things to go smoothly, disliking unpleasant surprises; Django a social bear, outwardly gruff and unconventional, inwardly shy. Physically very different too: Stéphane slim and elegant, the image of the man *qui sait se conduire*, Django broader, with a rustic air, sure of how to conduct himself only around music. Music, however, was what they had very much in common. Despite dissimilar backgrounds they had both begun with busking and gone on to an amazed discovery of jazz.

As a jazz fiddler, Stéphane was an oddity, but he was exactly what Django was looking for. The Hot Club Quintet's actual genesis would be almost off-hand, but something of the sort seems already to have been present in Django's mind. It isn't surprising that it was the gypsy who proposed such an eccentric concept; like Stéphane's father, he was impractical, temperamental and impulsive. But Stéphane well knew the practical difficulties of playing jazz on the violin. Why would a group featuring fiddle plus guitar – *two* instruments with amplification problems – be anything but twice as unsuccessful? For Stéphane, music was a way of making a living as well as a way of life, and you had to hedge your bets. Le Croix du Sud, where he was playing 'a bit of everything' – including even accordion from time to time – reflected professional reality.

Indeed he still regarded the violin as an instrument he merely 'tinkered with', and it says much for his talent that he still had a reputation for it.

Django, however, could afford music as a private passion because gypsy custom decreed that men were not supposed to bother with making a living anyway. So he could come innocently to Stéphane and propose 'starting a little orchestra'. But the violinist, already disconcerted by this apparition, wanted some musical substance. '. . . I asked him first to play me something, in order to form an idea of what he could do. As he'd brought his guitar to the Croix du Sud, there was nothing in the way, especially since André Ekyan and Alain Romans wanted very much to take a break.'

Stéphane told one interviewer that Django was playing banjo-guitar (a banjo with guitar tuning) at this time, for the usual reason: '. . . he was playing without a mike – he had to be heard.' As he later recalled the informal audition, however, the gypsy was already playing the instrument on which he would become a legend: 'Django began playing the guitar; I was incredibly fascinated by the style of this young gypsy, who dominated the guitar so well that Paganini . . . would have been pleased to listen.'

The feeling was promptly reciprocated: 'Neither did Django conceal his admiration when I played some jazz on the violin . . .' In the space of a few minutes, some talk and a little music, the two had affirmed kindred attitudes and mutual respect. But, though Stéphane may have been fascinated, he was not convinced enough to do anything as rash as throwing in his lot with his new, intriguing acquaintance. '. . . I could not make up my mind to give up my place in André Ekyan's band to follow this gypsy – who was, after all, strange and until then completely unknown, who certainly played the guitar marvellously – to go off toward an uncertain future.'

However inviting the musical possibilities might be, temperamentally it was not Stéphane's style. It seemed too much like one of his father's notions. Django remained an unsettling presence, one who 'didn't inspire confidence'. The pureblooded musician in Stéphane, however – the lover of jazz before anything – could not forget the experience. '. . . I was very troubled because I couldn't understand how a man could produce the sound he did . . .'

Django continued to drop in at Le Croix du Sud. They talked about music, particularly jazz, the musicians and records they admired. They played a bit too, most notably on one warm, memorable occasion which was Stéphane's first taste of Django at home in his caravan and their first duo performance.

'. . . One night he invited me to his *roulotte*. His wife prepared a meal. We ate, we smoked and we drank, and of course there is always a violin in the corner.' (Among gypsies, a violin is always 'of course'. Django played a bit himself, though no jazz.) Stéphane still felt somewhat rusty playing jazz fiddle 'but never mind – with a drink or two, I played my first time with him. I suppose we played "Honeysuckle Rose".'

It is a pleasant anticipation of the Quintet, reduced to its essence, Stéphane on Django's turf playing real jazz, the chance for which did not come too often. It came about now thanks to this wilful, greatly gifted gypsy who did not share his partner's qualms about what was practical. To him the only practicality was the best jazz they could play. On the other hand, there would be difficulties working with such a man that would require all Stéphane's tact, discipline, good sense and musicianship to sort out. No doubt knowing Django even slightly gave Stéphane an anticipation of that too. In any case, after a while their meetings ceased. Personally and profession-ally, the time for a partnership was not ripe. As Stéphane put it, 'True harmony wasn't yet created between us; little by little, we lost sight of each other.'

Easy friendship was not to be expected, though, as Stéphane said, they would become "more than close friends". He recog-nized that Django was 'a real gypsy – *real*', which meant immediately that he had to be judged by different standards. His birth in a caravan seemed symbolic of his mobile, mercurial nature. While he was never malicious, the whole point of gypsy life was that you did what you wanted, when you wanted to. Inhabitants of the workaday, nine-to-five world, living to schedules and routines, were regarded as 'peasants', and Django had been brought up to follow the sovereign whims of his personality.

He seemed predestined to perform. His birth, on the night of 23 January 1910, in the Belgian village of Liverchies near the French border, took place while a band of gypsies were making their yearly visit to entertain the townsfolk. But for her condition, his mother would have been taking part in the show. Famed as La Belle Laurence (though nicknamed Negros by the gypsies because of her dark skin), she was an accom-plished dancer and acrobat. She was also extremely indepen-dent, an early model of liberation. Jean Vées, another member of the troupe, had fathered Django, as he would Django's brother Joseph (known as Nin-Nin) in 1912. But Negros pre-ferred life as a single woman and parent; her sons took her family name, though Django was baptized Jean, after his father. As the names Reinhardt and Vées ('Weiss') indicate, both parents belonged to the tribe of German gypsies, the Manouche.

Django grew up with music and on the move. His father played violin and guitar as well as acting as instrument repairman and stage clown. Indeed the ranks of Django's numerous extended family were full of musicians, and his travels were full of melodies, spontaneous and constant. Negros took her children all over France before war broke out, performing, selling lace or odds and ends, and generally demonstrating a knack for foraging and fiddling that was more genius than talent. When war began she tried to outflank it, heading first for neutral Italy, then Corsica, and finally Algiers, before the family made its way back to France. When peace was declared, the Reinhardts returned to Paris.

Large gypsy communities congregated around the ancient city gates, trading in the local markets. Some of the old atmosphere – sounds as well as sights – remains today at the famous flea market near the Porte de Clignancourt. As British fiddler Bob Clarke observed, young violinists and guitarists still pour out their tunes there – 'little Djangos and Stéphanes!' But just after the First World War, while his small partner-to-be was recovering from four years of privation, the first little Django was living the life of a metropolitan Huckleberry Finn near the Porte de Choisy – playing pranks, practicing petty theft and, above all, not going to school. As a result, he would grow up illiterate, unable to take the Metro because he could not read the signs and unable to write – until that same future partner, tired of signing autographs for him and embarrassed at his signing contracts with an X, would patiently teach him to make the letters for D. REINHARDT, which he proudly wrote on every available space.

Instead of school, there were the movies, which remained one of Django's favourite pastimes, totally engrossing him. Even as an adult he would cry out in terror at tense, dangerous scenes. There was also billiards, another lifetime pursuit, which he cultivated in the cafés from an early age, and gambling – on anything – a compulsion which sometimes lost him parts of his clothing and earned him a maternal beating.

But the activity that began to fascinate him more than any other was music, a customary accomplishment among gypsy men. His yearning for an instrument was satisfied by a neighbour who gave him a banjo-guitar when he was twelve, and Django immediately devoted himself to it to the exclusion of almost everything else. He kept it by him literally day and night, exasperating his mother by plucking notes in the dark after he was supposed to be asleep. Like young Stéphane Grappelli, Django learned from his own ear (which Stéphane would call the 'ear of God') and watching older musicians. Unlike Stéphane, he had no access to the system of notation. Thus he remained musically illiterate too – but he made this liability an advantage. For him music would always be pure sound and expression, with no intermediary process.

His progress startled everyone. Expert players were happy to give advice and encouragement, and Django became so absorbed with one tutor-companion that he stayed away from home for several days. After frantic appeals to the police, Negros found him playing in a café at three o'clock in the morning and administered an epic beating – much to the disquiet of the older guitarist, who may have thought he was next. Django was better off staying in the family, and he was soon allowed to accompany his uncle on Saturdays to a cabaret near the Porte de Clignancourt.

But the family – even his far-flung network of uncles and cousins – could not keep pace with the young guitarist's talent and ambition. Before he was thirteen he was playing as a professional in a *bal-musette* with the celebrated accordionist Guérino. It was an ideal job for a gypsy, as ideal for Django as the cinema was for Stéphane. The *bals-musette* were a Paris institution – sweaty dance halls frequented by working people out for a raucous good time, with a sprinkling of prostitutes, pimps and small-time hoodlums. The music was hearty and infectious, with a certain piquancy as well. The special genre of the *bal-musette* style was the waltz, a mixture of ethnic strains from the Auvergne, from the gypsies, and from Italian traditions imported by the immigrants who arrived during the *belle époque* with their accordions and violins. It had its own swing, and French jazz historians look back to it as a distinct source of what – when mixed with black American music – would become a native brand of jazz. Certainly its instrumentation, with its emphasis on accordion plus strings, identifies it as European, compared to the brass traditions of early American jazz.

Django took to it as if he had been playing such music all his life – which, in a way, by osmosis he had. He was discovering the pleasure of making money at music too, though the music was one thing and the money another. It meant he could indulge his gambling habit – or would have, if Negros, who met him every night after the *bal*, had not confiscated his earnings. Another discovery was the new American music with its new kind of rhythm; the jazz revolution was catching him too, just as it had Stéphane. He would often go to Pigalle to stand outside the club where Billy Arnold's Novelty Jazz Band, from America, was playing. And it may well have been on such a trip, with some busking thrown in, that Stéphane recalled seeing the distinctive figure of the tall, swarthy gypsy boy.

Django received his musical education at the *bals*, impressing everyone he worked with. Another noted accordion player, Jean Vaissade, recalled hearing him in 1925 or 26, when 'he was already carving out a style that was different from anyone else's.' Also different was his penchant for experimenting with the American style, not a normal part of the *musette* repertoire. But since he performed it so well, with such fire, no one complained.

Jean Vaissade took the young manouche into his group and was soon getting a lesson in the gypsy style of life as well as music. Django was the soul of dependability for the first week, but after that unfamiliar faces began to appear in his place. They were all, they said, his cousins, and Vaissade concluded that eventually 'the whole family passed through'. Django, meanwhile, was off minding his business, whatever that happened to be.

With Vaissade Django make his first records, in 1928, accompanying first a slide whistle and then a xylophone. Vaissade recalled that the recording director for the slide whistle date was 'horrified' at Django's volume. The industry was not used to dealing with that kind of native power, tutored only in noisy dance halls and gypsy camps. It also was not used to artists who could not spell their names. The studio personnel listened carefully to what the banjoist said he called himself in his idiosyncratic French, and then did their best on the record label. The discs came out with accompaniment by 'Jiango Renard'. (It was not the last time this would happen. An attempt by another company later that year created a banjoist named simply 'Jeangot'. Fame would standardize the proper spelling, though the first Hot Club posters advertised Jungo Reinhardt. By a final irony, his tombstone reverted to the old approximation, rendering him as Djengo. The casualness seems fitting though, since with Django it was always the sounds, not the letters that mattered.)

By whatever spelling, he was making a name for himself, which was just as well, because at eighteen he was apparently a married man. (The wedding had been formalized according to gypsy custom, not legal statute. Django had gone off for a few days with a girlfriend, which made them husband and wife in the eyes of tribe.) He was playing now with another accordionist at a *louche* cabaret, and one night when the guitarist himself – not a cousin – was on the stand, an elegant man in evening dress appeared with an equally elegant lady on each arm. They were as out of place as Django would be three years later at the Croix du Sud, but word soon spread that the gorgeous interloper was Jack Hylton, the famous English leader of a Grégor-style orchestra. Indeed he would soon poach trumpeter Philippe Brun from the Grégorians to cries of patriotic outrage from their leader. At the moment he was interested in this extraordinary banjo-guitarist, and it was subsequently said that Django had actually agreed to join Hylton's ensemble.

However, the offer became academic after the accident of 2 November 1928, which not only transformed Django's life but almost ended it. His wife had filled their caravan with artificial flowers which she intended to sell. On his way to bed, Django dropped a cigarette or a lighted candle among them, and they went up instantly in flames. His wife escaped with singed hair, but Django was briefly trapped in the blaze. By the time he reached safety, the right half of his body had been badly burned, as well as his left hand, with which he had been holding a blanket to protect himself. He was rushed to Lariboisière, coincidentally the same 'hospital for the poor' where Stéphane was born. The surgeons saw no hope of saving his leg, but Django adamantly refused amputation, though he was in great pain. In a few days, with talk of amputation still in the air, his mother and cousins came to the hospital and spirited him away.

Safe in a nursing home, he began a slow, painful recovery. It was feared he would not walk again; it was certain he would never play since the third and fourth fingers of his left hand were paralysed in a bent position. Yet after eighteen months of patient, determined effort – assisted, as Stéphane said, by 'God and some herbs from the gypsy women' – he did both. He had to relearn the guitar completely. It was, to say the least, a daunting task to make up for the loss of half his capacity to cover the fingerboard, but Django found a way because, as his partner-to-be said·admiringly, 'he was so clever and so tricky'. He discovered he could use even the paralysed digits for chords on the two highest strings, and for single notes and runs, and Stéphane believed, being able to use only his two strongest fingers gave his playing even more power and clarity than before.

It was a feat of heroism, impelled by pure desire. After his long convalescence, Django went back to full-time playing, busking in cafés at first and astonishing listeners, especially musicians. Stéphane Mougin, who had had a hand in introducing Stéphane to the Paris scene, did the same for Django, hiring him after hearing him at a café frequented by musicians. After this, Django became more and more devoted to jazz; for him, the *bal* was over.

The process of conversion would be completed sometime later in the south of France. He had eloped there with a new wife, Naguine, and they took to the roads without anything much in mind and no means of support. Naguine, of course, tried to look after her man like a good gypsy wife; Django did not even have his guitar. But his brother Joseph met him, and they began making the rounds of cafés in Toulon playing for drinks on borrowed instruments. At the Café des Lions, they were heard by Emile Savitry, a bohemian photographer and jazz lover lately returned from the South Seas, who was amazed by Django's ability and intrigued by his demeanour. Savitry invited the brothers to his room and played them some of his records – Armstrong, Ellington, Joe Venuti and Eddie Lang. Now it was Django who was amazed, at his first real contact with the masters of American jazz. As Charles Delaunay relates, Armstrong particularly overwhelmed him: as he listened, Django sat head in hands, sobbing, 'My brother'.

The chance encounter became a house party, with Savitry happily vacating his room to the Reinhardts, and first Naguine and then – all the way from Paris – Negros joining in. The women looked after things, with Negros performing her usual miracles of procurement. The brothers absorbed Savitry's records and tried the new ideas on their guitars.

As it happened, also in Toulon was the man who would bring Django and Stéphane together, providing the occasion for the Hot Club Quintet. Louis Vola has claimed that he discovered Django in Montmartre even before his accident, and recorded with him. It is at least certain that he heard the brothers in Toulon and invited them to join the band he was putting together for the Boîte à Matelots at the Palm Beach club in Cannes. Simply keeping track of Django was a constant trial, as was getting him to the club every night. The difficulties multiplied in direct proportion to the number of caravans bearing cousins that regularly pulled up at his bungalow. As in a Marx Brothers movie, bodies, confusion and litter proliferated, until the distraught Mayor of Cannes implored Vola to do something. Mercifully it was almost the end of the season, and customers, musicians and cousins were soon on their way.

Vola took Django back to Paris, where a metropolitan version of the Boîte à Matelots was opening. The band created a stir among musicians, principally because of Django's solos. Django himself was as hungry for music and especially for jazz

51

as ever. He sought out fellow players, and it was now that he met Stéphane at the Croix du Sud. He began to spend time as well with André Ekyan, Stéphane's partner, who remembered clearly that 'face of a Calabrian bandit' which had appeared one night. Subsequently, Ekyan worked in the band supporting Jean Sablon, who was beginning to make his reputation as 'the French Bing Crosby'. Sablon was a very musical, intelligent singer who appreciated jazz, and it was not long before he heard Django and realized that he was something unique. Aided by Ekyan, he tried to persuade the guitarist to become his regular accompanist, 'regular' being the sticking point. In order to ensure his attendance at rehearsals or jobs, Ekyan had to pick him up and drop him off every day in Sablon's new car, which thus became more Django's than Sablon's. Even if he was delivered safely to work, distraction could always strike. Once he vanished from the Rococo club. When Alain Romans found him sitting oblivious on a bench outside, Django said dreamily, 'How beautiful the moon is, my friend.'

Django's partners put up with such aberrations because his playing was beautiful too. Accompaniment has always been one of the central arts of gypsy music-making, and it made him an ideal foil for Sablon. The singer used him everywhere, took him on tour to the south, recorded with him. Django too was beginning to get to know 'the good things of life', though they made absolutely no difference to his character. He developed an affinity for flashy cars, particularly American, which he drove erratically, having taught himself with the first one he ever owned. The story went that no one had told him about the need to change the oil or perform similar kinds of maintenance, and when the abused auto seized up at last, Django simply walked away, saying 'this car's no good.'

He retained a childlike confidence, the result of the absolute, carefree security he had always known among the gypsies. There he was protected, even cossetted, especially by his womenfolk. On chilly days Negros would run a hot iron over his trousers to prevent any discomfort when he put them on. When there were muddy stretches on the ground, Naguine would carry him over them on her back to save his shiny shoes. But in the outside world, among the peasants, things were mysterious and uncertain. Sablon had signed for a tour of England, but ran into a hitch with Django who would go neither by plane nor boat. 'There are spies,' he explained cryptically.

Carrying him over those murky social patches was a sometimes exasperating, sometimes amusing challenge to his colleagues. The more the esteem of popular stars like Sablon

exposed him to cultivated audiences, the more he was compelled to cope with the 'vagaries' of conventional modes of
behaviour – like hygiene, for instance. Django was a command-
ing figure; it is often said that he had a naturally regal bearing.
But he had still not been convinced of the value of soap or the
function of the toothbrush. For him there was no question that
a comb was very useful: its largest tooth made a passable guitar
pick. Gradually, by tact and persuasion, his fellow musicians
and friends introduced Django to the virtues, or at least the
habits of 'normal' society. But he would always remain basically
unconverted.

No one would have more extensive experience of minding
Django than Stéphane, and, while the guitarist was sampling
the fruits and penalties of success, the pianist-violinist-
saxophonist-accordionist was maintaining his own profitable
course. Starting in October 1932 he was back with the sublime
Grégor, who had been able to return to France as a result of
the traditional amnesty that followed a presidential election.
(In fact Grégor needed two amnesties, one for the auto accident, one for his flight from prosecution. By an uncanny,
wholly Grégorian twist of fate, he got them in rapid succession
when the newly-elected President Doumer was assassinated.)
However much Grégor admired Stéphane's hot fiddle playing,
he valued his pianism even more, since, as Léo Vauchant said,
there was no doubt that 'he played piano very well for the jazz
stuff'. Unprotestingly, Stéphane went to the keyboard. The
violin chair fell to his old flatmate, Michel Warlop.
   The band travelled the same kind of lucrative circuit that
Django followed with Jean Sablon – shows throughout France,
a featured part in a gala musical at the Olympia theatre (with
a nubile chorus line called the Olympiettes), recordings, and
a tour to Zurich, Lugano, Milan and Rome. But despite tireless
efforts to innovate and please, and the quality of the band, the
depression was beginning to take its toll. The payroll for a big
group was harder and harder to meet, and for the 1933 season
at St-Jean-de Luz, Grégor pared the roster from sixteen men
to ten. Stéphane had been one of two pianos. Now he was
alone, and Warlop was gone.
   After that season, even the flamboyant, optimistic Grégor
had to admit financial defeat. The band broke up, and Stéphane
returned to Paris. Ahead of him was a date with destiny in
the shape of an unlikely, perfectly Parisian combination of
elements: the modish clientele of the Hotel Claridge, a fervent
group of young jazz fans and a brilliant gypsy guitarist who
was just learning to wash his hands.

HCQ Strut

Meeting Django, Stéphane had been impressed not only by his playing, but by his commitment to jazz: he 'was a true enthusiast, and jazz enthusiasts were rare in Paris then.' The fraternal sign was a record collection. Like Stéphane, after his introduction the gypsy bought what was available, absorbing Ellington, Armstrong, Beiderbecke and the Chicagoans, through an old-fashioned *pavion* or horn speaker, with a wind-up turntable.

Django's discriminating taste in records also impressed a visitor to his *roulotte* in the spring of 1933. He was Pierre Nourry, secretary of the recently founded Hot Club de France, an ambitious scheme to give the small jazz brotherhood a local habitation and a name. The club was the brainchild of some university students who had suggested that Hugues Panassié and Jacques Bureau of *Jazz Tango Dancing* use their magazine to propose an association of French jazz lovers. They envisioned a nation-wide network of clubs, subsidized by the government. Less grandly, but more practically, they intended to sponsor dances, both for the sake of the music and for the interesting ladies that might attend.

The response to the idea was not overwhelming, but Panassié, Bureau and their fellow devotees took it up, and began

presenting concerts, both of records and live jazz. A hunt for
native talent brought Pierre Nourry to Django's caravan: the
gypsy's mentor, Emile Savitry, had recommended him as a
potential concert attraction. However, Django being Django,
he was momentarily without a guitar, so his well-selected
records were the only evidence that he recognized, at least, the
real thing.

That he could produce it too became obvious at a later
session at Savitry's studio. Nourry, impressed, looked for an
opportunity to present the guitarist at a Hot Club function
and got one, accidentally, when the three trumpet-players
scheduled to perform on 4 February 1934 failed to appear.
Django, profiting for once by somebody else's unreliability,
filled in and triumphed. *Jazz Tango* called him 'the revelation
of the concert' and declared, 'We now have a great improviser
in Paris.'

Meanwhile, not for the last time, Stéphane Grappelli's reputation had been overshadowed by his abilities as an all-rounder,
a talented, dependable musician who could adapt smoothly as
required. In a way, he suffered from a lack of Django's wilful
single-mindedness. Never forgetting the lessons of his childhood, he was cautious about taking chances. He liked to leave
himself as many options as possible and was content to embrace
whatever opportunities came along. No doubt he would have
preferred to play real jazz, but since there was little of that
available, he would not insist.

Shortly before Django's Hot Club debut, on 15 January
1934, the future partners made their first record together. It
was a Jean Sablon date with André Ekyan as musical director,
and the two tunes that it produced represent typical sides of
the Parisian popular scene. 'Le Jour où Je Te Vis' is very
French, very romantic, half-talked, half-crooned in Sablon's
most engaging manner. It features Django in a good if comparatively thin solo, showing traces of Eddie Lang's influence.
'Prenez Garde au Grand Méchant Loup', however, is the latest
American import, taken from a Walt Disney cartoon. The
English title expresses the cheeky defiance of three little pigs
toward a big bad neighbour, and the Sablon version is a merry
affair, with the band joining in to sing the key line. Stéphane's
personal contribution is a bit of fleet-fingered fiddle accompaniment. It is a performance tinged with enough jazz feeling to
make it sound modern but not so much as to be distracting.

Other recordings, with Jean Sablon's *chanteuse* sister
Germaine, followed in the winter and spring, but on these
Stéphane returned to the piano; the violin playing, along with
the arranging and conducting, was handled by Michel Warlop.

55

Later in 1934, however, he had a chance to pick up his bow once more, when Louis Vola hired both him and Django to play in the *thé dansant* band he was leading at the smart Hotel Claridge. It was not a long job, only from five till seven and was made even easier because Vola's band, which was in charge of the straight popular music, worked in relays with the inevitable tango ensemble. This meant there was plenty of time for the musicians to hang about between sets – thus furnishing the conditions for the creation of one of the legendary groups of jazz history.

The story of the Hot Club Quintet's genesis has often been told but, in its details, not always the same way. In the biography of Django published by Roger Spautz in 1983, Stéphane recalled the circumstances like this:

'As we played only once or twice an hour, we used the rather lengthy intervals to drink a beer or smoke a cigarette at the bistro on the corner, before returning to the stand. But Django never came with us. He stayed seated, all by himself, in a chair behind the heavy curtain we played in front of when we were on, and improvised on his guitar, while the dance orchestra was at work in the hall. He always said he didn't feel like going to drink or smoke, and preferred to stay at the hotel. But the reality is that he didn't like to move and could stay for hours or days without budging from his chair – unless he took up his favourite pastime: billiards. For a gypsy, it was an attitude (to say the least) unusual.

'One day, just before we were due to go on, a string broke on my violin . . . I put on a new one, but couldn't tune my instrument properly because the tango band was still playing and would drown out any other sound . . . So I withdrew behind the curtain, where Django and Louis Vola were waiting for our stint. I tuned my violin and at the same time improvised a chorus which just passed through my head. This music seemed to impress Django, because he took his guitar and accompanied my improvisation.

'We took to this mutual game and, every day, when the others left for the bistro during the break – I didn't particularly like killing my free time in a café either – Django and I would find ourselves behind the curtain at the Claridge and improvised whatever came to mind. Sometimes Django would come up with a theme, sometimes me. Our fellow musicians soon seemed to take an interest in our daily improvisations. One day Joseph Reinhardt arrived, called to Claridge's by Django to fill in for him. . . . He was intrigued by our duo, unwrapped his guitar from its newspaper covering and accompanied us. Now we were three and had, without intending it, laid the groundwork for the Quintet of the Hot Club of France, which wasn't long in coming.'

Some twenty years before, Stéphane had given an account to Charles Delaunay for his biography, *Django Reinhardt*, which at least presents the events in a different light: 'Django used to get behind a screen,' he told Delaunay. 'You know what he was like. He'd retreat into a corner and leave the communication of his thoughts to his guitar, I suppose. Sometimes he would pluck the strings as his fancy took him. At others he would lean on his instrument, and stare thoughtfully into space through an open window with that melancholic look of his. I still didn't know him very well. Sometimes I'd sit down at his side to listen to him. One day, to amuse myself, I picked up my violin and started to play with him. He asked me to play a little riff that he'd just put together. The effect pleased both of us and we went on to play some other tunes. The next day we waited impatiently for the intermission so that we could go and play backstage again. It was "Dinah" we played, I can remember quite clearly. We went on and on! Maybe we played for half an hour or so. Roger Chaput, an artist if ever there was one, soon hastened to join us, followed by friend Vola, inquisitive as a caretaker, as always, who had gone off to fetch his bass.'

Though in outcome there is no difference to these versions, Stéphane's later recollection gives more of a sense of Django's inertia, while the Delaunay passage emphasizes his dreamy, romantic side. Again, with Spautz, the broken string introduces an element of chance, and has Stéphane initiating the music, improvising an idea to be taken up by Django. Without the broken string, in Delaunay, it is Stéphane who joins in, for pleasure, and the tune is Django's. The effect of the Spautz version may be to increase Stéphane's role in the encounter, to tilt the serendipity a little more in his direction. Between 1960 and 1983, Stéphane must have got very tired of hearing the Quintet described as 'Django's group', and felt inclined to redress the balance.

This is not a question of misrepresentation, more of nuance, and there is a balance to be redressed. Whether there was a broken string does not matter much, though it is by now jazz lore, and the most famous of all broken strings. (In a couple of interviews Stéphane has said maybe that's how it happened, but he really doesn't remember.) Nor does it matter who the first rhythm guitarist was. It could easily have been Chaput because he was a member of the Vola band. On the other hand, it would have been equally natural for Joseph in good gypsy fashion to come to deputize for his brother. At any rate the final Quintet contained them both, because Django protested to Stéphane that the violin solos had two guitars for accompaniment, while he had to make do with one; hence the second rhythm guitar. On occasion, however, Stéphane has said he thinks Django's motive was nepotism, or gypsy clannishness, a way of getting a series of cousins into the band.

Whatever the actual events, the sum of the various versions and recollections seems to indicate that the Quintet came about when Stéphane joined Django. That sequence is significant because it accords with the real spirit of the group. The violinist and guitarist were co-leaders, but Django was the motive force. It had to be that way because of his compulsiveness, which showed itself in music perhaps more than in anything else. Certainly he was compulsive in his indolence as well, but when he thought about music that was all he thought about. It was his proper language. Stéphane's image of Django apart – retreating to a corner and communicating only with his guitar – captures his essence. But no less revealing is the slightly arch tone of his description. Stéphane was just as pure a musician as Django, but had a broader, more civilized view of life. He too had a reputation for being somewhat aloof – Charles Delaunay remembers him coming into the musicians' favourite gathering place, the Alsace à Montmartre, almost always alone – but one has the feeling Stéphane's solitude was devoted to seeking refinements he could not find in the company of jazzmen.

The energy, the ego behind the quintet were Django's. He looked on it as his natural instrument, an extension of himself. As Delaunay put it to me, 'Django thought he was the star. And in some ways I think that was right, since musically Django was the inspiration of the Quintet. They did the arrangements together; Stéphane might suggest something from the piano. But musically Django was the inspiration because he was always searching with his guitar. Even when there were no rehearsals . . . The guitar was his way of corresponding, of expressing himself.'

But if Django led, Stéphane more than followed. Django's confidence and natural absorption in music acted as a release for his partner, a source of power. As he told Roger Spautz, the violinist took heart simply from Django's conviction that the gentle guitar could play jazz with the impact of any other instrument. 'I was still hesitating to make modern music on the most classic of instruments: the violin. His genius swept away all my fears.'

The gypsy's headlong commitment to jazz and to his own way of playing it freed Stéphane from other constraints too, particularly the attitude natural to a professional musician that the public comes first, that he is being paid to provide a social service whose value will be determined by his listeners. With Django throwing caution to the winds, Stéphane could too, to the full degree of his talent. On the other hand, Stéphane could (would have to) enforce a necessary discipline on Django, reminding him that though the public might not come first, they had to come somewhere if a group was going to continue to exist, and that a real devotion to music and the group sometimes meant putting personal whims second, if music was going to be made. Not least, Stéphane's superb technical command was invaluable to the illiterate Django, who would otherwise have had great difficulty bringing his ideas to fruition.

Thus the dissimilar dialectical pair made a perfect, almost predestined combination – freedom and discipline, power and control. Together they created a unique musical shape that required both their efforts. The engendering impulse may have been Django's, and he may have captured the lion's share of *réclame* at the time. But the artistic and historical fact remains: no Stéphane, no Quintet.

The link between the little group amusing themselves under cover of the tango band and the Hot Club of France was not long in coming. In circles as small as that of the lovers of real jazz in Paris in 1934, word travelled fast, and in September Pierre Nourry and Charles Delaunay visited Claridge's alternative *thé dansant*. They were excited by what they heard, especially because the Hot Club was looking for a kind of house band, since the American pianist who had been featured in several of their concerts, Freddie Johnson, had moved to Amsterdam. They were also hoping to make more use of native musicians. French players had performed in some of their concerts, but the overall roster was American, reflecting the French prejudice that only Americans, and particularly blacks, could play jazz. For his part, Django still had dreams of his pet project, an all-string band 'sans tambour ni trompette' – without drum or trumpet – though Stéphane does not recall Django mentioning it to him since the Croix du Sud.

All the signs seemed propitious for trying to make the Claridge unit a working group. But at first the musicians themselves resisted the idea. They were playing for the pleasure of it, and since jazz never made any money, if the group went public their innocent pastime would fail or be corrupted. Either way they would lose. (One imagines this argument coming especially from the worldly wise Stéphane or Vola.) The quintet's first commercial effort, also in September, seemed to confirm their apprehensions. Charles Delaunay arranged a record date with Odeon which almost collapsed shortly after it started, when Django overheard the engineers sardonically asking what kind of music this was. Their two titles pleased the band but shocked the producers, who found them 'far too modern'.

A second session, for Ultraphone in December, proved much more successful. (Once Django had arrived: Delaunay had to race to his caravan and drag him out of bed. He arrived an hour and a half late.) However, the Quintet's performance of 'Dinah' was almost spoiled at the very end when, as it is variously reported, Stéphane's bow struck his violin or the microphone, or Django banged his guitar against a table. There were calls from the control to remake the piece, but the musicians were delighted and took it as it was, with the small atmospheric blemish that is still audible today.

In fact they were delighted with the whole session. The money they made from it was meagre, but the sense of prestige was considerable. (In later years, however, Stéphane would feel ill done by because the record contract entitled Django to a royalty, while he received only a straight fee. This rankled mainly, he told me, as a matter of pride: he and Django had agreed they would be equal partners. 'We were an association, like Marks and Spencer, or Baucis and Philemon!') Only a few months after their first encounter, the new group existed officially. It received its public launch on 2 December 1934 at the hall of L'Ecole Normale de Musique. It was a relatively small room, with a capacity of about 250, but it was filled for the Sunday morning concert. The posters for the affair promised an orchestra playing a new kind of 'jazz hot' and, as Charles Delaunay said, 'hot was the word for it'. The crowd was enthusiastic, but they could not know how close they had come to receiving a vintage Django non-appearance. Before the event the gypsy star had been struck with an attack of nerves and had done one of his fades, having to be hunted down and virtually manhandled into the hall by Pierre Nourry.

Though the group was not yet dubbed the Quintet of the Hot Club of France, it became so by the time of its second concert, with the great American tenor saxophonist Coleman Hawkins on 23 February 1935. Its begetters hoped the group would fly the Hot Club's flag, and, with its records and concerts, it immediately succeeded. Everything about the band was novel. It proved that Frenchmen could play real jazz and do it on stringed instruments instead of brass. It also expanded the audience for jazz, another thought that had occurred to the Hot Club members. As Delaunay said, they had 'a feeling that maybe people who didn't like jazz with brass would like it with strings. And it worked exactly that way.' Most remarkably, it was not only jazz without drum or trumpet, but without concessions, consisting wholly of improvised solos on standards and original compositions. All in all, the group represented a real breakthrough. Speaking of those beginnings to me fifty years later, Stéphane himself left no doubt about the effect, and the reasons for it: 'The Quintet was quite a sensation in those days. It was absolutely new, playing jazz music with three guitars, violin and bass, like chamber music. And the way Django was playing too: it was like a *philharmonique*, the way he was playing.'

For, despite Stéphane's occasional exasperation with his partner's moods, there has never been, and never was, any doubt about his appreciation of Django's ability. At the time of the Quintet's first concerts and recordings, they were playing together in another band at the Stage B in Montparnasse, a club musicians loved because for once they could play what they wanted to. Since it was a noisy room, Stéphane was playing more piano than violin, but his place in the rhythm section gave him a particular opportunity to observe his guitarist partner. On one memorable occasion Coleman Hawkins sat in, prior to his concert with the Quintet. According to Stéphane, 'he sat down and played "Sweet Sue", and his interpretation lasted nearly forty-five minutes. He must have played about forty choruses on his own, and I think it was Django's accompaniment that made him play so superbly. . . . To my mind Hawkins was playing better jazz, but Django was the best accompanist I had ever heard. Louis Armstrong used to come in too, and he was obviously amazed at the harmonic possibilities in Django's work. From my piano bench I could see the obvious satisfaction Armstrong got from the way Django was playing.'

Not long afterwards, Stéphane witnessed the once-in-a-lifetime duo of Django and his hero Armstrong in a spontaneous private concert at Bricktop's in Montmartre with Satchmo singing: 'There were no discussions to decide what key they'd play in or what tunes they'd choose. Louis began and Django followed him in the twinkling of an eye. It was a revelation for me . . . I'll never forget that evening as long as I live.'

Despite the mutual respect and talent of the co-leaders, the success of their records and their growing reputation, the Quintet's actual employment was very occasional. For this they had partly themselves to blame, or rather Django, who was soon cementing his reputation for a fine carelessness. The group's first club date, for instance, was booked at the Nuits Bleus, a fashionable boîte they were going to open. Django celebrated the gala first night by staying at home, in bed, deep in sleep. During the rest of the run, however, the band had another kind of surprise, what Charles Delaunay calls 'a phenomenon: nobody danced. They just listened. And the owner came to the band saying, "You don't make the people dance!" He was mad. It was a new thing that happened, and he didn't think it was commercially worthwhile. So they only played for one month.'

Clearly, none of the customary assumptions applied to the Hot Club Quintet, and throughout its existence its members knew better than to make any assumptions themselves. The appeal of jazz lies in its informality, but there has never been a group of comparable importance that had such an informal intermittent history as Django and Stéphane's little troupe. Due to the guitarist's tendency to absent himself, unannounced, at any time, and to play only when he felt like it, the Quintet worked together comparatively little. It made him difficult to plan around, so the other members took other work. Stéphane did well, by his usual diligence, playing both piano and violin, accompanying, broadcasting, making a quite handsome salary as interval pianist at a theatre.

In the summer of 1935, his piano-playing and general view of music received a shock, when he was playing in a casino orchestra at Deauville. Relaxing in the sun one afternoon, he heard a staggering piano record over a loudspeaker on the beach. He dashed to the disc-jockey's cabin and demanded the identity of the pianist, to be informed it was a duo – 'Art and Tintin'! In fact it was Art Tatum, all by himself (the impression that Tatum was four-handed was not uncommon. When Miles Davis's great pianist Red Garland first heard Tatum's 'Tiger Rag' he 'thought it was a couple of guys'.) Stéphane described the experience as 'an atomic bomb'. Tatum immediately became his idol, not just for his fabulous technique and immaculate touch, but for his unparalleled harmonic imagination. The pianist epitomized what attracted Stéphane to jazz. He extended the possibilities of the chords of the standard tunes that Grappelli had loved from the beginning, and his overall conception was so allusive and subtle that it recalled Stéphane's classical heroes, Debussy and Ravel. Exposure to Tatum overwhelmed him and helped to resolve his old ambivalence toward the fiddle: 'I was so astonished and disturbed by his genius that I temporarily lost my enthusiasm for the piano and determined to concentrate on violin.'

But the pianist's inspiring example had indicated a new

direction for his music on any instrument, and illuminated some of the things he had been hearing in the Quintet. 'When I heard Tatum,' Stéphane once said, 'it helped me to play with Django.'

Musically the Grappelli–Reinhardt partnership continued to be marvellous, whenever circumstances and whims permitted a reunion. Though meetings were always haphazard – as Stéphane has put it, one fine day they would run into each other on a street corner and things would start again – the group was recording more and more, 'like a machine'. Singers enjoyed using them as back-up because of their light, swinging sound, sympathetic accompaniment and solos. They (or sometimes just Stéphane and Django) were a kind of house band – 'like a stock pot' – for visiting American jazzmen. The Quintet's own records continued to display the band's development and spread its reputation, serving notice that at last France and Europe had achieved something unique. American musicians were more than impressed with the group and especially with Django. As trumpeter Doc Cheatham said, 'The Quintet knocked me out . . . it was upsetting to hear a man who was a foreigner swing like that. Because they were swinging! I don't think there was a band in America to compare with them.'

But all the acclaim and brilliance did not mean that life with the Quintet was any less precarious. Records were one thing. Then all you had to do was make sure Django got up in time for the session, through a mixture of remonstrations and threats, coffee and croissants. But public appearances were truly something else; again, more like the Marx Brothers than Armstrong or Ellington. The stories became legion: the Quintet, specially invited by a singing star to appear with him, ruining his show by getting the giggles on stage; Django, trying to take a hand in business dealings despite his illiteracy, poring over a contract and then objecting emphatically to a clause that guaranteed the group first-class travel; Stéphane gently persuading Django that red socks were not worn with a tuxedo; Django disappearing from a luxury hotel room because the thick carpets hurt his feet; Django disappearing just before the Quintet was due on stage at London's Piccadilly Theatre, finally discovered outside gazing raptly at his name in lights.

Disappearance remained his speciality, and Stéphane learned to recognize some signs: 'He'd hear a bird and say, "Oh, it's the spring." Spring was my worst enemy because when the leaves came on the trees, no Django.' No doubt it was spring when he failed to meet the rest of the group for a concert in Zurich, having entrusted his guitar to Charles Delaunay. The promoter was adamant – no Django, no fees or travel expenses for anyone. Fortunately, though, he did not know what Django looked like, so in a twinkling Joseph Reinhardt became the world's greatest guitarist – applauded by the crowd and critics – while Delaunay, at Stéphane's insistence, sat in the back of the band, tapping the side of a guitar nervously and trying to stay as far from the strings as possible.

Afterwards, the group themselves might relish an incident like that, perhaps, or like the affair of Baron Rothschild's party. A silver cigar box rested on the Baron's piano, full of fine cigars, with which Django was steadily filling his pockets as he played. Mortified, Stéphane would rap Django's hand with his bow every time he saw it sneaking toward the box. But all at once the little contest was interrupted by a cry of pain, as Stéphane, preoccupied, delivered a sharp rap to the knuckles of a bemedalled guest.

It was not uncommon for the Quintet to move in such posh circles as their fame grew. For Parisian society, parties were an art form, and the group's sound – infectious without being obtrusive – suited their soirées perfectly. Once, as Stéphane recalled, he and Django were invited to no less august a place than the Elysée Palace by 'an important personality', for dinner and a short concert. Stéphane arrived on time, making typically charming conversation while, typically, everyone waited and waited for Django. At last his embarrassed partner offered to go after him, though he really had little idea where he was. Given the official Elysée limousine, the irate violinist found Django playing billiards and, after stopping only long enough to pick up his guitar, brought him back to the residence.

With a baggy suit, slippers and a two-day beard, Django looked like anyone's bad dream of a gypsy. But however ill at ease he felt, his remarkable pride never left him. As they entered the gate, the guard automatically saluted the limousine. 'Ah,' said the guitarist, 'they recognize me.' Arriving in the dining-room, when his hostess politely asked if he had eaten, Django, taken by surprise, simply said no, though everyone else had finished dining and had been waiting for him for well over an hour. When food was brought, those guests who may have been preparing to jeer at this derelict-looking figure gorging himself, were amazed by his natural dignity and self-possession. To Stéphane he had the aura of an Oriental prince: 'His exquisite politeness was a lesson for everyone.'

However, Django's imperious – indeed sometimes almost comic – sense of his own worth had its divisive side. He treated his brother Joseph like a lackey, demanding that he always carry Django's guitar. During an engagement at the club

Don Juan, Joseph staged a violent rebellion, which only their mother could quell. Soon, however, he resigned himself to acting as his brother's porter, though resentment could still flare up. In the middle of one concert, an enraged Joseph stalked out, noisily dragging his chair off stage with him.

For all his respect for Stéphane, Django was very jealous in matters of prestige. He did not mind sharing billing (most of their record labels read: 'Django Reinhardt et le Quintette du Hot Club de France avec Stéphane Grappelli'), but precedence for Stéphane was unthinkable. Indeed Django once tried to rig up a kind of guitar stand so that he would not have to play seated, which might give the impression that Stéphane was the star of the group. Playing at the Big Apple in 1937 – which was being run by the doyenne of the Paris night club scene, the American singer Bricktop – the Quintet accepted an offer to broadcast to America on the CBS show, Saturday Night Swing Club, the first time a European band had been invited. But an unforeseen hazard was lurking. As a way of circumventing a contract, the Quintet had made some records as 'Stéphane Grappelly and his Hot Four – 'the one time,' Stéphane said, 'that Django didn't object to my name appearing as leader.' These were some of the discs by which the group was known in America, and, on the night of the show, with the Quintet ready to make its live transatlantic début, they heard the announcer proclaim: 'Stéphane Grappelly and his Hot Four'!

Nothing happened. In a rage, Django refused to play, and the rest of the band, as usual, followed his lead. There was a fraught pause on the air as whispered pleas and explanations were made, and finally Django deigned to begin. He glared at the innocent Stéphane throughout the performance, did not speak to him for weeks afterwards, and, Charles Delaunay believes, never really forgave him.

Despite this acrimony, the Quintet's few months at Bricktop's were their longest and happiest engagement. It was the summer of 1937 and the normal spirit of Paris, if rather subdued by the depression, was elevated by the presence of the International Exposition in the city. Bricktop was one of the most popular figures in café society. She had come to Paris from Harlem, and her blend of wit, sympathy and salty common sense established her primacy in the city's night life for close to fifteen years. To Stéphane, she was 'one of the queens of Paris. She had such an incredible clientele. As in the 1920s, it was a dazzling mixture of titles and talent – royalty from all over Europe and popular composers like Cole Porter and Gershwin. At Bricktop's, Stéphane said, aristocrats pretended to be bourgeois, instead of the usual practice of the bourgeois pretending to be aristocracy. It was just the atmosphere for him, and he was delighted when Gershwin, in town to compose *An American in Paris*, expressed his pleasure at the way the violinist performed his 'Someone to Watch Over Me'.

The hours were the customary long ones, but at least the musicians were not treated as though they were merely hired help. Customarily, as Stéphane knew only too well, they were 'obliged to come in through the service entrance, take care not to touch the carpets and conceal themselves carefully behind the potted plants!' In addition, the musical atmosphere was stimulating. Since the room 'was small and filled with elegant people, it was possible to play,' even without a microphone. When the Quintet was not performing, Stéphane switched to the piano to accompany either Bricktop herself or a singer he especially admired, the great Mabel Mercer. Every night he asked Mabel to sing Porter's 'I've Got You Under My Skin': 'It drove me mad the way she did it'. The combination of sets with the Quintet and piano accompaniment meant Stéphane was working straight for seven or eight hours a night, but in a setting of such style, artistry and appreciation, the time did not matter. And playing the piano he could at least sit down.

But a chance for a break often presented itself in the person of Eddie South, the excellent black American jazz violinist who was in Paris for the Exposition. South, whom Stéphane regarded very highly, loved to sit in with Django and the Quintet. When he did, Stéphane would slip gratefully around the corner for a drink. Charles Delaunay took advantage of South's Parisian stay to record the remarkable performances – duos and trios with Django and Stéphane – that have become an historic part of the legacy of jazz violin.

Django enjoyed Bricktop and her club too. In her autobiography, the hostess recalled how worried friends had warned her about his reputation: 'If he doesn't like the color of your dress, he'll walk out. If he doesn't like the way a client is looking at him, he'll walk out.' But Django only absented himself twice – probably a record – once to bail a gypsy girl out of jail, and once because he had a toothache. He called Bricktop 'minou' (cat) and said he enjoyed working for her 'because she's a girl and has nice surroundings. I like the people around her.' Bricktop liked him despite the fact that he 'wore tan shoes with his tux', and she thought the band was 'the hottest thing in the world'.

Despite their success at Bricktop's the Quintet's continued activities remained erratic. Records continued to multiply. During the week of 21–27 April 1937 alone, they made eighteen sides, and the next day Django and Stéphane (on piano) participated in the famous session that included Benny Carter and Coleman Hawkins and created a legendary 'Crazy Rhythm'. There were short tours of Holland and Belgium, but basically work was sporadic: continuity was not in the Quintet's nature. Django held court in his hotel room in Montmartre with Naguine, his pet monkey and legions of cousins, and Stéphane played piano with the society bandleader Ford Harrison.

Of course Stéphane's life involved more than music, though it may have lacked the devil-may-care, improvisatory quality of Django's. It was around this time that the love affair occurred that produced his daughter, Eveline. Stéphane has been reticent about his personal life. He tried not to allow it to disturb his control over professional responsibilities, and, unlike Django, he largely succeeded. But as a later guitarist-partner, John Etheridge, observed, looking back from the eighties, 'I think the Stéphane Grappelli we have now is in some ways different from the Stéphane of forty years ago – the person. I remember once we were talking about being in love, and he said, "Oh, that's over for me, thank God. Once I had this love affair. For two years I cried every day. I was on stage playing, and tears were coming down my face. And everybody thought 'Oh, he is into the music.' But no – I was crying because of this woman."' Etheridge thinks Stéphane now 'has arrived at a suitable age', having 'been refined in some sort of fire,' and Eveline's mother may have been part of this process. Stéphane has said little about her; except to recount that she was 'a very good-looking woman, younger than me, but very *difficile*.' With the cautionary example of his step-mother behind him, they never married.

In the autumn of 1937, the Quintet was set to conquer new territory, in a move that would be especially significant for Stéphane. The *Melody Maker* magazine and a British promoter suggested a concert in London, to capitalize on the group's growing popularity in Britain, and it was duly scheduled for Sunday, 30 January 1938. The *Melody Maker* pumped out ballyhoo for weeks, and the atmosphere of its coverage seemed to indicate genuine excitement, more than simple PR. A New Year's issue headline warned that the 'MM Concert for Musicians (true lovers of hot jazz, not dilettantes) was rapidly selling out, and an article noted the anticipatory fervor of swing fans already familiar with the band through their records. Subsequent issues kept up the pressure, announcing that the Hot Club was sending over a large contingent of supporters, and warning fans who wanted to see 'the quintet that has put French dance music on the map' that 'further delay would be fatal'.

It would clearly be the jazz event of the season, and for once the outcome was everything that could have been wished. 'French Quintet Staggers Swing Concert Audience' blazed the MM's headline, and its review began, 'They came, they were seen, they conquered.' It went on to say that the Gallic visitors may have taken British attentiveness for disapproval at first, but at the end, 'salvoes of applause crashed over their deserving heads as they lined up in front of the tabs, grinning delightedly at their overwhelming success.'

The report's description of the Quintet at work is intriguing, partly for what it implies about the tricks and gimmicks that the public usually associated with 'jazz': 'the Quintet is curiously static as it plays. The three guitars, sitting in a slightly spaced line with Django in the centre, hardly bat an eyelid. The maestro occasionally cocks an eyebrow in concentration or permits an enigmatic smile to pass across his face, but except for an almost imperceptible rocking, there is no movement, no showmanship, no gallery play whatsoever. Grappelly, standing, works to the mike with great skill and experience. Unobtrusively he moves to the flank when he is tacit, a polished, good-looking, grave-of-face sort of fellow who plays like an angel.'

In the heady weeks preceding the show, there had been no question that the Quintet's soloists were co-leaders; the group was regularly referred to as 'Grappelly–Reinhardt'. The review took essentially the same line, but made an accurate distinction between them. The writer was overwhelmed by Django's 'enormous talents . . . his command of the instrument, his own self-developed technique, the subtle nuances imparted to every note . . . the terrific fecundity of his musical imagination all tended to exhibit him as one of the greatest guitarists of his day. He is, quite obviously, the main inspiration of the Quintet.' But the difference in effect 'in no way overshadowed . . . Django's partner, Stéphane. That beautiful tone of his, the facile technique, that delightful and moving phrasing judged by all legitimate standards are impeccable. So is the whole Quintet.'

The only question the reviewer had was the vexed one about what such jazz is supposed to *do*: 'Maybe it's good for dancing and maybe it's not. Who wants to dance to music which is so good as that? Who wants to dance to Ellington? If the Quintet doesn't play swing music it plays darned good music, and that's the last word on that.'

The triumph marked the beginning of a special relationship between the Quintet and Britain. This first visit lasted only long enough for a recording session at Decca, but it made them aware of a level of interest that would repay a more extended stay. On the group's return to France there were a few appearances, but in July it was back to England for a tour of variety halls. Originally planned for several weeks, additional bookings expanded it to four months.

The response in the provinces repeated the enthusiasm of their London debut. The *Melody Maker*'s critic spoke of 'the intense excitement' surrounding their appearance and noted that their playing was 'too well-known to require any comment . . . except to say that it was well up to their own very high standard. The thrill really was in seeing the boys in the flesh and noting the cool confident manner in which Django and his partners go about their work. To watch them one would think they were merely playing to amuse themselves, rather than for the benefit of an audience, such was their control.' Indeed that was what Django was doing, which meant that when it came to actual performance, whatever the trials preceding it, he was stability itself. Stéphane, on the other hand, has always been subject to nerves, but he 'was never nervous with Django. Playing violin with him . . . I felt as easy as though I was sitting in my own drawing-room . . . He was like the rock of Gibraltar, that man, always perfectly serene on stage.'

Indeed Bob Clarke, who knew Grappelli well in the sixties, thought 'Stéphane was jealous of Django' – or rather, envious of Django's insouciant calm, that cool capacity to cut loose, to go for what he wanted regardless of what an audience thought. 'There was skin and hair flyin' all the time 'cause Django didn't care. He liked the adulation . . . but he just loved his music – if you dig it, you dig it. I got the impression that Stéphane was more of a showman.'

Stéphane, at least, was concerned about what the audience thought because somebody had to be. But it is true that for many young musicians of the time, Django undoubtedly had the charisma. Humphrey Lyttelton was an aspiring jazzman then, and, as he told me, when he and his friends pored over the Quintet's recordings, 'it was Reinhardt we really focussed on. I think Stéphane really came into his own later, after he came out from Reinhardt's shadow.' Another young musician, the guitarist Denny Wright (who would play with Stéphane when he came into his own), remembered that when he saw the Quintet, its stage set-up reflected Django's status: he was literally placed on a kind of pedestal.

Overshadowed or not, Stéphane was clearly developing as a

player, as the records that the Quintet made during their London stay reveal. He was profiting from life in Britain in other ways as well, enjoying a range of experiences from the rather ridiculous – the Quintet sharing top of the bill at the London Palladium with the movie cowboy Tom Mix and his horse – to the quite sublime – playing 'Honeysuckle Rose' with its composer, Fats Waller, who was also touring the halls.

The Quintet returned to France contented and discovered that their *réclame* in Britain had caused a new flutter of interest at home. They were booked first at the Marignan theatre, where a raucous crowd expressed disapproval of their fourteen-year-old English singer, Beryl Davis, with chauvinistic shouts of 'Français, Français!' But at the ABC they were a hit, thus, as the *Melody Maker* reported with patriotic pride, 'tardily reaping at home the success they first achieved in England'. It was true, but it did not last, as *Jazz Hot* admitted: 'After scoring a big – and unhoped for – success at the ABC, the Quintet can find no work in Paris and is about to return to England where its popularity knows no bounds.'

Immediate plans, however, proved difficult to make. The members of the Quintet had gone their own ways again. Stéphane, due to play piano with the Willy Lewis band, became very ill and could do nothing for weeks. The *Melody Maker* could locate Django no more exactly than to say he was appearing 'at some night club'. Parenthetically, the journal explained that 'the Quintet as such has a very spasmodic, occasional existence, apart from its tours abroad.'

Those tours were being taken over by the English. When the group did a series of concerts in Scandinavia in February 1939, the trip was arranged by their London agents. (Or by one of them. During their 1938 tour they had aroused displeasure by blithely signing with two agencies at once.) Stéphane recalled that the tour was sensational, though 'Django was extremely annoyed when the garland for distinguished visitors was put round my neck instead of his.' Returning to Paris in April, the band performed for Duke Ellington at the grand opening of the Hot Club's new offices in the rue Chaptal – partly in hopes that it would inspire Ellington's manager to propose an American tour.

That might well have happened, because the international scene was clearly where the Quintet fared best. When they returned to Britain in August 1939, it was with prospects of proceeding to India and Australia. But other international events were determining the shape of everyone's future. The group arrived to preparations for war, though these did not diminish the rapturous welcome at the Kilburn State theatre.

The sublime Grégor at the Olympia Theatre, Paris 1933. The Grégorians include Alix Combelle, saxophone (second row, second right); Andre Ekyan, clarinet, and Michel Warlop, violin (right and left of centre), and Stéphane Grappelli on piano (left).

The reunion recording session with Stéphane and Django, 1946; Coleridge Goode on bass.

Following recovery from a dangerous illness in August 1941, Stéphane scans get-well notes in the offices of the Melody Maker.

Stéphane at home, London 1951. Pat Brand, editor of Melody Maker, *has presented him with a certificate of his victory in the magazine's readers' poll.*

Stéphane and Django jamming backstage with their English quintet of 1948.

Stéphane prepares to board his train for France at Victoria station, March 1954.

Paris, 1950s: Stéphane remembers Django Reinhardt with his widow, Naguine.

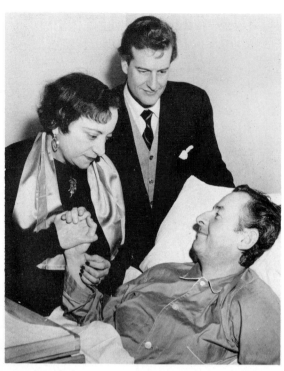

January, 1954: Stéphane is visited in hospital, following an operation, by Lord and Lady Browne.

Stéphane opens with his septet at the Club St Germain, April 1954.

Spring, 1954: Stéphane displays a copy of the Melody Maker *which claims he will open at London's Bagatelle restaurant. The wry observer is the great French writer and jazz-lover, Boris Vian.*

Stéphane in London , mid-1960s, with Lord Montagu (centre) and the pianist, Dill Jones.

Stéphane performs for a suspiciously well-behaved crowd at the Milroy Club, 1949.

On facing page:
Stéphane charms the dancers (and the camera) at 96 Piccadilly.

Stéphane checks over the score for the film Two for the Road *with its composer, Henry Mancini; December 1966.*

A graphic contrast in personal as well as musical styles: Stéphane records with Stuff Smith; Paris, May 1957: (left to right) Stuff, Jo Jones, Ray Brown, Herb Ellis, Oscar Peterson.

Stuff Smith and Stéphane during a break at their recording session in Paris, May 1957.

They were announced from behind the curtain to ecstatic applause, which swelled as they were revealed, white-coated, debonair and swinging. It seemed a most propitious beginning for a lengthy tour that might present new worlds to conquer.

But what it represented instead was hail and farewell to the old Quintet. On 1 September, air raid sirens broke the Sunday stillness. It was only a test, but Django panicked. Leaving everything he had, including his guitar, he appeared below Stéphane's window to shout that he was going straight back to Paris. Stéphane, ill once more, was in no mood to chase one of Django's wild geese. He took (mistakenly, as it turned out) a more settled view of events, and he did not share Django's reflex to seek the safety of the tribe. There were fewer bonds for him in France. Eveline's mother was still *difficile*, and his father had died the previous May (on the 16th, the very day of Django's death fourteen years later). So Stéphane told the gypsy to go ahead if he wanted; he would come later. Django did; Stéphane did not. They would not see each other for seven years, and things would never be the same again.

The Quintet, as we have seen, was always a sporadic thing, its real identity coming from a unique sound produced by the two rare individuals who were its leaders. That there was not a similar continuity to its professional existence was due to a large extent to Django's temperament. His energy gave the group its force, but Stéphane provided its polish, its finish. As their mutual friend Alain Romans observed. 'The relationship between Django and Grappelli wasn't easy, but when it came to making a record Django needed Stéphane more than the other way around . . . Stéphane was able to write down a lot of his tunes, and he enriched them too, because Django had a bad habit of starting things off and then not finishing them.' Romans concluded, 'They were altogether different characters. Stéphane was much more serious. He was very hard-working.'

How then does Stéphane look back on his association with Django? He too has described it as 'uneasy'. He has complained of 'the troubles he gave me' and even confessed, 'I think now I would rather play with lesser musicians and have a peaceable time than with Django and all his monkey business.' He has said that Django did not treat him simply as a friend, but more like a cousin or brother, confiding things he would not say to anyone else. And, uneasy or not, exasperating or not, there was certainly a deep relationship between the two men. Undoubtedly they had their differences. Stéphane has always had a respect for the social graces and practices them expertly. Many people have remarked on his wit and talent as a

raconteur. For such a man, Django's bearish taciturnity must
have been a trial. As Charles Delaunay said, 'Django was wood
compared to Stéphane.'

However, Stéphane was aware that Django's silence was due
to self-consciousness. 'Although he was terribly intelligent, he
knew he was ignorant, so he did not speak except to me. He
would ask me questions – "What means geography?" "What is
a square?"' He looked up to Stéphane both because he was
literate – 'You are instructed: you can read the newspaper' –
and because he was Django's elder by two years, seniority
conferring authority among the gypsies. At the same time, the
gypsy context also divided them. Stéphane liked his privacy
and objected to the constant retinue of 'cousins'. He was also
distressed at the temptations they – and others – presented to
Django. 'I saw a great talent going to waste . . . I said – I who
am as idle as you can be – "let's go somewhere and compose
something together, a fresco, something that lasts."'

Undoubtedly they shared a sensitivity to fine things. Of
course Stéphane has 'always valued elegance and beauty', and
he recognized that despite Django's caravan life, 'instinctively
he liked elegance'. When it came to expression in personal
style, Django inclined much more to flash and dramatic effects
(the red socks with the tux): Stéphane to subtlety. They were
the Oriental prince and the *boulevardier*, and a similar contrast
appeared in their attitudes to money. For Django, money had
meaning only as status, as symbol of the world's recognition
of his exalted rank. When once asked to name a fee for a concert
he replied, 'How much does Gary Cooper get?' Those were
his terms: a Hollywood star was a kind of royalty, and so was
he. Therefore the money should be the same. For Stéphane
money was the margin of life, and he was appalled at the
way Django's lavish wages vanished, in gambling or fantastic
purchases: 'Remembering my young days when things were
very different, I always managed to be a little careful. But
Django – never!' Perhaps the great difference was that
Stéphane had known what it was to be poor and alone. At
times in his life, Django may have had very little money, but
this did not mean he was destitute. He was a gypsy and of
noble standing in the tribe. Someone would always provide –
his mother, his wife, his cousins – and he gave not a thought
to the 'security' of bourgeois peasants.

Musically, they saw eye to eye at once. They had the same
values and heroes; they frequently attended classical concerts
together. Stéphane would have agreed at once with Django's
assertion, 'The harmonies, that's what I like best of all in
music: there you have the mother of music.' Django loved

Bach for the harmonic movement and emotion, but felt that 'Debussy comes closer to my musical ideal' because of his 'sensibility and intelligence'. Jazz appealed to him because of the 'formal perfection and instrumental precision that I admire in classical music, but which popular music doesn't have'.

These were all exactly Stéphane's attitudes, why he could complement Django's ideas with his own without anything needing to be said, and why he felt that playing with Django was 'the summit of everything that I had in my life'. Whatever the occasional disputes and frustrations, there was a unity of understanding between them that was more than musical. Charles Delaunay has spoken of the partnership as a kind of marriage, a bond that could survive spats and bickering. What they shared was great talent of an inexplicable kind. Critics have been fond of speculating romantically on the roots of Django's natural ability, why this gypsy should demonstrate an innate aptitude for jazz when nothing in his background could have indicated it. But exactly the same is true for Stéphane, with his busking, his *solfège*, teaching himself without even the support and example of gypsy musical tradition. As Charles Delaunay observed to me. 'He learned everything from everybody without a teacher; he made himself. And to become the purest playing that can be imagined, that way – that's what amazes me most.' It was a gift to him as much as it was to Django, and playing with each other, out of the possession of such a gift, brought it to new perfection in them both.

Moments of recollected pique aside, Stéphane has always known that, and recognized the nature of his relation to Django as something unique. As he said, they were 'more than close friends'. Some writers have believed that Stéphane resents talking about his partner because of the legends that have sprung up around him, to the detriment of a proper appreciation of the violinist's role in the group they shared. But, at London's 100 Club in April of 1984, Stéphane spoke to me of the guitarist easily, frankly and affectionately. If Django would come back now, there would be no question that he would play with him again, '. . . because Django would be playing something contemporary. He was always ahead of his time. Guitarists were terrified of him; they were *glad* when he disappeared.' As for his unpredictable character, 'Django was a genius, and if you're a genius you have to be crazy, because you're so involved. I'm not a genius, but I think I'm a little crazy too.'

Finally, essentially, they were two of the same kind, which is why their records express such an extraordinary integrity.

And for all the surface discrepancies of temper and background, there was something very clear about their relations,
something simple and deeply understood. Which is no doubt
what Stéphane meant in summing up his partner once to a
BBC interviewer: 'He was not a mysterious person. He was
absolutely a very straight and correct and clean person, you
see, Django Reinhardt.'

Swing
from Paris

Even in its heyday, the Hot Club Quintet existed mainly on records. No doubt hearing them in the flesh was a thrill, as reviews and personal accounts make clear, but the owner of a Quintet disc was at least sure that the promised performance would take place. He could enjoy the spontaneity of the music without worrying about it spilling over into the whims of the artists' behaviour. Partly because of those whims, the records convey a good deal of spontaneity. Other effects aside, the haphazard conditions of the Quintet's life meant that there was no chance of them getting stale, and their studio performances generally exude that excitement and discovery which is the soul of jazz.

Their distinctive style was present from the beginning. In his description of the band, the French critic Lucien Malson (after first observing that Django and Stéphane had equal genius) noted that 'Dinah', the Quintet's first work, 'contains in itself the whole essence of an original art.' And it is true; the formula is already there. Django plays a little unaccompanied introduction and begins the tune, but improvises on it at once, opening up with more and more freedom into his second chorus. Stéphane comes in for two choruses with Django behind him, not only playing time with a chunky shuffle figure but also dropping in rhythmic licks to spur him on. Stéphane's second chorus takes on the character of a climactic ride-out, with Django's accompaniment still more prominent, building tension finally released in a tender, out-of-tempo coda. A functional form, wholly suited to jazz: a lucid little arrangement gives a framework, but the emphasis is purely on solos from the outset, with even the melody stripped down to provide more improvising space.

Excellent on their own, the improvisations took on added impact from the blend of the players. Django's percussive attack – that simple intensity of sound no one had ever heard from a guitar before, the result of a high action off the bridge, steel strings, great strength and imagination – was answered perfectly by Stéphane's sinuous legato. Django provides drive and aggressiveness, Stéphane elegance and warmth. To adapt Charles Delaunay's domestic image, they represent an ideal marriage of the dual character of strings, the plucked and the bowed.

Against the unvarying, driving beat of the two supporting guitars and bass, Django flings off sudden angles and patterns, whirling chromatic runs, melismatic clusters, tremolos and those famous slashing octaves. You don't know where he'll start or stop, as he builds a solo out of surprises. Stéphane's approach is more continuous, riding the beat rather than challenging it, delighting in the simple mobility the bow provides. But at the same time, he has his quality of cut and thrust as well. He breaks up his lines constantly – leaping, in the middle of a descending passage, back up to where it started, hanging onto notes, throwing in tough, short riffs almost as asides, changing accents, slurring into and through blue notes, introducing trills and turns from the classical vocabulary, out-of-tempo chromatic runs like Django's, ecstatic riffs between the third or fifth and the tonic. These variations increase the momentum of a Stéphane solo; in fact they *are* the momentum, the twisting, tumbling flow of his inspiration. His solos seem almost to swarm sometimes, but however hot he gets, he never departs from taste or *justesse*. His essential quality is a wiry grace, civilized but with a basic gutsiness. It means he can balance – even at times redeem – the *brut* quality in Django's playing without being insipid. Which is why their ensembles are so attractive, and their *quintette à cordes* so satisfying, based not just on complementary instruments but complementary approaches.

Of course, the co-leaders were only two-fifths of the group, and occasionally the accompanying majority could cause problems. Stéphane told a *Down Beat* reporter, 'Those poor guys

were just boom boom and *finito* . . . ordinary musicians . . .
who were not up to standard.' (This is somewhat unfair to
Joseph who, after Django's death, recorded creditably as a
soloist.) He let Django deal with the guitarists, usually fellow
gypsies. But the tribal bond counted for nothing where music
was concerned. As Stéphane once said, for Django 'a wrong
note was an insanity. A wrong note put him in shock.' The
perpetrator immediately received the look known as 'les yeux
noirs' – the black eyes – with devastating effect. Charles
Delaunay, who supervised a number of Quintet recording
sessions, recalled that 'the others would be completely lost,
crucified, when Django looked at them.'

The band therefore went through frequent personnel
changes, not least in the bass department. On the records
the guitars generally sound all right, efficiently, if facelessly,
bouncy. But the bassists often produce tubby, indeterminate
pitches, thumping along two beats to the bar, making Stéphane
and Django sound even further ahead of their time by contrast.
This two-beat feel – even on ballads – is one of the unvarying
characteristics of the group (in the thirties), giving it a certain
jug-band quality, and like the all-string line up itself sometimes
making it suspect to jazz purists.

Indeed, even during the time of the Quintet's greatest suc-
cesses there were doubts about the 'authenticity' of its music,
corresponding to certain kinds of preconception about what
jazz was supposed to be. Max Jones, dean of British jazz critics,
told me how he and some other listeners of the day perceived
the band, in person and on records: 'I saw the group once at
the Kilburn State and didn't especially want to hear them again
. . . They were young Frenchmen fiddling and thrashing away,
and to be truthful the reaction was one of slightly putting
them down a bit. They were referred to as the Five Frantic
Frenchmen. They were considered to be frantic, and they
looked a bit like gypsies, and there was a fair bit of shouting,
as you heard from the records. By the time they got down and
Steph started swinging there were cries of "Yeah!", and it was
all thought to be good but not profound. In those days as
record collectors we had sorts of categories. Louis Armstrong's
"West End Blues" was deep; then a Goodman trio or quartet
– quite unjustly – we thought of as sort of cute. This group
came under the heading of cute rather than deep. That was
the reaction then.'

Max went on to say that by the time he met Stéphane in the
mid-forties, 'I'd revised my opinion of the whole scene and
realized they were much better musicians than I thought.' But
those original suspicions took some overcoming. The criteria

77

that, according to Max, jazz purists applied is revealing: Armstrong's 'West End Blues', an unquestioned masterpiece by the first genius of jazz, had the necessary insignia. It was a blues (the fundamental jazz genre) performed by a black man (a member of the creator-race) who played trumpet (at least well into the twenties the classic jazz instrument). By these standards, even Benny Goodman was somewhat second-rate. What chance did white Frenchmen have, bowing and plucking their feeble strings? We have seen that Doc Cheatham (another black trumpet-player) somewhat reluctantly admitted that the Quintet swung. But even he still felt 'it wasn't jazz'. Indeed a distinguished white European string player agreed with him. Svend Asmussen heard the Quintet's recordings as an aspiring twenty-year-old jazz violinist in Denmark. 'At the beginning I didn't even like it; I was amazed by Django Reinhardt, of course, his musicality, and Stéphane's beautiful sound, but I was so fixed on American jazz music that I thought it sounded somehow wrong – because it was far away from jazz in a way.' In fact Svend still doesn't think that Django and Stéphane's playing is jazz: 'It hasn't got the black roots; no blues in it.'

Not everyone shared these reservations. The black singer Adelaide Hall, another of the stars of the Parisian club scene in the thirties had created 'Creole Love Call' with Duke Ellington and brought Art Tatum to New York as her accompanist. She knew Django and Stéphane well, and for her, as for Bricktop, there was no question. 'No, that *was* the real thing . . . you know – real jazz. Oh, it was wonderful.'

Trying to define 'real jazz' in any but the loosest terms has the abstract futility usually associated with dancing angels and the heads of pins. It makes more sense simply to look at some of the Quintet's recordings to sample the kind of thing they were doing. 'My Sweet', for instance, has a special place in Quintet lore because of its bit of comic dialogue. After three scintillating opening choruses Django stops the group to inquire whether 'M. Vola would like to play a solo'. (In fact on the first try he asked M. Solo if he would like to play a Vola, but that take was never issued.) Vola slaps his way through sixteen bars and then Stéphane leaps in in fire-eating mood to charge through four choruses, the last of them propelled by a 'One more, Stéphane!' from Django. Django, however, was merely acknowledging a blazing *fait accompli*, since the violinist was obviously not stopping for anybody. Throughout he is playing at full stretch, but without losing a sense of pace or control. He comes in to finish off the last eight of Vola's chorus ('My Sweet' has an unusual twenty-four bar structure, in which the bridge seems to come last). His first chorus covers the full range of the violin, the second features a swooping riff figure and the third he attacks with passionate octaves. By this time he is playing so high and hard it would seem there is nowhere to go, but, with more furious riffing, he pushes the momentum to an ecstatic climax. There is, it must be admitted, 'a fair bit of shouting' during the performance, but it makes the listener feel like shouting too.

'My Sweet' is typical of one of the Quintet's most effective modes, the free-wheeling uptempo with the guitars pumping away feverishly, which critics found peculiarly French. But mere speed was not the point. As Stéphane told me, he and Django 'didn't play tempos, just rhythm', and one of the most remarkable aspects of these records is the sense of a rhythmic bond between the leaders. Violinist stimulates guitarist and vice versa, in a kind of spiralling rapture. At these times it is difficult to credit the stories of jealousy about which of them was the group's true star, and of Django resenting Stéphane stretching out in his solos. As Charles Delaunay put it, 'There was no reason. When Stéphane was playing Django was happy to hear.'

Another high-pressure classic is 'Them There Eyes' (which *Melody Maker* dismissed with a one-star review when it came out). Django solos in his best authoritative manner, inspiring Stéphane, where a lesser player might be intimidated. The violinist reels off three choruses, the last two in a quasi-clarinet style that may reflect his admiration for Benny Goodman – high wails alternating with digging riffs, while Django thunders along underneath, throwing in his inimitable heavy tremolos and octaves. The atmosphere is pure tumult, utterly intoxicating, this time wholly without benefit of shouts. Stéphane has often recalled Maurice Chevalier's advice to him that 'you must begin well and end well'. The Quintet's endings are usually in Stéphane's hands and they are never less than effective.

Other tempestuous titles include, very selectively, 'Twelfth Year', 'Runnin' Wild' and the later version of 'I Wonder Where My Baby is Tonight'. In the latter Django takes most of the solo space but Stéphane's chorus shows how to be both suave and intensely swinging, by the use of turns, trills and shifts in accent as his line unfolds. But such abandon is by no means the Quintet's only strength. There are straight ballads, like the early 'Ton Doux Sourire', with Stéphane's beautiful reading of the melody preceding a splendid Django solo, ballads with more of a beat, like 'It Was So Beautiful', ballads double-timed like 'Chasing Shadows'. There are medium-tempos, lilting like 'Swing 39', or rugged like 'Minor Swing', in which both Django and Stéphane surpass themselves, the violinist concluding with four declamatory choruses as Django musically and verbally urges him on.

In all, their performances illustrate what Stéphane meant when he said that, whatever personal disagreements he and Django had, 'there was something electric between us'. If this music is not jazz, it is hard to know what to call it. It is true that the blues element is less prominent than in American jazz, and there certanly are other non-American influences manifest in Django – his 'Neapolitan' trills, the dashing runs, flamboyant tremolos and tight vibrato that suggest flamenco, an occasional zither-like quality in sonority and voicing – the whole mixed inheritance that stamps his music as European and, above all, gypsy. Stéphane's distinctive contribution is the flavour of the French classical tradition. But jazz is still the central element in their playing, audible at once in its freedom, adventure and swing, focussing all its other attributes. Individually and collectively, their music is unmistakably 'the real thing', and through them jazz gained a fresh perspective and a new, international set of possibilities.

Just as the critics felt obliged to scrutinize the Quintet's jazz credentials, they also had to compare them with such similar groups as were available. Most obviously, this meant the various units headed by Joe Venuti and Eddie Lang. The Italo-American duo had a great transatlantic vogue: as the historian James Lincoln Collier has pointed out, 'If one has to choose the single most important influence on European jazz in general through the 1920s and 1930s it would be the Venuti-Lang combination.' This was due at least partly to the record companies' notion that their light, jovial approach might better suit continental listeners than the more unalloyed intensity of black artists. But even jazz purists approved of them. Lang was an excellent guitarist and peerless musician, with a well-developed harmonic sense, fleet fingers and an ability to swing, albeit somewhat delicately. Venuti, who could indeed claim to be the father of jazz violin, possessed a fine sound and technique, energy and a famous if rather coarse sense of humour.

They began their recording career with a few adroit duos, but their most notable performances occurred with the little bands known as Joe Venuti's Blue Four, or Five. Of course, Stéphane had heard these discs, but, as we have seen, while he respected Venuti, he did not consider him an improviser in the Armstrong sense. Writing of him in 1960 for the French *Jazz Magazine*, Stéphane said, 'He worked in what is called today a "novelty" style; his music evoked the sonorous accompaniment of silent films.' And, listening to the Venuti–Lang groups, one's prevailing impression is of catchy tunes, clever arrangements, fine musicianship and great fun. They really can not be compared collectively to the Quintet since their material emphasizes set-pieces rather than straight improvisation, and because the colours of the two groups are very different. Part of the fun of the Blue Fours and Fives arises from the contrast between Venuti's fiddle and bass or baritone saxophone (or, in the joyous 'Runnin' Ragged', bassoon) along with piano and guitar.* It is not by any means an all-string group, and the rhythmic feeling is completely different from the drive of the Quintet. Individually, though only a few years separate them, Venuti and Lang are from another era than Grappelli and Reinhardt. Venuti's playing feels almost like a ragtime – short, jumpily syncopated phrases and repeated patterns, instead of Stéphane's longer lines. Lang is a lovely player, as anyone can hear from his recordings with Bix Beiderbecke, but he lacks Django's force and new harmonic direction. There is no question that he was an influence on the gypsy, starting out, though Django soon followed his own course. When the Quintet was still a backstage duo jamming at Claridge's listener remarked that they sounded like Venuti and Lang. But, as Stéphane recalled the occasion, 'Django, with his customary frankness, could not help saying that there was nothing to be learned fom Lang.'

In spite of all this, and of weary reminders from readers that comparisons were not only invidious but meaningless, journalistic comparisons were rife. Some were intended as compliments, as when Stéphane was dubbed 'the Venuti of France'. Others were clearly hostile: after a long, passionate encomium to Venuti and Lang, a *Melody Maker* critic dismissed Grappelli and Reinhardt as 'merely averagely competent musicians who happen to play violin and guitar together'.

As far as the violin went, there were more fruitful grounds for comparison with two musicians who played side by side with Stéphane and Django, Eddie South and Michel Warlop. We have seen that South was in Paris for the 1937 Exposition. He had already spent time in Europe in the late twenties, studying the violin both in Paris and Budapest, where he was enthralled by gypsy music. Stéphane's old flatmate Warlop had made a busy if erratic career for himself as musical director arranger as well as violinist. In contrast with Grappelli, both South and Warlop had had extensive classical training. In fact,

---

* Stéphane himself added baritone saxophone to his group for a recording session during the war.

if race prejudice had not prevented him, South would very likely have remained in classical music. Warlop, on the other hand, for all his formidable achievements in the Conservatoire, wanted more than anything to devote himself to jazz. He deeply, almost despairingly, envied the natural ease of Stéphane's playing, his custom-made jazz style. And despite his great talent, Warlop never achieved it. Most unfortunately, he tried artificial means to help him relax – above all, drink. For much of his life he was an alcoholic, and he finally died of it in 1947, at the age of thirty-six. Both because of this pathetic waste and his great talent, an aura surrounds Warlop's name in France. As the critic François Billard told me, 'Nobody knows why he destroyed himself.' But for Charles Delaunay, Warlop's death was a clear suicide of frustration, at being unable to emulate Grappelli.

Biography aside, the musical facts can be assessed in a few recordings. The three men appear together on 'Lady Be Good' with the Quintet. Warlop's chorus is fascinating if unsettling. The effect is of expression under great pressure, struggling to break out into jazz. Part of this may be due to conditions: his nervousness at recording sessions was legendary. Whatever the reason, he seems to throw ideas at the listener pell-mell – repeated notes hacked out, plunging arpeggios, screaming leaps into the top register, with a stiff rhythmic feeling that verges on rushing. Stéphane, by contrast, spins out easy lines, putting together a nice bridge, and Eddie South wraps the solos up with an attractively cagey, languorous chorus that begins with wry double-stops.

In his duets with Stéphane, Warlop sounds more settled, particularly in 'Swinging with Django' and 'Paramount Stomp', but there is still a stiffness, still a sense that he is not fully at home in the language in spite of obvious talent and desire. He attacks boldly, as if trying to overcome the constraints of classical music by simply 'going for it'. Referring to him as 'my poor pal' Stéphane once told a *Down Beat* journalist that he did not think Warlop 'understood the meaning of jazz'. This is not quite fair, as a *Down Beat* reader wrote in subsequently to protest. There are solo Warlop recordings, like the relatively serene 'Taj Mahal', which have real jazz distinction. But he still represents a classic case of how unique an art jazz is, and how paradoxically difficult for such a superbly trained violinist.

Though black and brought up in Chicago, Eddie South had pursued the same kind of formal studies as Warlop, with some of the same effect. When I asked Stéphane if South had classical training, he said, with a small smile, 'Yes; too much.' But he wrote that he admired the American for his 'very clear sound . . . remarkable sense of development and great melodic refinement'. South's style is witty, sweet, now and then almost prim, but marked by both inventiveness and logic. These qualities are well displayed in his two best-known solos with Django, 'Sweet Georgia Brown' and 'Eddie's Blues'. (The latter track is much more convincingly bluesy than 'Stéphane's Blues', which Grappelli treats rather too rhapsodically.)

Stéphane and Eddie's duets, 'Daphne', 'Dinah' and 'Fiddle's Blues', are engagingly informal, with both men playing well and egging each other on, though at times, as at the end of 'Dinah', the proceedings slide into amiable free-for-all. Of course the most famous free-for-all is their recording of the first movement of the Bach double violin concerto – which in fact is two recordings, a 'swing interpretation' and an 'improvisation', two attempts to realize a fancy of Charles Delaunay.

As Delaunay explained it to me, the idea arose from his custom of spending tranquil Sunday mornings writing, and playing nothing but baroque music. He began to feel the rhythmic relationship between baroque and jazz (which had already been perceived by the twenties avant-garde at the Bar Gaya). In particular he found that the introduction to Louis Armstrong's 'Mahogany Hall Stomp' fitted perfectly in tempo and feeling with Bach's Concerto for Two Violins: humming one led automatically to the other. Therefore at the next recording session with Eddie and Stéphane, on 23 November 1937, he suggested 'an experiment: I put the music up on the music stand. They looked at it and said "It's difficult!" . . . I told them, "You do the introduction and then you improvise without the sheet music." But the first time we did that, they were so absorbed by the music they couldn't get out of the reading. So they did the first number like this, reading the music to the end.' It presents a diverting picture, the two jazzmen concentrating on old Bach's lines and getting into it all the same, throwing in jazz embellishments as they go. And the resulting record does have a certain nervous charm.

But Delaunay still did not have what he wanted. Two days later, when the violinists returned to do 'Fiddle's Blues', he had another try. '. . . I said, "We'll do it again. I'm sure you know the number." So they started, and immediately after the first chorus – if I may call that a chorus – I took the music away!" The moment when Delaunay's snatch occurred seems unmistakable: the unprepared fiddlers begin scrambling at once, while Django helpfully churns out his manouche continuo. In fact, outside an anecdotal interest in the panic, this version is less successful that the first, 'straight' one. There are a couple of interesting moments, but Eddie and Stéphane

83

sound mostly at a loss as to what to do. What they wind up doing is the same kind of 'jazzing up' they had done before, but with less security. Still, both records caused a stir, and one critic has called them 'perhaps unfortunately influential' – spawning, as they did, the whole idea of jazz–baroque and Bach plus rhythm section, to be popularized years later by Jacques Loussier and the Swingle Singers.

Not everyone approved of such irreverence: the records were subsequently banned both by the BBC and the Nazis during the Second World War. But Delaunay was very pleased, and at his home in Chantilly he still loves to listen to his Bach double. He acknowleges, however, that Stéphane was not amused. 'No, he said it was crazy – such a perfection cannot go into jazz. Nor Eddie South either – he was ashamed of himself. . . .' In retrospect, however, Stéphane seems to have been of two minds. He told an interviewer in 1975 that he was 'very pleased when somebody had the idea', and even took part of the credit himself. At other times he has called it 'folly' and 'an insult to Bach'. But in 1980 he lent himself to a much more dubious project with similar intent, in his *Brandenburg Boogie* album.

Of course Stéphane's recorded output in the thirties centered around Django and the Quintet, but his session with Bill Coleman (also in November 1937) shows he was perfectly capable of standing out in other company. The four performances feature a more conventional rhythm section – only one guitar (Joseph Reinhardt, giving a firm account of himself), bass and drums. They feel looser than the Quintet, particularly with the influence of the leader's lithe, swinging trumpet. In his duet choruses with Coleman, in the bold harmonic opening of 'Bill Street Blues', the relaxed double-stop riffing of 'Rose Room' and his spirited attack on 'After You've Gone', Stéphane shows he is his own man. Playing with Django had clearly developed his talent and confidence – good training for the war years, on his own in London.

Piccadilly Stomp

Late one morning in the autumn of 1985, sitting comfortably in bed in his favourite London hotel, sporting a red flannel shirt, Stéphane was musing on the course of his life. 'I have lived in obscurity for fifteen years,' he said, 'the light for sixty-two years.' In that long period, the illumination has been brighter at some times than others, but he has never left the scene, and he has never lacked work for long. The light is not fame – Stéphane is universally acknowledged to have no star complex whatever – but a life of security. It is the memory of the dark that drives him, those 'miseries that happened to me as a child'.

They may have loomed afresh in the autumn of 1939. Another war had uprooted him, just as the First World War had separated him from his father and left him to the uncertain mercy of charity. He was ill (a legacy of his early privations), and he was in a foreign land. The group that had brought him success and recognition, and seemed poised to bring still more, had suddenly ceased to exist. He had no work and little knowledge of the British musical scene.

But at the same time he was by no means helpless. He had talent, accomplishment, a reputation and a well-developed instinct for survival. He had friends as well, particularly the

family of Beryl Davis, the teenage singing star who had worked
and recorded with the Quintet and whose father Harry was a
singer and director of the well-known Oscar Rabin band. And
Stéphane could get by in English, though his command of the
language then displayed even more of the tentative charm
which delights his audiences today.

The Musicians' Union saw to it that he received proper
medical treatment, thus earning his gratitude and loyalty. As
for the musical scene, it was not long in finding him. As
Stéphane recalled it to Max Jones, 'One day I had the great
fortune to see pianist Arthur Young on a bike in Bond Street.
Arthur was an old friend of mine, and he asked me to form a
band with him at a place called Hatchett's in Piccadilly, where
I remained four years, in and out.'

Arthur's Young's group, called the Swingtette, was actually
already well ensconced at Hatchett's, but he was very glad to
have Stéphane aboard, and his acquisition made page one news
in the *Melody Maker*. The lead article for 2 December 1939
proclaimed that Young had made 'a big capture' in Stéphane
as a speciality attraction, and that the 'famous French hot
violinist' would be heard nightly, beginning the very next day.
Once again Stéphane had landed on his feet, and what would
be a lifelong special relationship with England had begun. As
he said, 'I always think of England as my second country
because I was welcomed during the war like a brother, and I
will never forget it.'

Hatchett's and the Café de Paris were the two famous dining
and dancing establishments of the day. The musical fare was
social and functional – swing-flavoured, but far from the
rampant impetuosity of the Hot Club Quintet. Max Jones was
a Hatchett's patron from time to time, though the prices were
a bit steeper than a young jazz enthusiast could afford too
often. 'It was very much polite swing for dancing. It was West
End music; it wasn't an all-out jazz gig. But it was written up
as one of the most stylish groups in town, and was about as
near to live jazz as you could hear in a public restaurant.'

Stéphane and the Hatchett's band went into the studio quite
regularly, the first session taking place on 29 December, less
than a month after he had joined them. The records reveal a
tidy unit of around ten men plus a vocalist – good musicians,
though Max's frank admission that 'in some cases it was corny'
is quite true. The performances guaranteed a certain amount
of corn simply because of the presence of the 'novachord', an
instrument much loved by Arthur Young and which provided
the distinctive sound of the Swingtette. It was a nasal electric
organ, a kind of proto-synthesizer, which wormed its reedy

way into all the band's arrangements, creating an infallibly bilious effect.

But offsetting the corn was Stéphane, as Max Jones was well aware at the time: 'In almost every case he is the outstanding jazz musician on those records, the one player who seemed to register on every track that he played.' As might be expected, he does not play with the abandon that characterized his work with the Quintet, where abandon was of the essence, but the elegance, the well-turned lines, the surprises and musical interest have their old distinction. As Coleridge Goode, the excellent bass player who would soon record with him, said, Stéphane 'was the only real violin player about . . . playing jazz, and in his style – he was on his own really.' He was reason enough for jazz fans to go to Hatchett's and mingle with the smart set, which now of course included a high proportion of officers and their wives.

But it was not long before going anywhere became problematic. By the summer of 1940 the phoney war was over and the Battle of Britain had begun. Though it would reach its deadliest level in September, an early attack injured Arthur Young, compelling him to withdraw from Hatchett's. The novachord was entrusted to the band's pianist; he was replaced on piano by a blind twenty-year-old named George Shearing, for whom a great future had already been predicted by the *Melody Maker* in 1937. Stéphane immediately recognized he now had an associate of his own quality. Indeed, he had noticed him before, in 1939. He has mentioned coming across Shearing playing accordion in a Battersea pub. An item in the *Melody Maker* chronicles another meeting, just before the outbreak of war at a party given for the Quintet at a club called the Nut House, where Shearing was the pianist. The festivities included a jam session, and the paper reported that George was 'playing some very interesting choruses with a vigorous left hand and using a trick of working in the treble with both hands, which made Stéphane Grappelly stop and listen with both ears bent.' The double-handed reference sounds like an early version of the block chords that would identify Shearing's popular quintet in America after the war. For the present, Stéphane's attentiveness was the basis for a partnership that would last while Shearing was in Britain.

Stéphane's first British record date under his own name occurred on 30 July 1940, producing a spritely arrangement of 'After You've Gone' for a second violin, vibes and harp plus rhythm section, with clean, swinging solos from the leader and Shearing. A session in February 1941 also shows Stéphane in somewhat experimental mood, this time choosing a backing of string quartet plus harp, vibes and rhythm. It is graceful 'light music', with additional interest when the leader and the pianist are on, which is no doubt what the mood of the time required. As Stéphane has said, 'In the war people liked to amuse themselves,' and by 1941, with the blitz at its worst, people were seeking what amusement they could. Going out was perilous, but so was staying at home. The clubs and cinemas went on during the raids and the blackouts, and clients took their chances, sometimes with disastrous consequences. In March 1941, a bomb destroyed the Café de Paris, killing, among others, its manager and several of the band.

Enemy action was not the only hazard. Max Jones remembers visiting Hatchett's with the streets full of shrapnel and going home to find that more shrapnel had punctured his roof. A tin helmet became part of the costume of any sensibly dressed *bon viveur*, which put a crimp in one's style, as well as emphasizing the constant risk. Max says, 'I didn't want to go out socializing with a tin hat on, but I think it was foolish not to go out with some protection. Because every time there was a raid, it wasn't what *they* did, it was our stuff going up – and what goes up wants to come down. So it wasn't a time for people thinking "We're going out to enjoy Stéphane Grappelli," or anyone else. People stayed at home in their shelter.'

Yet the bands played on. To Stéphane it seemed that the night raids were timed to coincide with the musicians' appearance on the stand: 'Always that bloody blitz started when we started.' Sometimes terror engendered macabre humour. Stéphane remembered accompanying a girl singing 'As Time Goes By': as the bombs came down, her vibrato got wider and wider, her voice out of control with fear. Another time, the bombs started to drop while he and George were in the middle of a set. 'I didn't want to disturb George, who was playing a solo, so I asked the manager of the club if we should stop. "Keep playing forever!" he shouted, and I didn't dare go because he had our cheque!'

After work, with the blackout in force, Shearing's disability turned into an advantage, as he guided Stéphane through the pitch-dark streets. But no one was really safe from the common danger. As Stéphane had said, the bombs – and later the rockets – could drop anywhere, and he suffered the kind of loss that afflicted so many in Britain when a woman with whom he had a close relationship was killed by a bomb.

However, in the late summer of 1941, Stephane's health put him in more immediate jeopardy than the Nazi planes. He was hospitalized and operated on for a kidney ailment and, as the

Melody Maker reported in 20 September 1941, his condition
had given more than a little cause for concern: 'Stéphane had
to undergo two operations inside a fortnight. After the second
operation, with a temperature of 105, he had seven doctors
around his bed, fighting for his life.' But the paper could also
reassure its readers than 'this great fiddle stylist is slowly but
surely taking the road to recovery, although it will be a long
time before he is in harness again.'

Dr Jack Harrisson, whom Stéphane had met at Hatchett's,
saw that he was well looked after, and the two men became
close friends. During Stéphane's convalescence, Dr Harrisson
and his wife Audrey invited him to their home in Devon. He
fell in love with that beautiful part of England, both for itself
and for its tranquil contrast to the danger and confusion of
London. He began house-hunting and soon found a cottage
not far from the Harrissons, in the village of Lustleigh. It was
called Underwood, and, when he resumed work, Stéphane
commuted to it as often as he could. As Audrey Harrisson
recalled in 1986, 'He would dash back and forth to London or
wherever he was playing. I seem to remember he had an old
Citroën, or my husband would go and pick him up at the
station.'

Stéphane's fondness for traditional elegance had manifested
itself as soon as he could indulge it. He furnished the house
with taste and scrupulous care. Mrs Harrisson remembers it
'filled with the most wonderful furniture and antiques'. To
make sure that things were properly attended to, even in his
absence, he installed a housekeeper who lived at Underwood
full-time – 'Mrs Coles, who just died a couple of years ago,
aged about ninety-nine!'

For Stéphane, the proximity of the Harrissons was one of
the amenities of the neighbourhood. He had a warm affection
for them both, and for Dr Harrisson in particular, as his wife
affirms: 'They were great friends, though completely different.
They were both very musical. Stéphane would come and play
our Bechstein, and I've never known a piece of music you
could ask for that he didn't know. He could play any piece,
even ones you couldn't name, if you just hummed or tapped
out a few bars.' Stéphane commemorated his happy times at
the Harrissons' with a piece named after their home, 'Yellow
House Stomp', which he scribbled down on a table cloth, while
lunching there.

They met in London as well, at Hatchett's, and the couple
invariably found Grappelli excellent company. 'He was delightful, very witty and amusing. I remember going to a French
restaurant where Stéphane pretended he couldn't read the

menu – '"I don't understand thees French . . ." Then for dessert, because of the war, there was a choice of either cheese or chocolate ice. Stéphane said to my husband, "You have the Louis Armstrong, I have the Fats Waller."'

'He used to tell a story about Django. They were in the country, walking through a farmyard one night, and Django hadn't been in England very long. He pointed up in the sky and said, "Look, they have a moon here, too." And then he caught a chicken and wrung its neck. "For supper," he said.'

In the years after the war, Stéphane continued to see the Harrissons regularly. 'He's a gorgeous personality, and his great success hasn't changed him a bit. When my husband died three years ago, I rang Stéphane. Because of touring he couldn't come to the funeral, but he said, "In my concert I will play 'Someone to Watch Over *You*'." And the next time he was over here, a friend of mine from Devon happened to hear him at Croydon, at the Fairfield Hall. During the programme he announced, "This is the first time I have played in England since a dear friend of mine died – Dr Harrisson, and for him I would like to play 'Someone to Watch Over You'." That was rather nice. And he still sends cards from wherever he is, signed "With affection, my darling Audrey, Stéphane".'

By the middle of the war Stéphane was both quite settled in England, which he loved, and on the move professionally. It is a Grappelli principle that 'musicians don't like to stay in one place too long,' and from the latter part of 1942 he was often more out of Hatchett's than in. He was doing increasingly well under his own name, broadcasting – a BBC studio in Bangor, Wales, was relatively handy from Devon – recording and playing with his own group. His band of course included George Shearing. It also frequently included Denny Wright, then an up-and-coming English guitarist who would star with the Diz Disley trio during Stéphane's resurgence thirty years later. As a teenager, Denny, like all other guitarists, had been mesmerized by Django, taking all the gypsy's solos off the Quintet records. But he had not been deaf to what else was going on: 'I wasn't just listening to Django. I was listening to Joseph and the other guy with them, and the wrong notes Louis Vola was playing. I'd listen to Stéphane. Django would make hard work of some things, but Stéphane would be so easy. You can hear it. There aren't many records where Django doesn't goof somewhere . . . Half the time you hear a goof, and you never hear one from Stéphane. You listen to it, and it's like liquid gold coming off.'

Surprisingly, since Django had a reputation as a player far

ahead of his time, Denny felt Stéphane was more remarkable in that respect. 'Let's be honest – Stéphane was much more modern than Django. Oh, yeah. Django thought 'modern' meant up half a tone and then down again. And the touch of flamenco, the Spanish influence. But with Stéphane it's entirely different. He had Ravel, Debussy. Harmonically he was more modern: Stéphane was more modern even in those days than Django was in 1953.'

For Denny Wright, Stéphane's exposure to George Shearing during the war was a liberation, freeing musical tendencies which the Quintet, with its monolithic basic accompaniment, had somewhat limited. 'His playing improved no end, because he was no longer tied to six bars of G7 and 2 bars of G. With Shearing, all of a sudden he got these beautiful full chords coming out behind him, changing key all over the place. And Stéphane's got a fantastic ear anyway, and suddenly he was hearing things he'd never heard before. And he just went with him.'

Of course Grappelli's response was just one more manifestation of his continuing absorption in music's harmonic aspect. However, his pleasure at the possibilities offered by Shearing's piano did not mean that he jettisoned the Hot Club tradition altogether. He and George did record a quite modern-sounding session with guitar, bass and drums in April 1941, but the rest of his work featured two guitars. This not only increased the firmness of the rhythmic pulse, but made it possible to evoke the Hot Club, a useful commercial asset in live performance.

Live performance, all over Britain, occupied Stéphane for much of the rest of the war. (His agent was Lew Grade, destined like his client for much bigger things.) He and the group played at military installations – bases and hospitals – and theatres, as part of a variety bill. Sometimes playing for the troops involved them more directly in the war than they had counted on. As they were being taken to an airbase near Ipswich for a concert, a dogfight raged overhead. Before they arrived, they had to make a stop to pick up a German pilot who had just bailed out of his disabled plane.

Variety was usually calmer. A poster from the Hippodrome in Birmingham, advertising a show in March 1943, gives the typical flavour. Described as 'the world's greatest swing violinist', Stéphane and 'his Hot Club Sextet' share top of the bill with his old Paris acquaintance Adelaide Hall, 'the crooning blackbird'. Supporting them are a cartoonist, a tramp cyclist, a cowboy humourist who also acts as MC, a 'character comedian', an American dance team and a vocal group. Denny Wright says the Sextet's part of the show always wound up with a Hot Club medley, the two guitars trying to stir up the old clamour. But as far as solos went, there was nothing for guitars at all. . . . The most I ever got with Stéphane was a middle eight bars. The other guitar player got nothing. . . . He was really playing with George Shearing.' Restlessness with unrelieved four-to-the-bar forced Denny at last to give notice. But he enjoyed the job, since the music was good and George Shearing was an old friend. They roomed together and settled grievances with pillow-fights in the dark, which George always won.

On the whole, Stéphane himself stayed aloof from palsiness, at least with the band. However, while doing a week in Dundee, he dropped in on a film called 'Reveille with Beverly', which included a sequence in which Frank Sinatra, backed by six violinists and six pianists, all women, sang 'Night and Day'. Stéphane was so enthralled by Sinatra's performance, and the arrangement, that he went back every afternoon just for that segment – taking George Shearing with him. 'The *location-naire* must have thought we were crazy. We turned up every day at five-ten – with George, blind, on my arm – and left at five-twenty!'

But most of the time Stéphane went off on his own expeditions, which no doubt included hunting for antiques for Underwood. He roomed alone and did not usually go to the pub. He wasn't unpleasant at all, just self-contained. Sometimes he would mention his former partner, and Denny Wright 'got the impression then that he really didn't like Django – not so much Django as he didn't like gypsies.'

However, it was what Stéphane called 'the extraordinary knowledge of the gypsies' that gave him the only information he received about Django during the war. Out of curiosity he once visited a gypsy encampment near Underwood and enquired about the guitarist. 'To my surprise they knew of me and knew the whereabouts of Django; he was in Lyons at the time, they told me.' Recalling the episode in the *Melody Maker*, Stéphane did not go on to say whether the gypsies also told him that Django had spent the war becoming the biggest thing in French show business, on a par with Maurice Chevalier. He was a kind of symbol, like jazz itself. Proscribed by the Nazis as 'decadent', the music was embraced by the French as an expression of the freedom the Occupation denied them. Django, as the greatest French jazzman, was celebrated everywhere and commanded huge fees.

On his side of the channel, if Stéphane had not achieved super-stardom, he had certainly made himself a comfortable and secure existence. Indeed, somewhat guiltily (in view of the war) he has called the period 'maybe the best five years of my life.' He was happy in England. He had a home and friends, professional status that guaranteed him steady work, and a musical association that kept him stimulated. Things were very much the way he liked them. The approach of the end of the war was bound to raise questions – principally, what, if anything, was he going to do about Django?

Nuages

As far as the French were concerned, the Hot Club Quintet had existed all through the war. In October 1940, it had made its first records with Django as sole leader. Like Stéphane, he made no attempt to replace his absent partner; he too opted for a new and more flexible sound. He could have gotten another violinist – Michel Warlop was more or less about – but he chose the young clarinettist Hubert Rostaing. To vary the rhythmic feeling, Pierre Fouad came in on drums and the second rhythm guitar dropped out, leaving only Joseph. The new group had a cooler timbre, but, propelled by Django and boosted by patriotic sentiment, it achieved immense success. Nevertheless, the Grappelli–Reinhardt union was still classic, and both men felt a natural obligation at least to re-examine it. Differences aside, they shared an undeniable bond, based on having inspired each other to the best music they were capable of.

According to Charles Delaunay, a reunion was proposed in a phone call to him from Stéphane in October 1945 (during which Delaunay was surprised to discern a slight English accent in Grappelli's French). In his biography of Django, Delaunay describes a delighted conversation between the guitarist and violinist, but recalling the event to me, he said they did not speak. Shortly thereafter, arrangements were made and, at the end of the following January, Django, Naguine and their infant son Babik left Paris for London with Delaunay. The Reinhardts evidently intended a long stay: they had divided all their belongings among their relatives, and Naguine had even left Babik's pram behind.

On the evening of 26 January, they arrived at Stéphane's very comfortable (and remarkably inexpensive) flat at the Athenaeum, overlooking Green Park. The violinist was working at Hatchett's, so the long-awaited reunion had to wait a few more hours. But when it came, it was fittingly emotional. (As if the occasion were not sufficiently charged, the 26th was Stéphane's birthday.) When at last, after midnight, Stéphane opened the door, he and Django just looked at each other, speechless. As Delaunay recalled the scene, 'There they were; they couldn't say a word. Then Stéphane opened his case, took out his violin and began to play the "Marseillaise", and Django immediately joined in. They couldn't speak.' The "Marseillaise" was obviously a natural choice, particularly for the exiled Stéphane, who had been deeply moved early in the war when he heard the anthem while in hospital, after an address by Churchill affirming Britain's solidarity with France. But for both of them the moment was, as Delaunay said, 'a wonder', and the perfect meeting for these two long-separated patriots of French music. After that, there were embraces, cries of 'Mon frère!', and a jam session till dawn.

The enterprising Delaunay quickly set up a recording session with some of Stéphane's English colleagues, including Coleridge Goode, his regular bassist on broadcasts. Coleridge was aware of the allowances that had to be made for the gypsy star. 'Once you got Django to the studio you were all right, but times had to be a little bit fluid to accommodate him. The session had to be pretty businesslike, because you had to get on with it while he was sort of in the mood . . . But it certainly was a great session, and it went extremely well.'

The records largely bear him out. At first hearing, the partners seem to have taken up where they had left off. In the two sessions on 31 January and 1 February, they did swinging standards – 'Liza', 'Django's Tiger' (a version of 'Tiger Rag'); ballads – 'Embraceable You', 'Love's Melody'; two of Django's wartime hits – 'Belleville' and 'Nuages'; and, at Delaunay's behest, a recreation of their spontaneous 'Marseillaise'. (Though this was cautiously re-titled 'Echoes of France', it still displeased French officialdom and indeed Stéphane maintains the original master was destroyed.) Both men are in excellent form, sounding strong and confident, and smoother than in some of the pre-war alliances. The sonority is still well-matched, with the angularity of Django's attack balanced by Stéphane's suavity, and they both swing, separately and together.

Yet something seems to be missing. Perhaps the guitar and bass backing does begin to feel repetitive, but certainly through no fault of the English players, who give distinguished support (and it is a pleasure to hear Coleridge playing swinging four-beat bass lines). Perhaps Stéphane, and Django too, had moved on from the kind of stimulation that feeling could give them, needing something more supple and suggestive. It had been six and a half years since the classic Quintet had ceased, and they had both had quite different musical associations since. The musical scene had changed as well. Though war conditions had imposed an artificial check on contact with the latest developments from America, it was inevitable that the music and its players would evolve. But perhaps these impressions contain something of hindsight, the knowledge that the old Quintet could not be recreated.

In any case, the shape of the immediate future was determined by Django's sudden illness. He went into hospital, the prospective tour and broadcasts were cancelled and, after a period of convalescence, he returned to France. As Delaunay says in the biography, 'the turn of events put paid to his expectations in England'; but they need not have ended all plans to refloat the Quintet. As Max Jones saw it, the causes were more basic. 'I did have a feeling that Reinhardt's first important thing was to return to France, to get out of England. I'm quite sure that I got the impression he didn't like it here. It was cold, and he couldn't speak. Several stories got around – he'd lost his guitar, [or] didn't want to play it. And then I think that everything was bother. I got the impression that he would have continued if Steph had gone to France and done it there.'

But Stéphane, for his part, did not seem disposed. 'I didn't get a very strong impression then that Stéphane really wanted to get the Quintet together. I think it was a commercial idea that was pushed on him by an agent. . . . So Steph was willing, as he always is, like any good player. But when for some reason they didn't get on or whatever, he just proceeded on his own, with the various bands. He was constantly playing.'

Indeed Stéphane told me the reunion was basically Delaunay's idea. In his memorial articles on the gypsy in the *Melody Maker*, Stéphane confessed that, after the war, 'I found another Django, mature, and yet more abrupt than ever. I was astonished at how changed he was.' Perhaps the warmth of their re-association had cooled somewhat. Perhaps it was bound to. Coleridge Goode was not alone in observing the old truth: 'Relations between them were always a bit odd, I think, because Stéphane was very sophisticated, and Django the complete opposite.' But Delaunay felt a more profound division. After the war, he told me, 'something was broken between them.'

Certainly Django had every reason to be more Django than ever. His wartime status satisfied almost all his fantasies, and he was going to have a chance to realize his greatest dream of all, to conquer America. What was more, he was being sponsored by the incomparable Duke Ellington, with whose band he would tour the country. He returned to London in October, en route to the States, full of grandiose prospects and childlike visions. The *Melody Maker* reported that Ellington was only the beginning: 'He intends staying in the USA for three years, and also hopes to clinch movie contracts with two well-known film companies.' How much does Gary Cooper get? For Django, Hollywood was his caravan's ultimate destination.

But he felt uneasy, too. Whatever his fantasies, he knew he would be on his own in a new world where the peasants did not even speak French. But his playing was as sensational as ever. Coleridge Goode remembers him sitting in at the Caribbean Club: 'My God, it was just fantastic.' At the same time, Django suggested he accompany him to the States. 'He said, "Why don't you come with me?" and that kind of thing.' Django and Stéphane got together and went out jamming, and, as usual, despite their differences, Django confided in his partner. 'Always in the difficult times he was there with me. He came to see me and he was a bit annoyed. First, he was afraid to take the plane, and he wanted me to go with him. He said, "I can't move, you see."'

In the event, the tour was a disappointment. Playing on an unfamiliar – and amplified – guitar (he had left his own behind assuming a guitar manufacturer would give him one), he received good notices on the road but suffered a debâcle at Carnegie Hall, where he almost missed one of his two concerts altogether. The critics were lukewarm, Leonard Feather, for instance, writing that Django could not 'hold his own as an all-round musician or as a jazz musician' with the top American guitarists. He played a month at Café Society and, when no other work turned up, he came home. The experience might not have been a total disaster, but for someone with Django's pride, it was close enough. Stéphane is not alone in seeing it as the beginning of the gypsy's decline: 'He was so affected by his flop in America, he was so affected.'

* * *

Django's difficulties were compounded by the fact that American musicians were speaking a new language which took Europeans, cut off by six years of war, completely by surprise. Bebop, pioneered by Charlie Parker and Dizzy Gillespie and the young players around them, created, according to Charles Delaunay, 'a real revolution in the mind; it turned the world upside down'. In Britain, Coleridge Goode was stunned by the stage of development the new form had already achieved: 'Suddenly you were presented with this thing which was so *mature*; it was all there. Not sort of growing up with it from the start to the state that it arrived in, you were hit with this thing – the tone, the harmonic structure and so on, and the terrific technique of the guys doing it. It was really amazing stuff.'

Stéphane, from a relatively secure position that linked jazz and entertainment, felt the same way: 'I must admit that we were all a bit disoriented.' And yet, as always, it was not long before he adapted at least some of the characteristics of the new style to his own milieu. In late 1946 he and a handpicked quintet – George Shearing and Coleridge, Dave Goldberg on guitar and Ray Ellington on drums – made a short film which gives a vintage view both of a Grappelli band at work and the musical climate of the time. They are all immaculately dinner-jacketed, presented in a set simulating the bandstand of a posh club. The film opens with a bit of Stéphane's theme song, 'The Stéphane Blues' – in fact an eight-bar adaptation of the blues changes, rhapsodic, romantic and a little gypsyish. The announcer introduces Stéphane as 'the world-famous French violinst and composer' and says his band is 'recognized as one of the greatest exponents of modern swing music'.

They began with 'Piccadilly Stomp', a pre-war Grappelli composition, which nevertheless receives a bright, boppish treatment, with the rhythm light and firm, and long-lined solos. The second piece is 'Wendy', written by Stéphane in honour of George Shearing's daughter, a pretty tune that the violinist reads beautifully. Throughout the set, there is no obvious showmanship, but everyone beams at the camera and reacts warmly to each other, much as they must have played to a live audience. This is particularly noticeable in 'Sweet Georgia Brown', a Stéphane standby updated to feature an oo–bop–sh–bam style vocal from Ray Ellington, who splits a chorus with Coleridge's singing and bowing à la Slam Stewart. At the end of the tune, Stéphane ever-so-casually twirls his fiddle, and the announcer observes, 'I hope drummer Ray Ellington feels better now, having got all that rebop off his chest.' The set concludes with what is described as 'one of

Stéphane Grappelli's best known compositions', 'Eveline', obviously written in honour of his own daughter.

The group comes across as slick, musical and modern,
paying attention both to what they play and to their audience,
appealing to their listeners as Stéphane has always done,
simply by communicating the group's own natural pleasure.
As the announcer says, bringing on 'The Stéphane Blues' at
the end, 'Well, these boys certainly seem to enjoy themselves'
– with some rebop, some swing, some elegant sentiment,
something for every sophisticated taste, impeccably done.

Like many others, Coleridge Goode sums up Stéphane's
musicianship as 'immaculate'. His ability and reliability gave
him the range for all kinds of work. Jazz was his first love, but
he could fit into any musical setting. In the spring of 1947, he
and George Shearing (who had just come back from a successful trip to America, where he would soon return to make a
famous career) teamed up for a tour of the variety halls as a duo.
The act was a great success, as the *Melody Maker* reported, with
the two 'wizards of *le jazz hot*' replacing their normal repertoire
with 'tunes they think the music-hall patrons will like'. The
reviewer was aware of possible cries of 'commercialism', but
had no apologies. 'Perhaps it will hurt some of their fans to
hear them trot out street-corner stuff like "The Old Lamp-
lighter" and "Open the Door, Richard", but it isn't *what* you
play, it's the way you play it that counts; and these two fine
artists are now winning the praise of variety-goers as they have
enchanted swing-addicts.' For him, the duo was 'undeniably
exquisite . . . so expressive and effortless', and the biggest hit
was 'their piano-duet, a sparkling bit of work which thoroughly
delighted the crowd'.

A month earlier, in March, Stéphane had made a brief visit
to Paris. The *Melody Maker* said he was there 'sounding the
French cabarets with a view to taking a British band over. . . .'
It also reported that he visited Django, who had a big band
working at Le Boeuf sur Le Toit, where Stéphane 'was given
a gigantic reception'. No doubt encouraged, the Quintet was
reassembled to record four sides and discuss future arrangements, but the violinist's busy schedule made that impossible
for the moment. It was not until 16 November 1947 that a
public reunion of the original Hot Club Quintet took place in
Paris's Salle Pleyel. Of course it promised to be a great occasion,
since Stéphane had been largely absent from Paris, and Django
had made his appearances with other combinations.

They were received affectionately, but again something was
missing. *Jazz Hot*'s review summed it up: 'Django has certainly
not played so well in public for many years. Some of his choruses

recalled the splendid improviser we once knew so well. . . . And yet somehow the old flame, the old urge to create seems to have left him. . . .' The Quintet was booked for the ABC in February, but their appearance was overshadowed by the furore attending the arrival in Paris of Dizzy Gillespie and his big band. The bebop controversy totally preoccupied jazz circles. Charles Delaunay and Hugues Panassié were locked in polemical combat over the issue, which would divide them forever and separate *Jazz Hot* (Delaunay) from the Hot Clubs (Panassié). In this passionate atmosphere, yesterday's novelties were definitely *vieux jeu*. Indeed, the promoters of the first International Jazz Festival at Nice, with groups picked to represent each country, 'overlooked' the Hot Club Quintet, only including them at the last moment when the mayor of Nice intervened. The Festival revealed that bop was not the only vogue of the day. The French artist making the biggest impact was Claude Luter, a leading exponent of trad, pure neo-New Orleans jazz. Henceforth, trad and bebop divided the jazz world between them. There was no third alternative, and players of the Quintet's generation found themselves without a niche.

The group responded by going to England, where audiences (if not always critics) appreciated them best. But even here there was a jinx at work. Within hours of their arrival, thieves made off with the luggage of Django, bassist Emmanuel Soudieux and second guitarist Challin Ferret. Django took the loss with hilarious equanimity, but the rhythm section, including his brother, knew an omen when they saw one and returned to Paris in short order. But after this shaky start, the tour went ahead quite successfully with three British players and was extended for a month in Scandinavia.*

That, however, was the last stand of the old line-up. Django went back to Paris and declining work, but Stéphane went there in September as leader of a twelve-piece band at the swank Sa Majesté night club, remaining through November. It was the kind of job that would have been impossible for Django, even if had wanted it, requiring not only skill but charm, flexibility and regular attendance. It suited Stéphane's professionalism perfectly. But he was still a jazz musician, and he welcomed the offer of a series of engagements in Italy, in January and February 1949, with Django.

---

* Denny Wright filled in on rhythm guitar for a couple of London concerts and got a taste of Django's superiority complex. 'He found out I'd played guitar with Stéphane during the war, and on the first tune we did he ripped through about seven choruses, just brilliant, and then looked at me, like, "Follow *that*."'

They were going as soloists, on their own, to play with local rhythm sections in Rome and Milan, with a date in between to open a cinema in Naples. At the Roman club, the Rupe Tarpea, they performed both for dancing and as a featured cabaret act. Things went well enough, though their rhythm section of piano, bass and drums was only adequate, and Django was less than happy with them. Nevertheless it was this group that would provide the backing for the final Reinhardt–Grappelli recordings. A local promoter arranged a number of sessions and the duo made a series of sixty-eight sides.

Like all their post-war recordings, there is something puzzling about them. There is no question that these are major league soloists, yet there is an incompleteness in the performances. They seem merely thrown off, which undoubtedly they were, but even so Stéphane and Django do not sound as if they are listening to each other. Individually Stéphane appears the more settled of the two, straining less and producing solos of greater clarity and shape. Django's power is still evident, but sometimes it seems more aggressive than penetrating. There is a fitful quality to his playing, as if he doesn't know quite what he is after. His accompaniments occasionally intrude (as they did in the '47–48 Quintet recordings as well), as if he were just throwing in plangent chords in an attempt to stir things up.

He also seems the more self-consciously aware of bop, using licks from the new idiom more frequently than Stéphane. Both of them are au fait with what has been going on in jazz: the Rome version of 'What is This Thing Called Love?' uses the bop line 'Hot House' as an out-chorus, and in a little over a year they recorded the boppers' national anthem, 'How High the Moon', four times. But Stéphane seems more to keep his own counsel. He employs much of his old vocabulary, but his playing has expanded, grown more fluent. It is centered, but it is not stale. Django, by contrast, though his immense talent is evident, is more abrupt, more obviously looking for something. As a duo, the difference between the feeling of the thirties and that of the forties is clear in their re-recordings of earlier material, which, generally speaking, are not improvements. The post-war works often feature excellent solos, but they do not have the pre-war freshness and eagerness. In the original Quintet tracks, Django and Stéphane were looking for something together, and the same thing.

After they separated following the Italian tour, Django went back to Paris and the electric guitar, with which he hoped to reclaim his thunder from the upstarts. The results were erratic because, as Stéphane said, 'He was playing it with the enormous strength he used on the acoustic guitar' – strength so enormous he would gradually bend an instrument out of shape. Also, Django took a childish delight in the simple volume he could achieve with his amplifier, sometimes turning it all the way up regardless of distortion, feedback or anything else.

But no matter what he played, as Svend Asmussen said, 'You could still hear it was Django.' The gift was still manifest; the obstacle was in his mind. As a gypsy and a genius, Django had grown up a creature of pure ego, like a favoured child, believing in a world of desire that would respond to his will. His effortless talent and the adulation it brought him were the proof of it. He played what he wanted, got what he wanted, was who he was. Music was not a *métier*, as it was for Stephane, a matter of love and money, a life and a living, something you worked at. For Django it was a normal condition, something you could do successfully whenever you felt like it. When he felt like doing something else – painting, billiards, fishing – he did that, with the same carefree absorption. It was his confidence in this customary order of things that his American failure had undermined, because he had done what he wanted without the expected success. He had been Django and no one much cared.

Thus his difficulty was not a question of framing a new musical style, but of replacing a world. What he did, in fact, was simply play less and less, and withdraw from the peasant world that had rejected him. That he could still play brilliantly was demonstrated in the early months of 1951, when he starred at the Club St Germain with a band of young musicians. He was on time for work every night, too, which he ensured by moving in, with Naguine and Babik, to the Hotel Montana right across the street. Coleridge Goode went to see him, and found Django had reduced his life to basic terms: 'He was in bed. You know, he stayed in bed, got up and went down and did his thing, came back and went to bed.'

Earlier, Coleridge had said Django's 'rough time' in America was due to his being 'such a free spirit' when he had to be 'cut and dried. . . . And he's not like that, not at all. He's completely inspirational. He does something when he's inspired: he does it, you see? If he's not, he doesn't want to know!' Even after his success at the Club St Germain, all Django was inspired to do was retreat to his little house on the banks of the Seine, play billiards and fish. There were occasional appearances, a few new compositions, but when Stéphane came from London in February 1953, bearing an offer to reform the Quintet for a tour of America, no one could say where the guitarist was. He had severed his ties with most people, including Charles Delaunay.

He told Naguine that no one understood him any more, that luck was against him. But in middle age his fatal innocence was finally catching up with him. As the French writer Yves Salgues put it, 'He never wanted to take the trouble to learn how to live.' Once again everything was bother – including Naguine's efforts to get him to see a doctor, the last thing a gypsy wanted, despite recurrent headaches and stiffness in his hands.

Django died suddenly of a stroke on 16 May 1953, after an afternoon's fishing. Charles Delaunay felt it 'the perfect end for Django.' Though saddened, he himself had suffered too often from the guitarist's whims to be really shattered by his passing. For his part, Stéphane was not surprised. 'I knew, more or less . . . I was not expecting him to die, but I thought it was the end of his career.' Speaking of another gifted player who died young, a veteran American jazzman once observed, 'He didn't take care of business, and baby, you've *got* to take care of business.' It was a lesson Django never learned: that Stéphane learned early and never forgot.

After You've Gone

As the pages of the *Melody Maker* reveal, the British music business in the late forties was more than a little precarious. Though the war was won, nationwide austerity meant money was still tight. Big bands were on the wane, partly through economics, partly through public boredom with the same old sound. Attendance at variety was declining, a trend which, as everybody could tell, the growing popularity of television would only increase. There were articles on 'the facts behind the slump', a 'slump symposium'. It was no better in France. After a visit to Paris, a British singer, while envying the 'stupendous personality-plus that every French man and woman seems to possess', reported it made no practical difference: 'business itself is worse than here. I heard that French bandleaders were having to sit in with other bands to make a living.' And from further afield a headline proclaimed 'Panic in States as Big Bands Fold Up', including among them names as big as Goodman, Shaw and James.

And of course the battle between the ancients and moderns, between trad and bop continued. Swing players with impeccable credentials found themselves accused on the one hand of impurity – having fallen from the state of grace that existed in

New Orleans – or reaction – resisting the wave of the future embodied in the music of Bird and Diz.

They were hard and tricky times. Yet, while Django had been dreaming and brooding on the banks of the Seine, Stéphane had been working harder than ever. Indeed Max Jones believed his career 'really took off a bit' after the war. Part of it was the little flutter of excitement provoked by the Quintet's reunion: a reviewer hearing Stéphane on the radio opined that 'the French fiddle wizard [was] inspired by his association with Django Reinhardt'. But mainly he made his opportunities himself, by professionalism and steady application of his talent. George Shearing's departure for the States had not slowed him down. As his new pianist he had recruited a friend of Shearing's, Alan Clare, who for twenty-five years, off and on, would provide rich harmonic patterns for the violinist to explore.

After Stéphane's return from his last engagement with Django, he opened at the exclusive Milroy Club in London's Mayfair, in May 1949, leading an eight-piece band. It was Sa Majesté all over again, with a line-up of three violins, two reeds, piano, drums, electric guitar and a singing bassist. To Max Jones and his wife Betty, the Milroy represented café society much more than a restaurant like Hatchett's. Max saw it as 'a pretty good up-market gig, and I think Stéphane could play what he wanted. It wasn't in any sense jazz. . . . You didn't have a jazz market; in such a place you never had. You could have a stylish band. I don't think the patrons were jazz-conscious, but they had some money.' For Betty it was 'the in thing to do: they admired musicians', and Max agreed that the Milroy crowd were 'the sort of beautiful people of the period, and their tastes could stretch. Of course they'd all heard Glenn Miller, and it was that sort of band, a swing band. . . . I don't know how Stéphane felt about all that. I don't think he bothered much.'

Probably he didn't bother, outside of assuring that he kept the customers happy. He played well for the people, whether they were jazz fans or not, whether he played jazz or not. Meanwhile, what was considered real jazz was going on elsewhere, with a different clientele. Trumpeter Humphrey Lyttelton was just beginning to make a reputation, and, as he told me, 'My generation of musicians really didn't have any contact with players like Stéphane. It was a transition time for jazz. I was part of the New Orleans trad revival; he was playing at those posh clubs with the funny names. . . . Our paths never crossed. Our audience were art students who would come to places like the 100 Club and throw themselves around.

They would have been thrown out at Hatchett's or the Astor.'

Thirty years later, of course, people would be packing the 100 to bob and weave to Stéphane and Diz Disley, but the violinist's post-war employers were not having any of that. Max concurred with Humph: 'Yeah, we weren't allowed in. They'd take one look at you and see you didn't have the bread. I could've got in but mostly it was in the daytime, to see the manager. . . . These were people who wore evening dress in the *daytime*.' 'Bloody crooks and gamblers,' Betty added darkly, 'ponces and people like that.'

Obviously no place for a Methodist. A diverting glimpse of this kind of night life, and Stéphane at work in it, appears in *The Flamingo Affair*, a feature film of 1948 (Stéphane appeared in two other forties features, *Time Flies*, 1944, and *The Lisbon Story*, 1945). In the film, an impecunious war veteran gets mixed up with a callous femme fatale with underworld connections. One of her regular haunts is a club she languidly describes as 'the highest of the low'. Two bands alternate in it: the kind of strings, horns and rhythm outfit in residence at the Milroy, and the characteristically Stéphane Grappelli quintet of Stéphane's short film, with George Shearing and Coleridge Goode. The group plays for the well-heeled patrons, and at the end of their number, Stéphane, with an arch glance at the camera, gives his fiddle the rakish twirl we have seen before. Later, beaming, he delivers a short bit of expert schmaltz at the *demi-mondaine*'s table.

Such a milieu requires a form of swank busking, and Stéphane obviously excels at it. Whatever the warring jazz factions thought of him, his status as an attractive musical personality was demonstrated when he was invited to appear in a revue at the Saville theatre also featuring Yves Montand. This was only a month after his opening at the Milroy, and for the run of the show he would go from his stint at the theatre to the club. In October he began an even more exacting double, when he took over the band at the fashionable 96 Piccadilly restaurant. In a front page report the *Melody Maker* confidently asserted that the new gig would 'not interfere at all with Stéphane's position at the Milroy club, where he will continue to shine in the late evenings after his sessions at the 96 are over.'

It was like a rerun of the thirties in Paris: eight o'clock till three or four, with a brisk stroll through Mayfair in between. (But brisk strolls were aleady part of Stéphane's regimen, as they have remained. On fine nights, after work at the Milroy he would walk more than a mile to his flat in Troy Court, Kensington.) It was a difficult arrangement, and it did not last long. The *Melody Maker*'s front page of 26 November announced that 'following his marked success at the 96 Piccadilly restaurant, French violin ace Stéphane Grappelly is giving up the leadership of the Milroy nightery.' But the only reason was conflict in hours; Stéphane said he would very likely be undertaking another late night job at a club run by the 96's manager, Frank Shaw.

In the event, that did not happen either. The reason this time was a clash of temperaments. Alan Clare describes Frank Shaw as 'a totally Philistine kind of guy, a real Raj Englishman. He gave Stéphane a standing order, something like "Grappelli, you must invariably play a tango as the first number when you return after an interval." And once, when Stéphane was on his way back to the stand, he got a request from a customer. So naturally he said, "Of course, monsieur," and played it. Well, Shaw said, "Send Grappelli to my table," and he sat while Stéphane stood, and they had a terrible row. Stéphane hit the wall and told Frank Shaw what he could do with his job, and that was that.'

A musician, not a flunkey. But while the Milroy and 96 engagements lasted, Stéphane developed the accompaniment of dancing and dining to a kind of art. While making a large contribution to the process, Alan Clare learned a lot: 'He taught me to play in places like that, how to force people to listen – the pauses, the silence. Everything that Stéphane played in those days was like a finished little production.' Ballad playing, inspired by Alan's chords, was already one of Stéphane's specialities. 'We used to cause people to get married at 96. We used to woo them . . . make love to them. He'd give a wicked wink and say, "We've got *those* two – they'll be the next." He used to make *me* cry.'

There were purely musical lessons as well. Trying out one of Alan's songs, Stéphane protested that the note he had written as an A sharp should have been a B flat, though on the piano keyboard they are the same. 'Oh, *no*,' he told the pianist, demonstrating the small but crucial differences in the pitches on the violin. So, as Alan says, 'When I wrote the A Sharp and it should've been B flat, he went mad. And he was right. He's got *fantastic* ears.'

The characteristic blend of musical and professional *savoir-faire* meant that, as usual, Stéphane slid smoothly out of the 96 and into the Empress Club (another of Humphrey Lyttelton's 'funny names'), where he opened in April 1950, to play for dancing of course. Later in the year, however, he moved his base of operations to southern Europe which he had visited most recently with Django in 1949. This time it was a mixture of opportunity and necessity: the medical debilities of childhood had reared up again, and, after surgery, Stéphane had been advised to seek warmer climes. In November and December he was in Nice at the Club d'Angleterre with a quintet, then in January at the Excelsior Hotel. Since Django was rumoured to be living in Rome – he had played and recorded there with André Ekyan the previous spring – there was speculation about a reunion. In fact the guitarist was living outside Paris and had begun his slide into semi-retirement.

By the next summer, Stéphane – 'now completely recovered from serious illness', as the *Melody Maker* reported – was working with the popular French pianist Jack Diéval at the L'Escale club in St Tropez – the same place where he had become an instant saxophonist twenty years before. As steadily employed as ever, he took a band of French and British musicians into Rome's Kiki Club in December 1951. It was a versatile group, the pianist doubling vibes, the guitarist trumpet, the drummer also a vocalist (the singing drummer was a standard feature of night-club bands). Stéphane had his eye on wide appeal, promising 'good dance music and plenty of modern swing'. He was sufficiently committed to the idea of modern swing to hope he could entice the first-rate American tenorist Don Byas to join, now that Byas was living in Rome. The choice shows Stéphane's eagerness to move with the times, since Byas, though originally one of the younger generation of thirties players, had thrown in his lot with the boppers.

The next spring found Grappelli in an even more stylish setting, the Shaker Grill in Naples, where he was playing both piano and violin for international names like Roberto Rossellini and Ingrid Bergman. However, in line with his policy of never staying too long in one place, he was preparing to return to London, after stops in Rome and Milan. When he did come back, he resumed his all-purpose round of activities, doing broadcasts, variety and appearing as 'chief supporting attraction' with Gracie Fields' stage show.

Max Jones welcomed him back with an interview in the *Melody Maker* of 15 November 1952, highlighting what Stéphane regarded as a great technical advance: the electric violin he had just acquired. Max thought it 'a curious sawn-off looking thing, visually unimpressive and extraordinarily heavy', but Stéphane was enthusiastic. 'It isn't easy to play well at first,' he admitted, 'but once you have mastered this fiddle it is *fantastic*. . . . It means that the violin can take a full part in the jazz orchestra at last. It's no longer a little voice, it's more like four fiddles!' All that power at his disposal at last recalled the old limitations: 'In the old days, you know, you had to have a special combination in which to feature the violin properly, such as we had with the Hot Club Quintet. Now with the amplifier it becomes possible to work with any band. You can even use the pizzicato against normal blowing instruments. . . . Yes, it is *formidable*!'

The problem of underwhelming sound had been a bugbear confronting every jazz violinist, even more than the supposed 'lack of attack' involved in a bowed instrument. Scratching away was no solution; even violinists hated the results. As Svend Asmussen said, 'As a rule I didn't like the sound of a fiddle in jazz. Myself included; I never liked my sound. I knew more or less what I was after, but this thin screaming sound – I hated it, especially if you had to play with bands where there were drums, and you had to play comparatively loud. Amplifying systems were poor at that time so you didn't get much help there. The result was you had to squeeze and scratch and work like hell to make yourself heard, with a screaming tone.' Stuff Smith, Svend's particular hero and the least classical of violinists, had gone electric as early as 1936, but a player as fastidious about sound as Stéphane was naturally slower to take that route. He had begun experimenting with an electric instrument at the Milroy; the new American fiddle he was praising to Max was a further development. Even so, he was only using it for dancing and jazz; for variety, where he was accompanied by pianist Yorke de Sousa alone, he still preferred the pure acoustic sound. He has continued to try out various modes of electrification throughout his career. But, as he confessed in 1983, all along his heart has belonged to the sonority that is his and the violin's own, unsullied by gimmicks: 'No, I don't like all these tricks, all these amplifiers, all these wires you catch your feet on. I like the true sound of the violin or of the guitar, or of any other instrument.'

Stéphane's interview with Max also brought out his response to that other latest thing, bebop, which by now was quite established. He declared he had to like modern music, even if he couldn't play it so well. Sometimes he became saturated with old heroes like Armstrong and Ellington, marvellous as they were, and wanted something different. 'I'm always interested in new techniques, new ideas. I feel like that about jazz. That is why I have to like bop, because it is advanced.' In a way, it was why he was experimenting with amplification too: you had to keep up with innovations to avoid being left behind. This was partly intellectual curiosity, partly good business, but in either case bop was really no more Stéphane's natural language than amplification was. In 1985, when I asked if bop had upset him he said, 'It didn't upset me, but I never

liked it much. I like jazz a little bit modernized; I like Art
Tatum or Fats Waller. . . . Bebop to me is good, but I think
it's one of those *characters* of jazz music. . . . I think it's more
mechanical than feeling.' It is not in Stéphane's nature to
criticize music, especially when played by people of talent, but
for him there was not enough emotion in the boppers who
merely ran chord changes (however harmonically 'advanced'),
and emotion was the essence of the music. He said as much to
Max Jones: 'What can you do without that? Jazz is not study
but feeling. It is a thing of the heart. If you have it, you have
it. The rest comes later.'

In the fundamentals, Stéphane has remained consistent
throughout his career, and in 1952 it was clear that music was
still a profession as well as a passion. Max observed that he
continued to be 'a fairly potent box-office attraction . . . despite
his long and devoted interest in jazz. Could he account for this
dual success?' 'Success?' Stéphane replied, apparently puzzled.
For him it was second nature. 'The truth is I like music of all
kinds. I must meet the public, so I play every type of tune and
like them all, even tangos. . . . Jazz is my life, but I cannot
be a real purist because I like good living too. I'm aware
you have to put water with the wine sometimes.' The only
musicians he said he 'heartily' disliked were those who kept
their heads buried in the music and did not communicate with
their audience. It was the principle of wooing, as he had taught
Alan Clare, and a musician did it with his manner as well as
his music.

None of this has changed, either. After a concert at the 100
Club in London I sat with Stéphane in the dressing-room as
he received a parade of enthusiastic fans. In the midst of them,
a musician from another band crept in almost furtively to drop
off his instrument. Stéphane nudged me. 'You see,' he said,
imitating the man's withdrawn, hunched-over bearing, 'this
one is no artist.' An artist performs; he gives himself to the
public and his art does not have to be cheapened in the process.
Even if it has to be watered, the wine stays wine.

Nowhere in the *Melody Maker* interview was there any
mention of Django. Strictly speaking there was no need. The
erstwhile partners had not met or played together in almost
four years; the Hot Club Quintet seemed to belong to another
era, kept alive by occasional reissues. Yet in February 1953
Stéphane made his trip to France to find Django, carrying an
offer from an American promoter for a Hot Club tour of the
States. Perhaps with Stéphane along Django could have had
his hoped-for conquest. But it was much too late for him.

Stéphane returned to London and, in April, left for a series of jobs in Italy, first in Florence, then Rome, Sicily and back to Florence, where a promoter wanted someone to play piano for American tourists – 'something besides Viennese waltzes.' He had been in Florence only a few days when a telegram arrived from Delaunay, announcing Django's death and asking Stéphane to return for a benefit concert he was organizing for Naguine and Babik. Saddened though he was, as he told Roger Spautz, Stéphane was unable to get away – especially because he was due to record with a symphony orchestra for Italian radio, and he felt an obligation to everyone involved in the project. (He also confessed in the *Melody Maker* that he 'hated flying', as well as being 'too sad to do it. I cannot feel like going into a happy atmosphere and playing jazz in tribute to a dead friend.')

But, as he told Spautz, as soon as he was finished at Florence, Stéphane came to Django's home in Samois. There, 'in the company of his wife and his son, I bowed my head at the tomb of this great virtuoso.' Naguine made her own touching commemoration of their relationship by presenting Stéphane with the red scarf in which Django had wrapped his violin, and which Stéphane uses to this day. In February and March of 1954 he paid formal tribute to Django's memory in a series of five articles in the *Melody Maker*, which are honest and affectionate. Stéphane begins the sequence by stating that however many fine guitarists there might be, 'there can never be another Reinhardt', and concludes with the conviction that music was 'the only thing that, to him, gave meaning to life, which made his early death all the more tragic.'

By the time the articles appeared, however, Stéphane himself had gone through another of his periodic medical crises. This time it was trouble with his gall bladder and, in contrast to Django, he took considerable pains to make sure he got the best treatment. As Max Jones recalls, he sought out the ranking specialist and then, instead of using the National Health Service, had the operation done privately. They were perfectly reasonable measures, Stéphane explained to Max: 'My dear, this is the only gall bladder I've got.'

The operation was a success, cards and letters from well-wishers cheered his recovery, and on 6 March the *Melody Maker* printed a photograph of him leaving England for Nice, and for good. Henceforth his centre would be in France, away from London's damp and fog. But there was no question that he would continue to visit his 'second country', where he had built up a following that would endure and, though no one could foresee it, grow extraordinarily in the future.

Undecided

After a short stay in Nice, where he was making his home, Stéphane celebrated his official return to France with a gala opening at the Club St Germain on 25 April 1954. Knowing their readers would be interested in the progress of their favourite Frenchman, the *Melody Maker* published an account of the affair, with a photo. But just before the great day, the newspaper had also published a page one item showing that the violinist was, as usual, on the lookout for options: supposedly he had accepted an offer to take an orchestra into London's posh Bagatelle restaurant in May.

Nothing came of it, and Stéphane stayed at the St Germain. Indeed, it would be a regular haunt of his for the next several years – a proper jazz gig in the heart of the Latin Quarter instead of the Mayfair nightlife he had accompanied in London. The St Germain was probably the best-known Paris jazz spot. It was there that Django made his brief comeback in 1951, and Stéphane stayed at the Hotel Crystal opposite the club, next to the Hotel Montana where Django had received visitors in bed. The violinist was otherwise occupied: another resident of the Crystal, the American writer and musician Mike Zwerin, recalls overhearing him practising Bach.

In the fifties the St Germain area was famous both for

jazz and existentialism. Inspired by the presence of Jean-Paul Sartre and Simone de Beauvoir, students debated meaningless- ness at the Deux Magots or Café de Flore, from which Babik Reinhardt had nicked rolls, sugar and the occasional spoon, much to his father's delight. The whole atmosphere was coolly intense, nonchalantly sophisticated, and the jazz at the Club St Germain reflected it. Stéphane opened there with a septet of clarinet, vibes and rhythm section, plus his violin – understated colours, quite like the sonority of the George Shearing Quintet, which had made a great hit in the States with the same instrumentation minus the clarinet and fiddle.

Of course it was very different from the old extrovert appeal of the Hot Club, though in the autumn Stéphane led a quartet at the Piano Club which featured the Django-style guitarist Henri Crolla. Despite the *Melody Maker*'s reference to him as 'resident leader' at the St Germain, versatility and mobility remained his motto. For two months in the summer of 1954 he accompanied his old thirties employer, Bricktop, at her new club in Rome, and in the next year played both there and for a season at L'Escale in St Tropez.

For all this diversity, it was hard to escape Hot Club associ- ations, especially with the renewed interest stimulated by Django's death and the first signs of the imminent flood of record reissues. In the summer of 1955 Stéphane told a reporter that he had been asked to reform the Quintet, but said he would only use two guitars and 'keep Django's place free'. He was not attracted by the idea of imitating the old style: 'We will try something different.' The project, however, did not materialize, and Stéphane continued with his regular round, which included not only jazz clubs and night-clubs, but trips to London for TV and radio broadcasts and records.

The resumption of his recording career coincided with his return to Paris. Discographies list no Grappelli recordings in the early fifties, though there may well have been some of the uncredited vocal accompaniments he has done regularly over the years, and a British fan recalled hearing a Grappelli record- ing of the novelty 'Hot Canary' on a German jukebox in 1952. The sessions in which he was subsequently involved epitomize the variety of his activities. For instance, his first album presented him on piano, with bass and drums – a record Stéphane regards as a mistake: 'Somebody asked me to do it.' But it is nothing to be ashamed of, and we can hear why he was perfectly capable of holding down the kind of piano jobs he did. That was May 1954; four months later he participated in a quartet session with his St Tropez partner, the pianist Jack Diéval, and just after Christmas recorded in another quartet setting, this time as co-leader with Henri Crolla. Under his sole leadership, there was a sextet session with vibes, along the lines of his first St Germain group, and then three quartets with piano, bass and drums. Stéphane very much tended to favour players of the new generation, including those, like pianist Maurice Vander and bassist Pierre Michelot, who had worked in Django's last bands. His repertoire, on records at least, did not diverge much from the standards he had always played, though in clubs he could become adventurous. He was also adventurous in the matter of instrumentation: on a couple of his quartet sessions, the pianist doubled on harpsichord. In a different mood, but one still altogether Stéphane, he did a series mostly of ballads, cushioned by a large orchestra and chorus.

After having gone largely unnoticed in the columns of French jazz magazines, Stéphane began receiving recognition in record reviews. Though the critic writing of the sessions with Crolla only specifically mentioned the guitarist (who 'brings back good memories of Django'), the whole group is praised for 'light, melodious interpretations in very good taste . . . which will unfailingly hold the interest of connoisseurs'. If his sextet sides were found to be a little monotonous, though good for dreaming to, Stéphane, as always, did himself credit. Every review, even of a record as 'frankly commercial' as the strings and chorus production, affirmed the distinction of his musicianship: 'Stéphane Grappelly plays . . . all those melodies with so much class that one is forced to admire.' The quartet tracks revealed that he was 'a great jazzman', despite being tied to an instrument of lower status than the trumpet or bass: "He astonishes constantly by his biting attack and the firm line of his phrases." He had kept up with the times as well, 'adapting very intelligently to a more modern form of jazz'. In sum, he was 'a marvellous soloist. . . . There is no violinist like him in the States.'

Nevertheless, it was a violinist from the States who helped earn Stéphane the attention of a feature article. In May 1957, Stuff Smith visited Paris for the first time with Norman Granz's Jazz at the Philharmonic, and both *Jazz Hot* and *Jazz Magazine* marked the event by addressing that jazz oddity, the violin. Stéphane appeared on the cover of *Jazz Magazine* in March. In April *Jazz Hot* printed not only an interview with him by André Clergeat (in which Stéphane declared that the older he grew the more he became interested in his métier and that music remained 'the great passion of my existence') but accolades from Charles Delaunay and the young pianist René Urtreger. The critic praised Stéphane for all his qualities and for staying abreast of the latest developments, and wished only that he would make a record that would truly display his talent. The musician hailed him for his unvarying love of playing, and a youthfulness that belied his legendary status. Urtreger's esteem was based on personal contact: 'Playing with you is the most beautiful experience for me; every time I have the chance, I profit from it.' He was amazed that Stéphane, instead of sticking to his old standbys, wanted to do bop tunes like Bud Powell's 'Parisian Thoroughfare'. He recalled Lester Young's tribute, 'Stéphane is my man; I love that music,' and concluded that Lester was speaking for everyone: 'Dear Stéphane, we adore you.'

It seemed that when the critic Frank Tenot, in a survey of violinists for *Jazz Magazine*, described Grappelli as 'beloved by everybody', he was only telling the truth. He too lauded the virtues of Stéphane's style, the incisiveness, logic, sensitivity and taste which made him 'one of the great masters of European jazz' and 'assuredly one of the most important figures of French jazz'. But, like Delaunay, he too wished for a kind of culmination, in Tenot's case not an ideal recording, but 'the supreme consecration' of recognition in America. He imagined the effect of Grappelli at the Newport Festival – an experience that was in fact twelve years away.

In the wake of all these accolades, Stéphane appeared in print himself, defending the man who to an extent had prompted them. Stuff Smith's appearance at the JATP concert had caused a small furore. His records from the thirties, like 'I'se a-Muggin'' and 'Youse a Viper', were classics, but French listeners were unprepared for his raw, rugged, wholly personal approach to the violin in the flesh. As the American trumpeter Peanuts Holland once put it, 'Stuff practically doesn't know how to play the violin, he uses it like a saw and he scrapes his strings with his bow.' He didn't care about beautiful sonority, or whether he hit one string or two.

It was too much for Europeans, even those sympathetic to jazz, who had grown up with a conception of how the violin should sound. With the best will in the world, they could not help shuddering at Stuff's slides, stabs and scratches, his wide, wobbling vibrato and his seeming indifference to the basic niceties of intonation. None of this bothered Stuff, who cared about swinging above all, and who had no doubt that 'you can swing more on a violin than on any instrument ever made'.

In his remarks on Stuff, Stéphane said the American had an impact on him like Django, Armstrong or Tatum and expressed astonishment that 'a great number' of Parisian fans seemed not to appreciate his style. Under a picture of him rather protectively embracing his fellow fiddler, Stéphane asserted, 'They should have liked my friend Stuff Smith.' On both sides of the double page spread are the comments of ten Parisian musicians, French and American. Significantly, reactions to Stuff split exactly along national lines. On the whole, the French – including Martial Solal, Alix Combelle, Sacha Distel and René Urtreger – while acknowledging his great ability to swing, cannot tolerate his lapses of taste and technique. Almost all of them specifically contrast him to Stéphane, whom they deem the best in the world. In turn, the two Americans, Bill Coleman and Mezz Mezzrow, reach just the opposite conclusion, regarding Stuff's lack of classicism as a virtue.

Everyone should have been able to make their comparison in short order, because Norman Granz seized the opportunity of Stuff's appearance in Stéphane's town to record them together. Unfortunately, the record was not released for over twenty-five years, the tapes, according to Granz, having been misplaced. As it stands, the disc, *Violins No End*, shows both players in strong and definitively contrasting form. An apologist for either player could find support for his arguments in the four tracks they share (the rest of the record is given over to Stuff's concert).

Stuff is undoubtedly the begetter of a true, native violin style, untainted by dreams of a classical career or playing the Bach Double. He honks like a tenor player, his buzzy, insinuating sound projected strongly by his electric fiddle. He plays incredibly far behind the beat, loves to dig in and hang on to notes, repeating them, twisting, them, turning them into riffs. He revels in the simple physical character of bow and strings, the scratching, scrawling attack they make possible. He seems to pull his lines *through* the strings; you can feel them bend. Indeed, physicality is the main impression of his style, texture its supreme attribute – the wails, the slurs, even the abrasiveness. No one could ever ignore Stuff Smith; no violinist was ever further from a palm court. The complaints about his intonation are, strictly speaking, sometimes justified, but that makes no difference to him. In a way, notes are only textures too. It could be said that he is more interested in the approximate colours of pitches – higher, lower, louder, softer – than in the exact tones of the orthodox scale. This freedom makes him sound harmonically 'advanced', though he has no theoretical conception behind what he plays. It is all part of the emotional effect he creates, all a function of swinging.

Slow or slow-to-medium groove tunes are his meat, like 'Don't Get Around Much Any More' and 'Chapeau Blues' on

Violins No End: he generates a heavy, grinding feeling of pure funkiness. On up-tempos – 'No Points Today', 'The Lady is a Tramp' – the same qualities may build excitement, but can also start to feel somewhat brutal or frantic, lacking a real melodic direction – the unrelenting character of the lines makes the ears buzz after a while. There is no question that Stuff is a mighty swinger – so mighty sometimes that he is almost a caricature of sweaty swing. For some listeners his style is marked primarily by 'crudities', as one critic put it; for others – like Svend Asmussen – he is the only violinist to capture the visceral essence of jazz on his instrument.

The contrast with Stéphane does not require much elucidation. On the slower groove tunes in *Violins No End* he tends to double-time and rhapsodize where Stuff digs in, but his two choruses on 'Chapeau Blues' are by no means flippant, exhibiting toughness as well as grace. On the up-tempos he is fully at home, sailing along, riding the rhythm section in his best style, spinning out lines that are elegant and full of surprises, as well as exhibiting some Stuff-like grittiness of their own. It is obviously very distinguished jazz playing. If it lacks the swingeing power of Stuff's approach, it is also less inclined to fray the nerves. Between them, Stéphane and Stuff have defined the two poles of jazz violin, 'European' and 'American', their descendants being on the one hand French players like Didier Lockwood and Dominique Pifarelly, on the other Americans like Leroy Jenkins and Billy Bang. However, young violinists on both sides of the ocean have chosen their models regardless of national lines.

As usual, the straight-ahead jazz session with Stuff was only one aspect of Stéphane's activities. He starred regularly at the St Germain; for much of 1956 he combined his work there with a long season at the Hotel Claridge, where the Quintet was born. He made records for dancing too, with a big band plus strings playing Quincy Jones arrangements, another light jazz session with his own quartet, featuring the harpsichord gimmick again, and another solo set backed by strings and chorus, playing Cole Porter.

On the surface he seemed, as Frank Tenot had said, beloved by everybody, and happily playing music for everybody's taste. But a few celebratory references in jazz magazines and even the respect of younger musicians did not necessarily indicate a fruitful career. When the harmonica virtuoso Larry Adler (who had recorded with Stéphane and Django in the thirties) went to Paris, he stopped in at Claridge's and found the violinist 'playing absolute palm court music'. What was more,

Adler got the impression he was not well known, and his presence was not considered of particular interest: 'He wasn't even advertised in the lobby.'

Bob Clarke, the British violinist who was a great fan of Stéphane's and who had met him in London, tells the same story. Visiting Paris in 1957 (where he would later have a very successful career as part of a music and comedy trio), he came to see Stéphane at the Club St Germain. The violinist remembered him and welcomed him warmly, with practical advice: 'He said, "Don't drink here, it's too pricey." And when I left he told me to be sure to keep my coat buttoned up because it was so cold: "You must be very careful."' He seemed in good spirits: 'He's a very funny man; I always found him with a good sense of humour.' But on the whole Clarke felt that Stéphane was getting by rather than flourishing. 'He'd do a month at the St Germain or Les Trois Mailletz for not so much money.' Like Larry Adler, he also didn't find much evidence that Stéphane had real status: 'You never saw his name on the posters.'

Steady but not stunning: 'I don't know if he'd made a fortune and was hiding it away, but. . . .' There was still a special difficulty for players of so-called 'middle jazz' from the thirties, as the devotees of trad and bop fought their ideological battle. In addition, the main thrust of jazz (in spite of the reaction of the Dixielanders) has always been forward; listeners are keen to discover the newest star, what the tenor saxophonist Bud Freeman called 'the kid of the moment'. Stéphane was no kid, nor could he, as yet, claim the mantle of elder statesman. It did no good for critics and young musicians to insist he was playing as well as ever, indeed was developing and improving. The jazz public wanted new faces, a new fashion.

Despite Stéphane's constant curiosity about music, bop did not really suit him, as he has said. It did not suit the violin either, since it was a particularly aggressive style, tailor-made for the hard-driving trumpet and saxophone quintets that were its standard line-up. Stéphane's lyricism, his basic elegance – as swinging as it was – was at a disadvantage, even with amplification. He was also somewhat old hat in his attitude to the audience. On the whole, the boppers were musical militants, demanding that their music be taken seriously on its own terms, shunning any association with jazz as entertainment, criticizing older jazzmen who, if not actually catering to the public, at least viewed audiences with benevolence. The boppers threw a barely-concealed challenge to their listeners, a gesture alien to Stéphane's character.

His very versatility may have hampered him as well, as far

as promoting a career was concerned. Despite the enormous talent that all his colleagues recognized, to the public he could have seemed a journeyman, albeit a journeyman of genius. He did not promote himself as the giant he had a right to be considered. He was quite happy, as he has always been happy, to do the work that was available, content to make his living as it came. Daniel Humair, who met Stéphane in the late fifties and who would become both one of Europe's finest drummers and one of Stéphane's favourites, immediately recognized him as 'a monster musician – he's so musician it's frightening'. He appreciated the violinist's interest in younger players: 'He was one of the only ones of that generation that came to hear other people. He was always curious to know what was going on and what was good in the scene, and was always the first one to give advice when somebody asked him. And he never cared if somebody was an important name or something. He was there to help and to enjoy.' But Humair also saw what was, to him, a puzzling lack of self-projection in Stéphane: 'He's not a pusher *at all*.' And in the fifties – and increasingly in the sixties – with jazz and popular music in turmoil, a certain amount of self-promotion was vital.

Hints that Stéphane may have felt his own kind of disorientation in the contemporary climate emerge in two articles, one of which he wrote, the other in which he figured. The first was a retrospective view of twenty-five years of jazz in *Jazz Hot*, called 'Le Métier'. In it Stéphane talked about the rigours of the musician's life in 1935, with long hours, low status and an ignorant public. He thought modern musicians should seem more pleased to be playing than they did: 'One wonders why they seem so disgusted with life and so full of bitterness, instead of enjoying themselves as we used to, although the work was more difficult.'

The modern demeanour was existential, cool, hip. It definitely was not Stéphane. What was more, audiences showed the same tendencies: 'It isn't only the musicians who make long faces. I remember Louis Armstrong's concert in 1934. Everybody was radiant. Going there was a treat. You would say that today people go to concerts to whistle or make noise. The fans are divided among themselves, and you find only malcontents.' In the battle of the ancients and moderns, 'Each one speaks to you of pure jazz.' He deplored the effects of such contention but made no bones about his preferences: 'In life one must go forward and live with his time. . . .'

At fifty-two, he was still committed to moving forward, but he had to regret the dour mood that had settled over jazz. In 1952 he had told Max Jones that 'basically jazz is a gay music.

Even the blues is fatalist rather than sad. Anyway, how can you be serious and studious when you're playing "I'm Just Wild About Harry"?' But in 1960 there was not much gaiety about. No self-respecting jazzman would have been caught dead playing 'I'm Just Wild About Harry', Louis Armstrong was derided as an Uncle Tom and the approved models for deportment – studiously correct and moodily withdrawn respectively – were the Modern Jazz Quartet and Miles Davis.

The other article fascinates in a number of ways, offering a view of the Paris scene in the late fifties, and an insight into Stéphane's state of mind as well as the state of his art, all from an American perspective. American writers seem to have been little aware of Stéphane's doings, as Frank Tenot had pointed out, but the writer Richard Gehman was a great fan of his from the Hot Club days. He was also a friend of the Dixieland player and entrepreneur Eddie Condon, assisting in Condon's autobiography *We Called It Music*. His 'Letter to Eddie' appeared in the *Saturday Review* of 17 May 1958.

Gehman begins by observing that the great days are gone. A Parisian friend tells him that 'Paris, which once leaped with jazz, now hardly hops.' Still, there is Stéphane at the Club St Germain. Gehman notes that he has heard one of Grappelli's recent records with strings, which is pleasant, 'but hardly indicative of what he can do'. Having heard him live, Gehman goes on, 'What he can do is swing, and he is doing that today . . . under severe handicaps. Behind him are an early Birdland drummer from the States who can but will not keep time, a bassist who hears some secret inner rhythm, and a fair modern-derivative pianist who might just as well be across the street for all the rapport he is able to establish with the other two. It doesn't matter. Grappelly pulls out a rhythm of his own, and above it he plays some of the most exciting jazz I've ever heard in my life.' Stéphane is playing electric violin, exhibiting 'a hard swinging attack' on the up-tempos, covering the full range of the instrument 'with such effortlessness it appears accidental', but which clearly is 'the product of an assured and authoritative intelligence'. On ballads 'he is overcome by romanticism. He turns down the lights and plays moodily and ruminatively, as though picking over some old affair. . . .'

Stéphane ('slender and grey-haired, delicately handsome and soft in manner') tells Gehman he has been 'jobbing around with various groups, staying six months here, six months there, sometimes longer.' He recalls Django with wry affection – the intelligent *sauvage* who took such pride in learning to write his name, who kept silent out of embarrassment at his ignorance.

Gehman concludes, 'I got the feeling that he misses his friend and musical companion much more than he will say. Perhaps that is what makes the sad tunes so astonishingly effective.'

Gehman's article creates a rather poignant sense of Stéphane in isolation – a little lost, sympathetic in principle to contemporary musical language, but unable to achieve a real rapport with its self-absorbed practitioners. It is not his scene; he is on his own. Gehman suggests that he might be better off with the American expatriate Kenny Clarke, who is playing drums with the other band in the club, but Stéphane says he is too loud for him: '"Kenny is a diamond . . . but one can live without diamonds."' In addition, though he is obviously at the top of his form, the records he is making, aimed at a commercial market, do not let him give all he can.

The contrast with the Django days is evident, and Gehman's inference about Stéphane's regret for his partner may be the most arresting item in the price. For Django was still bound to be an abiding factor in Stéphane's life and work. Even personal tributes could not avoid the connection. René Urtreger's letter of homage had identified him first as 'le légendaire Grappelly . . . Django, le quintette à cordes. . . .' An appreciative review of a record by his quintet commended 'the style of Django's companion'. His interview with André Clergeat was headlined, '"Django qui. . . ."' It was natural; the Hot Club group had been the most sensational thing in European jazz, and Django's death had only increased the aura surrounding it.

And the aura surrounding Django. Though he had been in virtual seclusion at the time, his demise had released the considerable eulogistic powers of the Gallic press. One journal declared that his death left the jazz world in 'stupor and disarray'. From the Académie Française, Jean Cocteau paid a characteristic tribute. Though basically ignorant of jazz, he responded to its liberating implications, as in the salad days of the Bar Gaya and Les Six. Django the gypsy especially appealed to him: 'He is one of those sweet beasts who died in a cage. He lived as one dreams of living: on the road.' Probably he had not seen much of Django, or bought many records, but the image was irresistible. Dead, Django had even more allure than he possessed alive. It made things awkward for the non-gypsy partner left behind, self-effacingly making his way playing six months here, six months there, often in conventional bourgeois settings.

For again, Stéphane's adaptability, even his very quality posed problems. Not only was he a member of the new lost generation of jazzmen, the players of middle jazz, but he had

the wrong credentials. As François Billard pointed out to me,
there is a quasi-political dimension to jazz appreciation in
France. To be considered authentic, you should be anti-
bourgeois and, ideally, black. (Being gypsy, of course, was an
acceptable alternative.) Stéphane, a poor white boy with great
regard for financial security, was on the wrong side of the line.
As François said, 'For much of the time in France, though
nobody would say it, Stéphane has been considered in those
sort of areas as a rightist, which is a crazy situation. You can't
imagine if you don't live in this bloody country that it's reality.'
And he was not the only one of his generation to suffer: 'In
those terms, at the end of his life Alix Combelle, who was an
excellent musician, was not considered at all.' It was one aspect
of what Stéphane himself called the 'snobbisme' that had
intensified in jazz after the war.

All in all, the reissues of the Hot Club recordings, which
began apace after Django's death, were a decidedly mixed
blessing for Stéphane. Of course, it kept his name before the
public. Or did it? Stéphane has often expressed the anger he
felt when these products of a partnership came out with new
covers giving Django's name alone. He also grew increasingly
exasperated at being regarded as a source of Django lore instead
of as a musician. As Charles Delaunay said, 'He didn't like it
when people woke him up to ask about Django.' He especially
disliked it when questioners referred to him as 'Django's violinist', to which he rejoined impatiently, no, the gypsy had been
his guitarist.

Without exception the reviews of the reissues took the form
of eulogies for Django – proving that, as Martial Solal observed
drily, 'It's always better to die. When you're young and you
die it makes a legend.' The usual attitude was that Django was
a genius, and had not played a single note to which one
could be indifferent. Stéphane's contributions usually received
recognition, but invariably each notice concluded with a pan-
egyric to his dead partner. Indeed Stéphane found himself
praised for his complementary skill, the talent with which, as
Charles Delaunay wrote in *Jazz Hot*, he translated Django's
ideas and anticipated his desires. As another writer said in
Jazz Magazine, Stéphane's 'profound melodic sense and . . .
virtuosity [were] stimulated by Django's feverish chords.' And
Yves Salgues, in his series of biographical articles on the gypsy,
stated that 'Stéphane and Django, separately, never had as
much genius as when they were together.' That may have been
fair comment in 1958, and in a sense it was a tribute to
Stéphane, acknowledging that the stimulation was not all one
way. But it left the violinist in an odd position, making it seem

that his best years were behind him. That was all right for
Django, being dead, but Stéphane still had plenty of music in
him, Django or no.

When the reissues appeared in Britain, reaction to Stéphane's
role was both more various and more one-sided. 'The rapport
between Grappelly and Reinhardt' was granted to be 'remarkable', and Stéphane was hailed for 'some of the smoothest
violin work I have ever heard', but another critic was bound
to declare that Grappelli could not 'really be considered as an
outstanding jazz musician'. Stéphane was defended, more than
a litte patronizingly, in another review: 'In no way the genius
as was Django, he nevertheless was a gifted musician, who did
much to help his guitarist colleague.' In a couple of cases he
suffered by comparison with Eddie South, who was regarded
as 'being of course one or two cuts above Grappelly' and, more
devastatingly, 'definitely the violinist most suited to Django in
style and invention'.

Perhaps the oddest and, for Stéphane, no doubt the most
galling aspect of the reviews was the way they wrote him off;
their sense that he had somehow disappeared with Django and
now belonged to the ages. 'Stéphane was a talented violinist,'
said one writer, with awful finality. Another acknowledged
that he was still active, but beyond the pale: 'Grappelly was
then far removed from the commercial bandleader we know
today. . .' This was the man who was presently playing some
of the most exciting jazz Richard Gehman had ever heard, who
was esteemed by all the musicians of the rising generation (as
Daniel Humair said, 'If somebody doesn't respect a man of
that importance, he's an idiot'), and yet who still had the status
of a well-kept secret. It was due partly to the musical climate,
partly to his connection with a legend, partly to his own
character. In 1962 a writer in *Jazz Magazine* put the case
exactly when in the course of reviewing a Quintet reissue he
referred to 'this great unrecognized . . . Stéphane Grappelly'.

Understandably, in the fifties and sixties, Stéphane did not
make very much of the Django connection, seeming rather to
avoid it. He contributed to two albums of homage and recorded
some of the guitarist's tunes simply because they were good
tunes – particularly 'Nuages' which he played on a strange
project called *One World Jazz*, in which musicians from several
countries overdubbed their parts. In 1961 he briefly joined
Joseph Reinhardt in a string quartet. Then, in 1962, at the
suggestion of Nesuhi Ertegun of Atlantic Records, he put
together a group for an album intended to evoke the great days
of the Quintet. Stéphane, however, declined simply to 're-do
some Django' and substituted a wide range of pieces for the

proposed sequence of QHCF greatest hits. They still did 'Nuages', 'Minor Swing' and 'Daphne', but included good standards like 'Soft Winds' and 'Like Someone in Love' as well as tunes from leading modern jazzmen: Sonny Rollins' 'Pent Up House' (which would remain a Grappelli favourite) and John Lewis's personal *hommage*, 'Django'.

Stéphane made the record his own, picking young players like Daniel Humair (because he was musical, could play soft and swing) and bassist Guy Pedersen. To suggest the Hot Club sound he brought in guitarists Pierre Cavalli for the solos (electric) and Léo Petit on rhythm, but the whole session feels modern, without any pervasive chunk-chunk-chunk. Humair and Pedersen produce supple grooves, Petit is firm but unobtrusive and Cavalli throws in chords like a pianist. They are tight in the best sense, and the leader responds with absolute mastery, as if this record were the Opus One of a new phase of his career. It is a real departure from the Hot Club, with Stéphane playing with increased freedom, confidence, logic and swing.

Treats abound – Stéphane's story-telling solo on 'Django', his embroidery of the melody and cadenza on 'Nuages', the *mysterioso* introduction to 'Daphne' which makes her seem a less innocent maid than she was in the thirties – but the *pièce de résistance* must be 'Minor Swing'. It was one of Stéphane's finest moments with Django as well, and here he delivers a stunning solo, sweeping through seven choruses that in themselves make a beautiful completed shape, but contain individual marvels besides. Opening with a marvellous, haunting figure, he turns out long slippery lines, suddenly holds back against the beat, drops in a gutsy aside and flows off again in a new direction. Never losing his momentum, invention or aplomb, he is always unpredictable, though what he does, when it happens, makes perfect sense. You can feel him creating, finding the shape as he goes. For instance, near the end of the fourth chorus, he throws off a kind of double-stopped smear that leads in the fifth to a heady patch of dissonant sawing of the sort usually associated with Stuff Smith, though with Stéphane it is perfectly under control, in perfect taste. All by itself, the seventh chorus is a gem, working artfully from the upper-middle register to the low by way of some especially sinewy, bluesy passages that are at the same time quiet, almost off-hand. As a matter of fact, Stéphane carries on into the next chorus, which I'm sure was intended to be a bass solo, but which turns into a duet simply because he could not stop playing. And indeed he momentarily plays into Daniel Humair's following drum solo.

It is a remarkable performance, particularly for a man who once said he does not like recording studios because they are 'cold and deprived of the essential thing: the public'. But as anybody who has heard Stéphane live knows, this kind of transport can occur anytime. He once told Whitney Balliet of the *New Yorker*: 'When I improvise and I'm in good form, I'm like somebody half sleeping. I even forget there are people in front of me. Great improvisers are like priests; they are thinking only of their god.' And so it sounds on 'Minor Swing', which is the real jazz thing. Though the 1937 recording is excellent, this version shows plainly that Stéphane has developed a new vocabulary, a new sophisticated mode of speech. And yet the old roots are still there. Such enriching mixtures are basic to his character. Daniel Humair once summed him up, using the French slang term for street-urchin: 'an aristocrat with roots of a *titi* Parisian: he can be delicate and earthy'.

In the sleeve notes to the album, however, Stéphane chose to present himself as the blandly satisfied professional musician, happy to be working steadily in 'night-clubs, concerts, radio and television. And I record – especially pop sessions. Sometimes someone will ask if I wouldn't rather relax and enjoy life. I answer that considering I started out by playing in courtyards, my greatest pleasure lies in having become and in remaining a recognized and respected artist who is looked after and . . . who is well paid.' Very frank, very business-like, in a way very Stéphane. But 'Minor Swing' came from somewhere else.

The album was released in France and America titled *Django* to capitalize on the Reinhardt connection. Significantly, it came out in Britain – reduced by two tracks – as *Feeling + Finesse = Jazz*. Apparently someone felt that in the UK Stéphane had enough of a reputation on his own without the Django link. In London, *Jazz Journal*'s reviewer listened to it with 'unexpected pleasure' – perhaps anticipating a QHC rehash, but finding music that was 'essentially up-to-date', revealing Stéphane as 'a musical Peter Pan if ever there was one'. He concluded his recommendation by pointing out that 'Grappelli's talents have long been obscured by the posthumous glory of Reinhardt, and perhaps this album will help to establish a reputation for originality and exceptional musicality which has long been deserved.'

But such worthy sentiments did not signal a change in Stéphane's direction. His next recording, three months after *Django*, was part of a series he had been working on featuring the harpsichord gimmick, now adapted to easy listening. The present set was the third volume of a sequence called *Dance on Your Memories*; it would be followed by a collection of

Edith Piaf's greatest hits. Outside of these sessions, Stéphane was continuing to take what turned up – location dates in and out of France, private parties, broadcasts. He had also been back and forth several times to Britain.

The music scene, however, was changing. By 1963, jazz had begun to move further out in terms of experimentalism, and further away from the tastes of a popular audience. Inspired by Ornette Coleman and John Coltrane, the post-bop generation of players were beginning to play what was called 'the new thing', which would soon lead to full-blown 'free jazz'. All connections with the dancing past were severed, as were traditional notions of harmony and a regularly stated rhythm. Total improvisation came to be the ideal, total freedom of expression without structural constraints the goal. Along the way, before the music went headlong over a cliff of self-indulgence, some exciting and mesmerizing jazz was created. Particularly captivating were Coltrane's experiments with modal frameworks, originally suggested by his work with Miles Davis, especially in the album *Kind of Blue*. Coltrane's 1960 album, *My Favorite Things*, caused a sensation in the jazz world and became something of a commercial hit as well. With the scalar character of his improvisations on soprano over the hypnotic chords of McCoy Tyner on piano and the barrage of cross-rhythms from Elvin Jones's drums – in three-four, but unlike any waltz ever heard – the effect was intoxicating, timeless.

Stéphane became an avid Coltrane fan, admiring not just the saxophonist but McCoy Tyner as well, with whom he has said a number of times he would like to record. No doubt it was the spell of the harmonies again, Grappelli bending his ears to new, expanded possibilities. He had no sympathy, however, with the stage that quickly ensued after Coltrane – musicians who had none of Coltrane's technical preparation but were simply enthralled by the liberating effect of what he played. The modes, which offered a much freer harmonic framework than the standard system of chord sequences, were soon abandoned in favour of no system at all. Players simply poured out what possessed them, individually or all at once, while rhythm sections smashed away as the headlong spirit moved them. The old demanding disciplines of the jazz musician disappeared, driven out by a vision of jazz freedom, the price of which was forgotten or rejected. Free jazz was almost certainly the only movement which Stéphane, with his tolerance and curiosity, utterly deplored. His pithy appraisal was, 'What a horror!'

What a horror too for the jazz business. The mid and late

sixties saw a true crisis in the clubs, corresponding to the crisis in the art. Few people wanted to spend money to hear musicians dispense what sounded like chaos, however 'intense'. Philo- sophically, though, much of the burgeoning youth culture was in favour of it. It was doing your own thing, as the phrase was coming to be, with a vengeance. Looking back, with fifteen years of hindsight, a critic in *Jazz Hot* identified 'the great myth of the epoch: everyone can make music. A variation on Rousseau's myth of the Noble Savage, with the idea that the Noble Savage is us.'

To a degree, the condition of jazz reflected the social turbu- lence of the sixties, but the most compelling musical mirror of the time turned out to be rock. Jazz, sliding from complexity to chaos, almost ceased to matter as rock came into its own. From being merely the preferred genre of twisting teenagers, it became the *vox pop* of a generation – more than a music, a state of mind, a faith, a political stance. It was a worldwide phenomenon, beginning in the States, leaping the Atlantic to the Beatles and the Rolling Stones.

The new mood had little to do with Stéphane. In 1960, in an interview with him subtitled 'The Art of Being Elegant', Lucien Malson had declared: 'There is nothing in the Grappellian language of magnificent modern chaos, of the fascinating movement of a mad *logos*.' In 1960 no one had had any idea of how magnificent chaos could become, how mad the *logos*, or how out-of-date the mainstream traditions of jazz.

The effects began to be traceable early. In February 1963, in Paris, Stéphane made a three-fiddle record, arranged by Duke Ellington for Frank Sinatra's Reprise label, the other soloists being Duke's own Ray Nance and Svend Asmussen (on viola). It is a record of considerable charm, demonstrating the typical Ellington virtues of looseness, spontaneity and invention; languorous sophistication laced with barrelhouse. (In spirit Duke was a *titi* Parisian too.) Yet the disc was not released until 1976. The recording business has its vagaries, of course, but it is not unlikely that *Duke Ellington's Jazz Violin Session*, as it finally became, was shelved as being out of fashion.

Stéphane's subsequent recordings also attest to the change in climate. There would be no records under his name alone until 1969; those he did make emphasized the specialist fiddle connection and were aimed at the European market. *Two of a Kind* resulted from an appearance with Svend Asmussen on Danish TV in December 1964. Not surprisingly, the duo were a big hit – both for reasons of musical quality and novelty – and they were into a Copenhagen studio a few weeks later. The

session (which included the nineteen-year-old Niels-Henning
Ørsted Pedersen on bass) sounds very sympathetic, with
Svend's and Stéphane's different styles complementing each
other well. Svend is in particularly good form, leathery and
aggressive on both violin and viola, hooking and jabbing like
the tenormen he admires. Stéphane, on the other hand, dominates the up-tempo 'Parisian Thoroughfare' with his usual
high-powered fluency. A notable treat is simply the way the
two men play the tunes together, feeling and phrasing them
in perfect unison – a slow, luscious 'Honeysuckle Rose', a
loose-limbed 'Twins', a sidelong 'Satin Doll'.

By contrast, there are no unisons in *Stuff and Steff*, the
Grappelli–Smith rematch made in June 1965; that kind of
homogeneity was not Stuff's style. But the two players dance
around each, providing counter-melodies and commentaries.
They do their separate specialities well, Stuff infectiously jivey
on 'Skip It', Stéphane sensitive but bluesy on 'Willow Weep
for Me'. (The piece tests the effects of a risky injury Stéphane
suffered in 1964. In a fall, he broke a bone in the little finger
of his left hand. He was unable to play for several months and
found when recovered that he could not sustain notes with the
finger for as long as he had before. He has said this has made
him play faster, but on 'Willow Weep for Me' his sostenuto
still sounds rich and fine. He has also said the injury is 'like a
souvenir from Django to me. If he could take it I can take it
too!')

Stéphane's next record, *Violin Summit*, brought together
not only Svend and Stuff but also the new boy of jazz violin.
With an extensive classical background, Jean-Luc Ponty had
been influenced first by Stéphane, who met and encouraged
him, but then by Stuff Smith: 'I went crazy over him – he was
the most revolutionary; he played the violin with so much
punch.' It became clear early on that it was that punch Ponty
was after, coupled with an uncompromisingly contemporary
approach. He wanted 'to sound like a trumpet or a horn'. He
was listening especially closely to Coltrane, and soon, as the
critic Joachim Berendt has said, 'found the violin's equivalent
to Trane's vaguely "Oriental" sound.' He was equally modern
in his view of amplication, which was not, as it was to Stéphane,
a necessary evil, but a positive advantage. 'The tone I was
getting through the amp was so different, and I got a kick out
of it, I liked it. It helped me play jazz, actually, because it took
me away from the traditional violin sound.'

Speaking to *Jazz Magazine* after his very successful appearance at the Antibes Jazz Festival in 1964, the twenty-one-year-
old Ponty was already clear about the essential difference

between him and Stéphane, though he admired him as 'not only a jazzman, but also an artist in the full sense of the term. . . . He utilizes the effects of the violin more, he plays with a purely violinistic sound, while I'm trying to make jazz on the violin since it happens that's my instrument. But it could just as well be a saxophone.' Jean-Luc compounded Stuff's example, all the musical influences of the moment, and, above all, great talent, determination and technique. He made the instrument relevant to a new, young audience, so that, as Matt Glaser observed in *Jazz Violin*, 'Jean-Luc Ponty is largely responsible for the renaissance of jazz violin.'

Made live in Basle, Switzerland on 30 September 1966, the *Violin Summit* record has the excitement of a kind of ritual combat. We are hearing the future of jazz fiddle, and it works. This does not in any sense mean that the old guard is vanquished and dismissed forever, but Ponty clearly announces the arrival of a new school. He knew exactly what the occasion signified, as he told Matt Glaser: 'They were all established jazz violinists, and that was the beginning of my career. To be on stage with those masters was an incredible thrill for me, and at the same time, a chance for me to burn, and prove myself, to them and to the audience.'

Which he did. But the record's main impression is simply of the difference in mode, not quality. Ponty does have a very high-voltage style, and on 'Summit Soul', for instance, a jazz-funk tune of the 'Watermelon Man' type, he plays a teeming solo with straining octave stops, piled-up asymmetrical runs and glissandos, all delivered with his penetrating vibrato-less sound. It is exciting, and excitement is its main intent. On 'Pent Up House', which he and Stéphane play together, Ponty is much more frenzied than Stéphane, interested, as he said, in burning. But a sense of the distinct harmonic character of the tune comes across much less in his reading than in Grappelli's. The aim of the school of players absorbed in modal playing and the new thing – and even more in rock – was to turn the tune into a vehicle for a certain kind of declamation, to tear a passion to tatters. Stéphane is more concerned to keep the structure of the tune, to use it, to expose it to the listener; to show its specific properties and values.

It is very like the differences in the way the two violinists approach their instrument. Stéphane never forgets, as Ponty said, that he is playing a violin, an instrument with a certain sound and a distinct character. It can be turned very effectively to the uses of jazz: its character becomes part of Stephane's jazz vocabulary which he explores and refines, but within whose limits he is content to stay. Ponty, however, puts his expression before the instrument. Though he plays the violin marvellously well, it is only a means to an expressive end – and in fact its limitations are an impediment to expression. Hence the amplification which becomes a sound in itself – amplification which throughout his career has become more and more elaborate, more and more pronounced.

Thus, from this point of view, the tune and the violin are fair game, to be sacrificed, if necessary, to the primary end of the player's feeling. This is not automatically to be condemned – the history of jazz is the history of musicians searching for their voices – but it is also not to say that the more traditional view of tune and instrument has exhausted its possibilities. Ponty's work on *Violin Summit* is powerful, that of an ambitious young voice obviously to be reckoned with. He brings the house down with a fiery, riffing solo on 'It Don't Mean a Thing If It Ain't Got That Swing'. But Stéphane's solo has it own quality, more discerningly examining the harmonic contours of the tune, digging in and following its flow, turning up surprises. And the piece he has to himself, the ancient, innocuous 'Pennies from Heaven', is an excellent performance, one of the high points of the concert, earning bravos if not cries of animal ecstasy.

Stéphane's art is simply different in kind. In terms of wattage he may be outgunned; musically he is certainly not outplayed. The arrival of Jean-Luc, however, was another sign of the times, his aggressive approach to the fiddle an example of the change in the contemporary character of music. Not long after the *Violin Summit*, the rock guitarist Jimi Hendrix caused a sensation at his début concert at the Olympia in Paris. His playing was devastatingly amplified, mind-blowingly loud. His stage manner was less showmanship than psychodrama, his guitar more sexual object than musical instrument. It was music as spectacle, rock as tribal rite, the performer as priest or shaman. His young audience was overwhelmed both by him and by their reactions to him: this was *it*, naked emotion, taking them out of themselves and oppressive reality. The next summer, the 'Jimi Hendrix Experience', as his trio was called, reached a peak at the Monterey Festival. After enflaming a vast crowd with a set supercharged by nine amplifiers and eighteen speakers, he capped the display by actually setting fire to his guitar.

On 10 December 1966 Stéphane, visiting London to play on a Henry Mancini film score, was briefly interviewed by the *Melody Maker* (which was devoting less and less space to jazz). He mentioned the *Violin Summit*, and a duo appearance with Jean-Luc at the Berlin Festival. He confessed he still regarded amplification as a necessary evil, because it distorted the violin's tone and made it sound like a clarinet: '. . . personally I don't like it.' Summing up the current state of his career, he said he did not play clubs much any more, preferring private parties, concerts and 'how do you call them, gigs'. He referred to the inevitable proposal to reform the Hot Club Quintet, but said that, if he agreed, the line-up would have to include a drummer. 'Maybe I play a bit old-fashioned, but I like to play with a modern rhythm section.'

Something about the interview sounded weary, as though he were no longer so sure that in the current climate he could represent himself as 'a recognized and respected artist who is looked after and well-paid'. Perhaps he felt out of place in the brave new world proclaimed by the spray-painted slogans of the counter-culture. At any rate, next year, when the Paris Hilton offered him a residence leading the dining and dancing band in its Le Toit Club, he took it.

Parisian Thoroughfare

Stéphane's five years at the Paris Hilton provoke different reactions from different people. His tenure there was either 'soul-destroying' or quite painless, a dead patch in his career or a valuable period of retrenchment from which he would launch the great advances of the seventies. On the whole, British observers take the more negative view, but some French musicians have been uneasy too, or perplexed. Career-conscious himself, Daniel Humair has often felt 'amazed' at Stéphane's lack of ambition, at his general willingness simply to take what came along, and at his acceptance of the Hilton residence in particular. 'I never understood that thing of Hilton: this guy that was a star was playing for dinner. He was playing concerts, he was always travelling, he could have made a career. He could have worked any place – all the time people asked him to play, and I don't know why he went to this Hilton. Did he need the people? . . . It was the way musicians worked during the war: was it a nostalgia for that time? Did he do too many of those jobs to understand how *dépassé* it was?' For a serious young musician it would have been unthinkable. 'No one of us would have gone to play at the Hilton. If you asked me, maybe I would sub for one night just to see what it is, but I wouldn't take a week at the Hilton – even at that time, when I needed work.'

In the mid and late sixties, with great changes occurring in popular culture, work for jazz musicians was often in short supply, especially for musicians playing older forms of the music. A stubborn dedication was necessary if you insisted on devoting yourself to that and nothing else. As the romantic image of art required, you had to suffer, and, as Humair says, 'Grappelli's not a sufferer' – which is perfectly understandable if you are nearing sixty and know first-hand what suffering is. Thus, while Stéphane was not without engagements (though one Australian acquaintance thought he was 'on his uppers') the work was not as plentiful, or as easy, as it had been. Bob Clarke, who had returned to Paris to begin what would be ten years of successful, profitable appearances at the Lido and Crazy Horse with his comedy trio, remembers Stéphane referring to the Hilton offer as ''a good proposition'.

Clarke well knew the lot of the travelling soloist. 'It's a hard life for those guys. . . . He was working maybe a couple of months in Italy and then a month at Les Trois Mailletz and then a guest spot. So I got the impression that he was over the moon at getting the Hilton gig . . . In other words, a long-lasting gig instead of living out of a suitcase.'

Of course, Stéphane's subsequent years of fame would bring a great deal of suitcase-living, but on his terms. As it was, the Hilton offered security, albeit at a price. Bob Clarke often went around to see him there. 'It was called 'Le Toit de Paris', on the tenth floor. It was just an orchestra in a restaurant, and there was a little dance floor if you wanted to get up and dance around . . . As you walked in, the bar was on the right; then a few metres down was the restaurant, and the bandstand was at the bottom of that again. So it was a regular U-shaped restaurant. If you just wanted to go up for a drink, and you wanted to hear Grappelli, you couldn't do that: you had to sit at the bar, or have dinner. But if you went up at say, ten-thirty, eleven, you could go in and sit at a ringside table.'

As far as he was concerned, the clientele was unworthy of Stéphane. 'There were knives and forks clattering around. Nobody knew who he was. . . . It wasn't a jazz crowd, it was people who lived in the hotel going up and having a nosh. It was only people like me who'd go gee them up. It must have been soul-destroying at times . . . How can you play jazz? Jazz is an atmosphere. You've got to feel it. . . . But it was the right money.'

Stéphane's band was the kind of quintet he had often worked with in Britain – violin plus four rhythm. The mandatory vocals were supplied by the guitarist. At times, there was also a saxophonist who would relieve Stéphane as the lead instrument, and occasionally a pianist to play at intermissions. Often, however, the intermission pianist was Stéphane himself. The group is preserved on *Le Toit de Paris*, recorded in January 1969 – the first LP Stéphane had made since *Violin Summit* in 1966 – and sounds competent and pleasing, but not particularly gripping. Though Stéphane plays well, there is no sense of risks or discoveries. Aside from a couple of up-tempos, the emphasis is on ballads and tunes with a polite, unobtrusive beat. You can almost hear the clink of silver, the swish of gowns, the witty chatter.

The ambiance recalled the old days of the Milroy and 96 Piccadilly, but Alan Clare, Stéphane's pianist at those rooms, worked up a fine British indignation when he visited his old leader at the Hilton. To him it was 'that bloody torture chamber', and as far as he was concerned, Stéphane *was* suffering, because 'the French are the worst listeners in the world. They're the most loquacious listeners. They *talk*; they listen with their mouths, and it used to drive Stéphane mad. . . . They used to sit right on top of the band and then complain about the noise. And Stéphane would say, "But I can't move. I must stay here. *You* can move."'

On the whole, Gallic observers are less exercised. For Michel Chouanard, who became Stéphane's French agent after he left Le Toit, Stéphane was happy simply because he was playing: 'The moment he makes music, the moment he plays, he's always happy . . . He likes playing and giving pleasure to the spectators.' Obviously it is preferable if that pleasure comes from people who are actually paying attention, but since the money was right, Stéphane was willing to make certain concessions. For him, coming from the old school of musician-entertainers, contentment is professional. Daniel Humair, coming from a newer school, puts the difference neatly: 'He's a musician for the audience, and now I think it's time for the audience to be for the musician.' So, as usual, Stéphane played both to please, and to please himself. Once, thinking of the Hilton, I asked him if he liked everything he did. 'Always,' he replied firmly. And the people danced? 'Of course. But I didn't take any notice.'

Obviously he has a highly developed and subtle sense of self-preservation, part of which is his sense of humour, his ability to take amusement where he finds it. Sometimes Bob Clarke would sit in when Stéphane was playing intermission piano: 'I'd pick his fiddle up and play a couple of wee tunes . . .' Once the wee tunes were a medley of Strauss waltzes, which

Stéphane jams in the beer tent at the 1973 Cambridge Folk Festival, the scene of one of his greatest personal triumphs.

At the 100 Club, London, late 1973. Spreading joy are Len Skeat, bass; Denny Wright and Diz Disley, guitars, and the maestro.

Stéphane and his admirer and protegé, Nigel Kennedy.

Stéphane and Diz at My Father's Place, New York.

*Stéphane at the Haymarket Theatre, Leicester, 23 November 1973. The Diz
Disley trio is composed of (left to right) Diz, Len Skeat and Denny Wright.*

An almost-punk Stéphane in 1976, with Diz Disley (left) and John Etheridge (right).

Celebrating the award of Stéphane's Legion d'Honneur at the Paris Hilton, 1975. The group includes (from left) Marc Hemmeler, Daniel Humair, Alix Combelle and (far right) Diz Disley.

Ovation at the Albert Hall after Stéphane's 70th birthday concert: (from left) Diz Disley, John Etheridge, Phil Bates, Brian Torff, Niels-Henning Ørsted Pedersen, SG, George Shearing, Julian Bream, Didier Lockwood.

Stéphane in a mood of fatherly pride after his duet with Didier Lockwood at the Albert Hall.

Stéphane at the Kool Jazz Festival, New York 1984.
Stéphane filming for French television with (left to right) Oscar Peterson, Kenny Clarke and Niels-Henning Ørsted Pedersen.

Stéphane reunited with his wartime colleague, George Shearing, at the Albert Hall.

Previous page:
Yehudi Menuhin compares notes with Stéphane, 1980.

Stéphane acknowledging the cheers of his 70th birthday crowd at the Albert Hall, 1978.

Bob came in to find Stéphane rendering in the best Viennese manner. He joined in helpfully, only to find that Grappelli was having a little joke, playing along innocently in awful keys like Db and Gb, the worst and most constricting for a violinist.

The pianist for the last three years of the Hilton residence was one of Stéphane's favourite musicians, Marc Hemmeler, for whom it was a very pleasant job. Granted, in terms of volume, 'the Hilton was a soft place, but we had a good time.' Though it was not a true jazz gig, it was also not destructively commercial. Marc had played other jobs with Stéphane, and for the Hilton, 'we didn't change, really. . . . We played jazz, slow foxtrot, bossa nova . . . sometimes we played 'Charmaine' or 'Always' as a waltz – a very English waltz.' But it really didn't matter what they played, simply because of Stéphane's way with any tune. 'He makes all kinds of music sound. I mean, I hate "Strangers in the Night". Sometimes at the Hilton we had to play it, and he has this sound, so pure, so marvellous, that if you do nice chords behind, "Strangers in the Night" is a nice melody – played by Stéphane.'

That is certainly one of the violinist's secrets – never playing down to the music or to the audience, always doing as much with the material as he can. As Marc said, 'Tunes played by Stéphane always arrange themselves. He changes the meaning . . . A very small melody with him, you know, in his hands sounds different.' Not only was the music worthwhile, but so was the atmosphere. 'It was a nice place, very *chic*. All Paris came. Stéphane knows a lot of rich people. . . . It's phenomenal all the duchesses, all the counts he knows, from all over Europe, rich English people from forty years ago, and they all have great respect for him. . . . All those people from the thirties, when Paris was tremendous.'

One of Stéphane's principal recollections of the Hilton is how indispensable Marc was, not only musically but socially. As he told me, with a laugh, 'Hemmeler was really conducting the business; I was just there to smile and say hello. We would be in the middle of a tune, and he would say "watch!" – it's odd that we were all French and he (though he was Swiss) was speaking French, but he would say "watch" in English – and then he would switch into another tune, because he had seen some guy come in who requested that tune six months ago, and he'd remembered that. And of course the guy was so pleased that he would immediately order champagne for the band!'

There were numerous American tourists too, and not just businessmen. 'All the musicians came after concerts. Basie used to be at the Hilton, Errol Garner, Stan Getz, Dizzy,

Gerry Mulligan. They came to eat, have a drink and play.'
This was late night sitting in, after the diners had cleared
off, taking the waltzes with them, though some of the more
free-spirited dancers may have remained. It all makes the
Hilton seem a very mixed bag, which is natural, since throughout his career Stéphane has been a man of so many musical
parts. He played the job for what it offered at the moment. It
meant security, some reputation, musical challenges that other
players brought or that he created himself. But inevitably his
old restlessness began to assert itself. He told Whitney Balliet
that the one sure lesson he learned at the Hilton was: 'It is
stupid to stay in one place so much.' He told me that pretty
quickly he was 'in and out'. 'I was there maybe one year and
then I started to vanish.'

Some of the places he vanished into were recording studios.
There is a definite quickening of his recording activity in 1969,
beginning with two superb albums made in two days in June.
His partner was the American guitarist Barney Kessel, who
was visiting Europe, and who had made the customary
musician's call to the tenth floor of the Hilton. Stéphane
played on two tracks of a Kessel album, and less than a week
later the two got together in earnest for *I Remember Django*
and *Limehouse Blues*. Like the earlier *Feeling + Finesse =
Jazz*, these albums have the feeling of a beginning, a declaration; unlike that album, they were to lead rapidly to others
and a gathering momentum.

They are extraordinary first of all because of their wonderful
freedom. Genuine blowing sessions, they still possess that
concision and shapeliness typical of Stéphane. Well as Barney
Kessel plays, Stéphane is the star of the show, reeling off one
hungry solo after another, a delighted truant from the Hilton,
the knives and forks, duchesses and counts. He feels no need
to change repertoire; he had been playing the likes of 'Honeysuckle Rose' and 'I Found a New Baby' for forty years, and
yet he goes after them as if they were the latest heads, full of
tantalizing possibilities.·

The structures he creates from them possess that amazing
integrity we expect from him at his best, like his seven (or
eight) choruses on the 1962 'Minor Swing'. Each one of the
four choruses on 'Honeysuckle Rose', for instance, is complete
in itself, and it seems an unanticipated bonus when Stéphane
plunges on into the next one. Yet that one turns out to extend
what went before as well as having its own character. As in the
best jazz solos, you can hardly believe what happens next. It
is logical and surprising at once, and yet it occurs seemingly
without thought, certainly without hesitation, simply flowing

and flowing on. Stéphane has said that he has an image of pure
fluidity in mind as he plays: 'The movement is like water, you
see; you don't know where the water goes. I always visualize
that.' And that is just how it sounds, that spontaneous and
free, the music finding its natural course.

His tone is remarkable as well, not just pretty in a banal
one-dimensional sense, but the perfect vehicle for his fluency
and variety. The alterations in vibrato, the bits of ornamen-
tation, the colours and nuances are all part of the expressive
momentum. Of course it makes the ballads like 'More Than
You Know' and I Can't Get Started' especially absorbing, but
the same subtlety informs the up-tempos. Stéphane never
merely runs changes; every note says something in terms
of sound, harmonic function, rhythmic placement. Without
intending to be, it is a full vindication of the violin as a jazz
instrument, because in Stéphane's hands the characteristics
that have made it a supreme instrument of classical music turn
out to be valid for jazz as well. It is simply a question of the
form of jazz and quality of the player.

Stéphane's performance also brings out the rich character of
acoustic instruments. Barney Kessel is a world-class player, full
of drive and conviction, but the basic sonority of his guitar seems
monochromatic next to Stéphane's playing. That difference in
the range of available colour is expanded by the difference in
vocabulary. Barney was one of the first electric guitarists and
beboppers, and bop, flavoured with a *soupçon* of country twang,
remains his basic language. But Stéphane absorbed so much
music from so many sources that he cannot be categorized. He
has simply continued to become himself. To call him a swing
player is nonsense: no swing player ever spun out lines like these,
with their teasing harmonic shifts, their rhythmic guile. Yet at
the same time, in 'Tea for Two', he can happily, unselfconsciously employ four repeated quarter-notes, bent downward, a
famous King Oliver lick from fifty years before. That passage is
not an anachronism; it too is just a part of Stéphane's vocabulary,
distilled from all the music he has listened to and loved. In the
same way, parts of 'Willow Weep for Me' sound like Art Tatum
transcribed for violin. Perhaps guitarist John Etheridge
summed it up best when he said the violinist simply plays 'pure
jazz, neither old nor new'.

No doubt some of the range and resourcefulness of
Stéphane's language is due to the harmonic interest he brings
to a linear instrument. Reflecting on how he structures a solo,
his sometime partner Martial Solal said, 'I think he tries to
make a melodic line; it's normal for the violin.' At the same
time this is a violinist who loves the piano, who has said himself

that his approach is not 'violinistic' (guitarist Ike Isaacs has called him 'a pianist on the violin'). The line he makes has rich vertical and horizontal scope, with every chord offering myriad choices. His form of musical discourse incorporates a plenitude of asides and allusions, commentary and cross-references, any one of which can provide a whole new direction. Returning to his favourite image, Stéphane says, 'The water goes where there is a possibility for it to go,' and on any given terrain, the possibilities can seem infinite.

Finally, some of the terrain will be forever French. Daniel Humair observed to me that, unlike Django, Stéphane has 'a Parisian approach . . . a French way of playing American standards.' For Daniel this is right and proper: '. . . we are all inspired by American musicians, but our background and our freedom and our way of living should influence the music and we should let go. Personally what I'm looking for is to have a totally jazz approach with an intellectual concept of European tradition. . . . I like to burn but I don't like to be obvious; I don't like the first degree.'

That seems to me to define Stéphane's style admirably, particularly as embodied in the records he began to make in the late sixties, the records of his maturity. Nothing he does is obvious; he is both swinging and intelligent. It is not mixing a metaphor to say he both burns and flows (one recalls Denny Wright's reference to 'liquid gold'). For all its purity and direct appeal, his style is immensely sophisticated, the product of a musical instinct developed and refined over decades of experience, which continues to ripen and grow.

Word of somebody playing this well was bound to get out sooner or later. In America, *Down Beat* magazine noted that Grappelli and Kessel had recorded together. Before this, Stéphane had been duly mentioned there in a February 1967 survey of the history of jazz violin, which praised his mixture of the French tradition and jazz as exemplified in *Feeling + Finesse*, though his earlier recordings were out of print. A year later the magazine reported on a memorial concert for Stuff Smith in Denmark, comprising his three colleagues from *Violin Summit*, Stéphane, Svend and Jean-Luc. The reviewer admired Stéphane's '*esprit* and noble masculinity', but contrasted his approach with that of young Ponty, who was 'exciting in a way usually reserved for tenor saxophonists'.

Indeed Ponty's electrified/electrifying Coltrane-style fiddle had been causing a stir for some time. In 1966 he had won the International Critics Poll despite the fact he had not yet had a record released in America. Certainly he raised American consciousness of the violin; as Matt Glaser said, in general he was responsible for the instrument's public renaissance. To Daniel Humair, Ponty was specifically responsible for Stéphane's renaissance in America: 'Though it should be the reverse, Ponty made Grappelli happen in the States . . . this breakthrough with this French violin player. Then Stéphane came and people said, "That's the master of it."'

At any rate, Stéphane was ready, and the event that Frank Tenot had hoped for in 1957 – that he would be 'consecrated' by American acceptance in the form of an invitation to the Newport Jazz Festival – came to pass in July 1969. (The advance listings of the event in *Jazz Hot* show that Stéphane had now resumed the final 'i' in Grappelli.)

That the actual experience turned out to be less than a consecration was not Stéphane's fault. Newport has had a history of extra-musical excitement, usually brought on by youthful crowds indifferent to jazz but devoted to beer. In 1969 young emotions were at flood tide, incited not by such old-fashioned stimulants, but by the spell of the counter-culture with its opposition to authority (epitomized by the government and the Viet Nam war) and its dedication to humanity breathing free (rock, drugs, mass manifestations). Unwisely, the guiding lights at Newport decided jazz would benefit financially from a piece of the rock action, and for the first time the 1969 bill included rock and jazz stars side by side. Indeed, the crowds materialized but turned out to be uncontrollable. Holding the attitude that all art – all everything – should be free to the people, the hordes simply pushed in wherever they wanted to go. The result was close to chaos, inside the grounds and out. As *Down Beat* reported in a scathing review headed 'Newport 1969: Bad Trip', 'thousands of "kids" ranging in age from mid-teens to late twenties were milling about, doing their thing and blocking traffic. We were informed that all parking lots, including the official one, were "full", meaning full of human litter refusing to move on.' Inside the festival, listeners were 'blown out by the noise and squeezed out by the milling throngs – 22,000 people compressed inside an area normally limited to 18,500, all of them wanting to be up front.' Jazz lovers were appalled to realize that music meant something different to the rock culture, who were there not so much to listen as to be over-whelmed. As an outraged Ira Gitler reported, 'Amplifiers and speakers are as important, if not more so, as the actual instruments played by the musicians.'

It was the high tide of Jimi Hendrix, which meant that Stéphane, aiming for a more civilized form of excitement, was at a disadvantage. Still, he was a *succés d'estime*. *Down Beat* reported that despite having 'his American debut marred by the unfortunate circumstances [he] impressed in a set including "How High the Moon", "Nuages", and a swinging "Pennies from Heaven", his tone full and sweet but not cloying, his mastery of the instrument evident throughout.' Importing Grappelli had been one of the festival's good ideas, they declared, but their general advice for next year was 'leave rock where it belongs: in the kindergarten'. In fact a month later the rock culture found its spiritual homeland in the fields of Woodstock, in upstate New York.

Stéphane's reaction to the débâcle was mixed. A year afterwards he told a BBC interviewer that the festival was 'a great revelation for me, not only for jazz, but pop and rock, which were very interesting in my opinion'. But several years later he said, 'It was not a concert, it was a revolution.' Though he had been invited back for 1970, he had declined to go: 'Never again do I want to be faced with a *difficulté* like that.' In 1985, talking to me, his objections were more muted and general: 'I was not very pleased. It was cold, it was raining all the time, it's a crazy place. I played twelve hours late, and I don't like to work like that.'

What he did like was the reaction of a trim black man who came up after his set to compliment him. Stéphane thanked him and inquired politely if he was a musician. 'Yes,' said the fan, 'I'm Miles Davis.' Stéphane also very much liked the playing of Gary Burton, the young vibes star who he later described as 'of the same strength as Tatum or Django Reinhardt. . . .' As he returned to Paris, perhaps somewhat shell-shocked by his experience of America, he was hoping to arrange a record date with him.

Word of Stéphane's desire reached the proper quarters, and wheels began to turn. However, his first visit to a studio after his return from the States brought him, on 22 October 1969, face to face with the godfather of jazz violin, Joe Venuti. They had never met, and the encounter was bound to produce sparks both of inspiration and competition. Venuti was an aggressive character who, one way or another, liked to make his presence felt. Bob Clarke, acquainted with both men, was present for the session, and he knew, though Stéphane did not, where Venuti stood: 'When I met Joe in Las Vegas, he said, "that punk" – he didn't reckon Grappelli.' Stéphane, for his part, had never expressed anything but admiration for the older player (nor would he), even though he always maintained he had developed his own style independently.

But when the music started, Stéphane took off. For Bob

Clarke there was no question of the result: 'Grappelli played the ass off Venuti. He really laid right into it, he *wailed*.' Though an admitted fan of Stéphane, Bob is no blind partisan. He is quite ready to recall times when Svend Asmussen, for instance, had the edge on the Frenchman. But on the record that came out as *Venupelli Blues*, there was little doubt what was what. Joe plays with drive, but his tone and attack sound strident, almost querulous. His phrasing is stiff – hot, perhaps, but more hot-cha than swinging. At times, Stéphane plays musical rings around him, more inventive, more coherent, his confidence and aplomb unruffled by Venuti's belligerence. Reactions may be affected, of course, by listeners' tastes. Venuti stood clearly on one side of the fiddle fence, being for Stuff Smith and against not only Stéphane, but Eddie South: 'I like a man who swings,' he said once, implying that South didn't. But for Bob Clarke, when confronting Joe, swing was what Stéphane did. 'He surpassed Venuti on that session. . . . He'd probably been saving it all up, all those years – WHAM!'

The session with Gary Burton came up two weeks later, on 4 November. Though the vibist was in Europe on tour, and available, the meeting had not been a foregone conclusion. For young Burton, Grappelli, Newport or not, was part of the past. He requested an audition, and Stéphane, probably more amused than anything else, complied and passed with flying colours. For the violinist, the making of *Paris Encounter* was memorable not only for Burton but for the presence of bassist Steve Swallow. He had never played with electric bass before and had not liked what he had heard of it. But Swallow, both as musician and composer, bowled him over: 'What an artist!'

The record itself has moments of distinction without quite gelling. Stéphane is in fine fettle: his headlong solo on 'Daphne' alone would be worth the price of admission. But the Burton group has a cooler, more introverted quality than that best suited to Grappelli, and some rather restless drumming does not encourage him to stretch out. However, the session gave him a chance to engage the new jazz repertoire, and produced beautiful readings of tunes like Miles Davis's 'Blue in Green', Swallow's 'Falling Grace' and Mike Gibbs's 'Sweet Rain'. Especially beautiful is his performance of 'Here's That Rainy Day', one of the loveliest of all standards, which, after only a few bars of melody, he begins to explore, expand and celebrate. On the whole, however, he seems somewhat under wraps.

By contrast, he comes busting out all over on *Stéphane Grappelly and Friends*. Except for Marc Hemmeler, all the friends are British, and, though he had appeared in London – most recently for the BBC at Ronnie Scott's – this was the first full-scale recording he had done there in years. It involved two men who would soon play significant parts in his life: Alan Clare, his pianist from the days of the Milroy and 96 Piccadilly, who would begin to arrange concerts with him in Britain, and guitarist Diz Disley, who would reunite him with strings.

Whether it is the atmosphere of homecoming or simply a successful chemistry in the studio, the record has at times a feeling of almost giddy abandon. On tracks like 'I Can't Believe that You're in Love with Me' and 'Taking a Chance on Love', Stéphane is playing flat out, with awesome results. On 'Can't Believe', he delivers a fiery opening solo, then piles up three stunning choruses at the end, leaving his mates unsure of how long he might go on. (The last chorus, by the way, contains a hair-raising Grappellian version of Coltrane's 'sheets of sound'.) The same sort of thing occurs on 'Taking a Chance', with an amazing double-stopped passage before Stéphane drops into the melody, giving it a reading so tantalizing it becomes a natural extension of his solo. Nothing illustrates the unbuttoned mood of the proceedings as clearly as the group's hilarious version of 'Darling, Je Vous Aime Beaucoup', in which Stéphane, as vocalist, takes revenge on all the 'fractured French' singers that plagued the thirties. As he sings, he quickly gives up any attempt to keep a straight face, while behind him his friends fall about, uttering little shrieks and fracturing some French of their own.

This was also Stéphane's recording début with Marc Hemmeler, who was by now established on piano at the Hilton, having replaced Raymond Fol, who had recorded the *Le Toit de Paris* album. Stéphane has always admired him deeply, once telling an interviewer he was 'packed with talent', and their recordings show their affinity. Further fruits of their partnership appear on Stéphane's next three records, made between October 1970 and March 1971. The best may be *Stéphane Grappelli 1971* (which also includes Alan Clare on a few tracks), the first in a three-yearly series made for Pye records. It shows Stéphane not only at the height of his powers, but trying out new directions. Not all of them succeed: the disc contains a rather gooey, echo-chamber version of 'Blue River', a tentative bow toward rock. Even here, however, Stéphane's taste comes through, and another contemporary experiment, James Taylor's country-style 'Sunny Skies' works well, thanks to Grappelli's dark, tender sostenuto and Hemmeler's idiomatic, slightly twangy accompaniment. Most ravishing is 'The Folks Who Live on the Hill', which shows Stéphane's ability to create a ballad mood not only moving but thoughtful – or rather, moving because thoughtful.

A pleasant curiosity is the record's retention of Stéphane's comments between takes: 'Ah, non, mes enfants . . . We must do it again; it is difficult, you see.' But the performances sound as if they went off without a hitch. Among the up-tempos 'Peanut Vendor' is notable as a Stéphanic response to yet another prevailing current. Originally a kind of pseudo-South American novelty, the group transforms it into a Coltraneish modal piece, hypnotically rhythmic. In fact a closer model would be tenor saxophonist Charles Lloyd's 'Forest Flower', whose light Latin groove was a hit in the late sixties. Whatever the specific inspiration, Stéphane speaks the modal language like a native – the real McCoy, you could say.

Overall, the sheer variety of the record is remarkable, evidence of Stéphane's openness to whatever was going on in music. Perhaps the most dazzling performance is the twenties warhorse 'Runnin' Wild', also brought up-to-date, its melody reworked with stop-time rhythms in the manner of Miles Davis's 'So What'. The tempo is blazingly fast – indeed it rushes – and Stéphane roars through four choruses in irresistible form, impulsively riffing behind Marc before adding one more at the end for the sheer exuberance of it. But even at this tempo it is clear that Stéphane's great quality is emotion. I once asked Marc if Stéphane particularly liked up-tempos, like 'Runnin' Wild'. 'It depends on the people,' he started by saying. 'If he plays fast they like it; but he touches me more in ballads or mediums –' He stopped abruptly, then continued, 'No, he touches me in *everything*.'

This is why they continued to play so well together, on *I Hear Music* and *Afternoon in Paris*, both examples of the high standard Stéphane was maintaining. The first album includes his tributes to several jazzmen, among them Coltrane and Ben Webster, as well as 'A Flower for Kenny', a feature for drummer Kenny Clarke. Grappelli once thought him too loud, but he plays with exemplary taste and push throughout the album, and on his solo he opens up handsomely, painting the kind of posey associated with Van Gogh. *Afternoon in Paris* has some lovely ballads and a delicious quasi-baroque duet between Stéphane and Marc on 'Undecided', the kind of witty, tasty counterpoint that is still a feature of Grappelli performances.

Of course, all the time these records were being made, he and Hemmeler were holding forth at the Hilton. His vanishings, however, were growing more frequent, encouraged by friends like Alan Clare who were still disturbed by what they considered the disrespectful treatment he suffered there. Alan began to arrange trio concerts in London, to show him the kind of reception that was available and fitting for him. According to the pianist, it was only Stéphane's old 'horror of poverty' that kept him at Le Toit. 'He used to say "It's a safe job; they never give me the sack." But I told him, "You're a great artist; people are queuing to see you. They're going to pay you a lot of money from now on." So he never went back.'

According to Hemmeler, Stéphane's departure was inevitable: 'He had too many propositions to go do concerts. At the end, he was at the Hilton two days a week. He had a lot of Saturday gigs, and Saturday was important at the Hilton too. That's the principal reason.' As Michel Chouanard saw it, enough was simply enough. 'When you are young you must change; only old people don't want to change any more, and Stéphane is always young. He has the vivacity of his music.' Indeed, age is irrelevant to Grappelli. When Bob Clarke once referred to 'the old pianist' who was playing at the Hilton's coffee bar, Stéphane was startled: 'Old? He's the same age as me!'

Whatever the factors, by late 1971, when Stéphane and the Alan Clare trio recorded the excellent *Stéphane Grappelli 1972* live at London's Queen Elizabeth Hall, he was ready to leave his tenth floor sanctuary. A decisive stimulus may have originated in a surprise phone call from the BBC in December. It was an invitation to take part in the special Christmas television show of Michael Parkinson, who, as Stéphane described it to me, 'liked to do some funny *mariages*'. The *mariage* in this case would musically join Stéphane and Yehudi Menuhin. In a letter to me, Michael Parkinson recalled that the project came about when a researcher went to interview Menuhin, who was already scheduled to appear on the show, and noticed a record by Grappelli on his desk. It turned out 'that the record had been sent by a music company and that Menuhin had little knowledge of Grappelli's playing. He had heard he was exceptional but had little idea of the style he played in. When the researcher reported this we decided to try and arrange a meeting between the two on the air. Both Menuhin and Grappelli agreed providing they could get together and rehearse beforehand.'

Over to Menuhin, who, in the notes for the sixth duet record that he and Stéphane were to make almost fifteen years later, recalled his original reactions. 'I was more than hesitant. I felt it would be rather sad for this contemporary embodiment of thousands of years of fiddlers . . . to be saddled with a useless colleague who had never played jazz and could only remember one tune from the rhythmic point of view: "Jalousie". . . . Yet the challenge was tempting.'

For his part, Stéphane was a little dismayed by what

Menuhin considered 'jazz'. 'Mr Menuhin chose a tune that I
must confess I'm not very keen on. . . . It's not my type of
music.' 'Jalousie', the archetypal tango; it was Paris in the
twenties all over again. But he was, as ever, accommodating.
'. . . I thought if Mr Menuhin, that great violinst, liked it,
why not me?' In fact, the prospect of playing anything with
the legendary virtuoso, whom he had heard in Paris when
Menuhin was a thirteen-year-old prodigy, was more than
daunting. All his diffidence about not being 'properly trained'
came to the fore, as Parkinson clearly saw: 'Stéphane was
terrified before he met Menuhin for their first rehearsal.'

They awaited Stéphane's return, worried perhaps that the
prospective union was not to be, but in due course 'he arrived
with his face wreathed in smiles. When we asked him why he
was so happy, he replied, "I was frightened of playing with
the maestro. However, three bars into 'Lady Be Good', tell
me who is the maestro?"' Indeed it was Menuhin who was
invading Stéphane's turf and had more reason to be nervous.
For him the experience was a revelation: 'For the first time
ever I played with a rhythm band. I was amazed at Stéphane's
originality and fascinated by the fact that the soloist can
improvise without ever losing rhythm. It was (and still is) an
adventure and an inspiration to play with such complementary
talent to my own training.'

There was no question of the show's success on 19
December 1971. As Parkinson put it, 'The television programme was wonderful – two great musicians meeting in
mutual respect.' Stéphane thought it was one of Parkinson's
'best plans, one of his best achievements'. And, as Menuhin
observed, the public effect was immediate, with a hint of the
future: 'The very next day French television sent a team for
filming, and from then on we collaborated and developed and
our first record followed.'

In December, that record was some months away. But the
whole Parkinson/Menuhin experience was bound to give a fillip
to Stéphane's sense of his public potential, and make him even
more inclined, on the eve of his sixty-fourth birthday, to go
back on the minstrel road.

I've Got the World On a String

Public response to the Parkinson show was so enthusiastic that it ultimately had to be repeated. On a personal level, its two stars were mutually impressed. Responding to an interviewer's question about Menuhin. Stéphane said, 'Ah, I was so lucky to meet him – such a great musician, such a human *extraordinaire*.' For Menuhin, Stéphane embodied qualities he had long admired and variously pursued – a natural approach to music, a gift not shaped according to conventional academic prescriptions but which flowed out freely and personally, without constriction. What the classical virtuoso has called his 'lifelong journey toward spontaneity' had already taken him to musical associations with the sitar master, Ravi Shankar. Stéphane was a logical if unexpected further stage on the way.

Since the partnership augured so well, it seemed a shame to sever it after one meeting. EMI records clearly saw that a large public would be interested in a record by the duo, and preparations were duly made, with musical arrangements by Max Harris, who had done the work for the Parkinson broadcast. The first session took place on 14 June 1972. By this time Stéphane had left the Hilton, encouraged by developments on a range of fronts: in addition to the Menuhin possibilities, the work Alan Clare was getting with his trio, similar work in Paris with Marc Hemmeler and an offer from the singer-guitarist Sacha Distel to take part in his stage show. At the time of the Menuhin session, Stéphane was appearing with Distel at the Duke of York's theatre in London. Adroit as usual at changing hats, he composed three original pieces for the next day's recording after one night's stint on stage.

As initially conceived, the record was to consist of 'Jalousie'-style duets on one side, backed with jazz-influenced classical works of the type produced by Les Six in Paris in the twenties. There would have been a certain appropriateness about that concept, since it embraced music from the time of Stéphane's own awakening, but the two fiddlers got on so well with the repertoire of popular standards that the more legitimate side of the enterprise was shelved – for good, as it turned out. More arrangements were needed, so the completion of the full disc was postponed, the final recording occurring in March 1973. More important, Menuhin and Grappelli got on famously. As Stéphane expressed it to a *Newsweek* reporter, 'We were kissing each other like mad.'

On his own, Stéphane continued his upward, forward mobility. Hardly were the first Menuhin sessions over when he was back in the studio with a British rhythm section (plus Marc Hemmeler on a few tracks) paying a distinguished *Homage to Django*. Consisting of tunes connected with the old Quintet, the album is part tribute and part declaration of independence. The invited comparison with the previous versions shows how much Stéphane has developed in confidence and daring, sound and fluency. There is no question it is the same player, but he has come fully into his own. The grace and accuracy have opened into a new looseness and punch. His sonority is still beautiful, but more rounded and flexible. On ballads, like 'Tears', his vibrato takes on the deliberate expansiveness of Ben Webster; he is at once agile, heartfelt and reflective. The up-tempos are a stream of inspiration, demonstrating his amazing rhythmic and harmonic surefootedness, carrying the listener along, dazed and delighted.

The sense of strain that occasionally appeared in the Django recordings has vanished, and the feeling of playing under pressure has matured into easy resilience and strength, with no loss of excitement. As it became clear from performances and recordings like this that Stéphane Grappelli, former 'commercial bandleader', had become a startling new jazz musician, journalists attempted to increase the drama of his re-emergence by deprecating his powers in the Quintet. One, while extolling his July 1972 appearance with Alan Clare at Ronnie Scott's, said that anyone brought up on the early records might have dismissed him 'as a man who can take a chorus now and then'. This is pure and silly rhetoric. Anyone with ears knew how much Stéphane had contributed to the Quintet. But now he had clearly arrived on his own: he was in no one's shadow. For him, life really had begun at sixty.

The interview with *Newsweek* shows the extent to which his creative surge was being accompanied by public recognition. Other signs that appeared in 1972 were his presence at the Royal Variety Performance, after which he met Queen Elizabeth, and his invitation to appear on Roy Plomley's *Desert Island Discs*. The Grappelli selection of eight records included, as we have seen, old totems by Armstrong and Beiderbecke; his first love, Debussy's *Prelude à l'Après-midi d'un Faune*; tracks by Ben Webster, Art Tatum and John Coltrane, and his own 'Gary' (for Gary Burton) from the *I Hear Music* album. His choice of a luxury object and a book have a certain significance. For his object he took the Koh-i-Noor diamond, no doubt feeling that if pure luxury is what you're after, you should go the whole way, but perhaps also reflecting the love of clarity and colour that is central to his style. For the book he requested an atlas, to remind him, cast away on his island, of how many other places there were.

Though no one could have predicted it, the opportunity to see those places was forecast in a Queen Elizabeth Hall concert with the Alex Welsh Band. Reviewing it, the *Melody Maker* critic professed himself 'usually impervious to Gallic charm', but found Stéphane delightful, 'a veritable Ben Webster of the violin'. For one number only, however, the Alan Clare trio were replaced by a special line-up: 'Nostalgia had its day when compère Diz Disley and fellow guitarist Jim Douglas joined Stéphane for a limp recreation of the Hot Club Quintet.' Obviously the critic was impervious to nostalgia too, but he had to admit that 'the audience loved it'.

Though a one-off event, the meeting was prophetic, implying that Diz Disley was already having visions and dreaming dreams. He had taken the proper measure of the public too. Every review of Stéphane in person mentioned the infectious happiness he communicated with his music; he was 'a phenomenal crowd-pleaser'. His playing with the guitars only increased the effect, for a surprisingly large number of people. As one fan wrote to Diz years later, though she had no doubts about the excellence of the Alan Clare trio, 'It wasn't quite the right sound, and I cannot have been the only one present in 1972 whose heart leapt with joy when you joined Stéphane to produce something much nearer what I had cherished in memory.'

But even more surprisingly, there turned out to be a large number of potential listeners who cherished no memories of the old Quintet and who had been exposed to very different kinds of guitar playing. For a number of reasons, the musical and social climate was changing. The issue of the *Melody Maker* which reviewed Stéphane's concert featured Jimi Hendrix on the cover – still influential, but dead in 1970 of a drug overdose. The week before, the magazine had contained an article in the wake of the US presidential election which declared that 'Nixon's victory has finally stripped away any illusions that rock could produce a new culture.' The counter-culture's hectic blend of idealism, innocence and arrogance was beginning to pall, along with the notion that one could be deafened into consciousness. It was possible that music, apprehended purely and personally as music and not as tribal rite, might reappear.

Although its recorded products had yet to emerge. Stéphane's association with Yehudi Menuhin was burgeoning, and it brought him before another kind of young audience, with little experience of rock. One of Menuhin's most important experiments had been the founding of a school for talented young musicians in Stoke d'Abernon. The violinist was so impressed with Stéphane that he invited his jazz colleague to play for the students there. Among the school's prize pupils at the time was Nigel Kennedy, who would go on to become the renowned concert violinist he is today, and one of the few classical musicians who feels at home playing jazz. That dual interest had already surfaced at the Menuhin school, somewhat to the discomfiture of his teachers.

It had started, Nigel told me, with a pile of 78s at the family home. He began listening to them as an escape from his usual regimen: 'After I'd been practising I didn't want to listen to classical any more.' He discovered the jazz classics – like Fats Waller, Louis Armstrong and Jack Teagarden – and his reaction was typical of an interested conservatoire fiddler. 'I thought, "This is great music", but I never thought of playing it.' Then he discovered the Hot Club, which changed everything. In a way, his reaction to the group was typical too – 'Suddenly there was this music. It didn't sound at all like Fats Waller to me, the Hot Club. It's not the same; it doesn't belong to that period of American jazz at all. It's a totally different concept of music. I didn't think it was really jazz, but on the other hand there was something I really liked about it. And whoever was playing fiddle was playing in a way that no

149

classical bloke has ever got close to. It just brought out a whole
new spectrum of what the violin could do for me.'

He found out very quickly who was playing and started
joining in – 'playing along with the records, and learning one
or two licks of his.' It all made the prospect of Stéphane's visit
to the school enormously exciting. 'He came with Alan Clare
and Lenny Bush. They didn't bring drums, because there were
no mikes, and they just played acoustic.' Stéphane was 'really
nervous playing in front of classical kids', but it made no
difference. 'It was great. It was a revelation. It was the greatest
day of my life. I was about fourteen at that stage, and it
brought music alive to me. . . . It was a huge thing, because
he was definitely the man I admired the most of any musician.'

Better was yet to come, to make the Cinderella tale complete,
and Nigel was ready for it. 'At the end of the concert, he said
as a joke, "Does anyone want to join in?" It was only a joke,
but I had my fiddle there, under my chair and already tuned,
and I got up before he could say no, and I just joined in. . . .
I knew all of the songs 'cause I was really into it, and he was
into it that a young guy, a different generation, was into the
music. It was only meant to be one night, but after that, we
went around and played a lot in clubs and concerts.'

Nigel was not the only one who was captivated, despite
the distinct negative predisposition of the school. 'What they
thought of jazz was totally different to what they thought of
Stéphane as soon as he arrived there, because he's got a
personality which will win anyone round. You know, I used
to be practising jazz in my practice time when I should have
been practising the Brahms Concerto, and be getting into a lot
of trouble about it. But once he came there, everyone loved
him.' However, the authorities still had reservations about
Stéphane taking Nigel off to iniquitous dens like Ronnie
Scott's. 'I'd of course have to get special permission from the
Menuhin School to go have this experience, and they were
very worried about me drinking too much beer and all that
business. . . . It wasn't what they called a healthy existence.
It was fun; I wouldn't have missed that for anything. It's been
one of the most valuable learning experiences I've had and one
of the most enjoyable.'

Though Menuhin himself was pleased, on the whole it didn't
seem that so much had changed since Stéphane Mougin had
ruffled owlish feathers at the Conservatoire by playing 'Tea
for Two' fifty years before. With a foot in each genre, and
acquaintance with each man, Nigel's reaction to the Menuhin–
Grappelli records has a special interest. The first of the series
appeared when he was performing with Stéphane and, with a

chuckle, he describes the project as 'a blunder'. 'Pretty shocking, I think . . . really disgraceful. But I think it made [Stéphane] more money, and he deserves some money, so it's all right. It's the only time he's been paid royalties when they come in, without having to chase them up. Classical labels are much more organized than jazz labels.'

Nigel's response is typical of most musicians, particularly in the jazz camp. No one would begrudge Stéphane some financial recognition for a lifetime of playing well. His own reactions to the records have been polite and politic, stressing his admiration for Menuhin and his pride at working with him, but not concealing the commercial genesis of their collaboration. He described the events following the Parkinson show to an interviewer accordingly: 'You know, business is business. A recording firm asked me and Mr Menuhin to make a record, and I am very, very pleased, because there is a very nice copyright with it, which helps put some butter on my spinach.'

The music, though, is another matter. While acknowledging that the Menuhin partnership was 'a great strike of luck' for Stéphane, Svend Asmussen leaned into my microphone to emphasize that the result was 'a series of recordings which I would dare to call completely ridiculous, and I know that Stéphane will agree. Mr Menuhin shouldn't have descended to making himself believe that it's so easy to play jazz. He can fool the people, but not the musicians.' Daniel Humair is more tolerant. 'They get along; it's a good gimmick. But Menuhin, as good as he is, has nothing to do with the jazz scene. I respect him, and several others, because when they do that, they do it with respect to jazz music – with humility, and that's why I accept it. Commercially it's great, but musically, jazzistically speaking, it's a joke, because he can't improvise . . .'

The notes accompanying the records, in fact, are coy on this question of improvisation, just as they are vague about what they mean by 'jazz'. There is a flavour of the twenties about the whole project, in its sense that jazz is bouncy, slightly arch and fun – a light, raffish mood that can accommodate 'Jalousie' as well as 'Lady Be Good'. The arrangements are witty and stylish, the atmosphere polished and professional. Stéphane is in his element, tossing off bits of choruses and counter-melodies. Menuhin does his manful best, but from time to time does show the difficulties of adapting a classical technique – with its wider dynamics and longer bowing – to the more quicksilver idiom. As the young French violinist Didier Lockwood observed, 'Sure, Menuhin's a great violin player, but it's so different. Jazz time, you know, it's moving. You never have time to be a little back. . . . He's scholastic, in a way.'

At their best, the records convey harmless merriment, what a reviewer called 'a sort of brilliant daffiness'. At their worst they feel strained and facetious. Listening to one of the *Jalousie* tracks, the American jazz violinist Leroy Jenkins thought that Menuhin sounded 'out of his league', and, as we have seen, from the beginning the classical player worried about simply getting in Stéphane's way, fully aware that it was he who was venturing on foreign terrain. He did it out of genuine fascination with the fluent artistry of jazz in general and Stéphane in particular, whom he likened to 'a wonderful juggler who throws plates and pots into the air and miraculously catches them again.'

It is not Menuhin's fault that the records' producers made him seem to claim abilities he did not possess. The liner notes refer to both him and Stéphane playing 'jazz solos'. Aiming to disarm criticism, the annotator of *Jalousie* declares that 'Menuhin makes no pretension that he can improvise with the ease and brilliance of Grappelli.' Indeed; in fact he has never made any pretension that he can improvise at all. Everything he plays on the records is written. To imply that he is actually improvising is to misrepresent what the records are like. 'Jazzy' they may be, jazz they are not. Not appreciating the difference comes close to trivializing jazz, an attitude that Daniel Humair attacked as 'making like a little entertainment: "Let's have fun and play jazz." Jazz is not fun.' But he acknowledged that 'Menuhin wasn't doing that.' Stéphane, of course, is more willing to see jazz as fun and to humour people who want a little entertainment. For him, the records were a fruitful episode in a lifetime of adaptations. As always, he took the opportunity and did what was required, as well as he could; at least he wasn't dancing the Charleston and playing the saxophone. He earned the esteem of a good man and great musician, and, as he told an interviewer, their duets 'sell like hot cakes all over the world'.

The Menuhin sessions comprised only one of some eleven appearances that Stéphane made on record in 1973, easily his busiest year, and another sign of the acceleration of his career. They also demonstrate yet again his versatility. Most of the settings find him with piano, bass and drums. In February he recorded in Paris with an all star trio featuring Oscar Peterson, Niels-Henning Ørsted Pedersen and Kenny Clarke. Niels, certainly one of the world's greatest bassists, remembered the session as another example of Stéphane's singular jazz qualities: 'There's a bite to the way he plays; it's absolutely fantastic.' He regards one track, 'Blues for Musicdisc', literally as a model performance. 'I use it as an example for some of my students to demonstrate that you can swing on a violin. . . . Stéphane really gets into it.'

There was a final session with the Alan Clare trio on which Stéphane played a piano solo, 'Emotion', which he introduces as 'my latest composition'. In fact he told me that he 'composed' it sitting at the piano with the tape rolling. It is a nonchalantly elegant performance, with bows in the general direction of Waller and Tatum and a specific reference near the end to a passage from his well-loved 'In a Mist'. With Alan Clare alone he made a lovely set of ballads, *The Talk of the Town*, using Alan's 'beautiful chords' to full advantage. With his French trio – Marc Hemmeler, Daniel Humair and former Hilton bassist Jack Sewing (who still plays with him in 1986) – he made an exhilarating album live at the Montreux Festival in July – an argument for those who say Stéphane is best captured in person. On the other hand, in a London studio he responded with conviction to the Americans Roland Hanna, George Mraz and Mel Lewis, and the resulting album, *Stéphane Grappelli Meets the Rhythm Section* (known in America as *Parisian Thoroughfare*), earned a five-star rating in *Down Beat*.

In December he summed up the distance he and jazz had travelled in two Paris albums. The first was a warm meeting with his old trumpet-playing colleague Bill Coleman, the second a jazz-rock fusion encounter with Jean-Luc Ponty (who, as Stéphane observed regretfully, would soon be 'lost to jazz') with high tech and disco rhythms abounding. Finally, just over the line into 1974, he recorded the music he had written for the film *Les Valseuses* (distributed in English as *Going Places*), an assignment he very much enjoyed, including a love scene of which he was especially proud.

It was the most remarkable year so far, the most extraordinary since the Quintet days. And finally it was the echo of the Quintet, the first flowering of Stéphane's celebrity, that would complete his new ascendancy. The guitarist Diz Disley was aware of his growing prominence, but Diz's interest in him had much older roots. As a fourteen-year-old, he had met the Hot Club on record and been smitten for life: 'I liked the rhythm sound; I just liked that nice, twangy sort of a plangent and rolling noise. I thought that was fucking wonderful. Still is – it's still the greatest.'

Diz became the complete Djangophile, mastering the guitar in the great gypsy's style and adopting some of the Django view of life. He grew up an intriguing combination of Yorkshireman (though Canadian-born) and Manouche, free-spirited but with a distinct capacity for hard-headed organization when it was required. He built a reputation as a cartoonist as well as a musician, with a nice line in comedy songs besides. In 1956 he founded the Soho String Quintet, a group patterned after the Hot Club that became his main interest, the medium of 'the one type of music I've preferred above all others'. And at one stage, as an act of specific homage, he organized a Django club that met in a pub every Thursday.

He was heavily involved in the fifties skiffle scene, that curious British mixture of trad jazz, blues and folk which was in some ways a forerunner of rock – The Beatles, as Diz points out, started as a skiffle group called The Quarrymen. In the fifties, all the West End 'clubs with the funny names' that had sported swing combos during Stéphane's war time residence put in espresso machines and hired singing guitarists who imitated Leadbelly. After a couple of heady years of 'dark roast and down home', rock took over. Half the skiffle bands threw out the washboards, brought in drums and went electric, now aping Little Richard. The other half went pure folk, plighting their troth to acoustic instruments.

Scornful of electrification, Diz went folk too, though as a freelance compère with the BBC he also had the honour of presenting the new model Beatles to London for the first time in 1963. Through the late sixties, while Stéphane was lying low in the Hilton, Diz was touring the extensive network of folk clubs that provided an alternative to rock throughout the UK. He was MC, singer, comedian and guitarist, appearing solo or with a bassist and sometimes a voilin. The music was not purely folk. Since acoustic stringed instruments were the real essence, it was easy to throw in old Quintet classics like 'Sweet Georgia Brown'.

Diz had met Stéphane briefly in 1957, when the violinist had come to London for a BBC broadcast, but was disappointed to see his old hero playing an electric violin. They met again in 1964 at a Reinhardt festival in Liverchies and then later in the sixties, when Diz's trips to Paris to see his friend Bob Clarke at the Lido or the Crazy Horse would include a visit to Grappelli at the Hilton. Then came the *Friends* record of 1970 and the Hot Club recreation of 1972.

All this time Diz had been aware that the folk clubs augured a potential market for Quintet-style fare if it were presented not as jazz, but simply good, lively music played on acoustic instruments. Listeners in the clubs agreed generally with classical guitarist Julian Bream, who described the sound of the electric guitar as 'the most boring, lifeless, phoney, vulgar noise that could have ever been contrived by humankind on this planet'. Diz, an old friend of Bream's, wholeheartedly concurred, believing that 'somewhere there had to be an audience of people who were tired of being deafened. There had to be an audience of more discerning people who were driven away by all the decibels.'

He got his chance to test the theory in March 1973, while playing the Cambridge Folk Club. One of his old Cambridge friends was Ken Woolard, who organized the Cambridge Folk Festival, one of the biggest events of its kind. After work at the club, Diz mentioned to him that he was going down to London to hear Stéphane at Ronnie Scott's and went on to suggest that Grappelli would be a likely candidate for that summer's Festival. Woolard was enthusiastic, and that night at Ronnie's, Diz broached the proposal to Stéphane, who accepted. The contract was signed soon after and the only, momentary hitch ensued when the violinist asked who would be playing piano. (Stéphane's only experience of folk had been 'Hobo's Blues', a short duo track he recorded in 1971 with the guitarist Paul Simon.) Diz had to explain that there would not be a piano 'because we're playing out in a field. It all takes place outside – they've got tents and things.' Stéphane had been around, but he had never played in a field, and he agreed to leave it to Diz. He also left to Diz the matter of other work, and the guitarist began utilizing his folk contacts, ringing up clubs and arranging dates for the group around the festival. 'In the end, I fixed up a solid block of two weeks' work, with the Cambridge Festival in the middle, like a currant.'

Stéphane appeared in July, ready for their first engagement at Solihull. He had insisted on the importance of a rehearsal, so he and Diz drove up early on the 23rd. However, characteristically, as Diz was to learn, Stéphane's appetite took precedence over his need to go over the programme. Once on the way from London to Birmingham, and again on arrival at Solihull, he requested a stop for a 'sand*weech*' – which metamorphosed each time into a multi-course meal. It was Diz's introduction to Stéphane's legendary relish for food, a certain capriciousness and a musical instinct that got along very well without rehearsing. They never did rehearse during those first two weeks. As Diz recalls, 'It was just, okay, Denny Wright would do four bars in, and we were off, galloping away.'

The results were sensational. Denny Wright, reunited with his old boss after twenty-five years, was as amazed as anyone. 'He said, "Allo, Denny. What shall we play?" I said, "What do you fancy?" He said, "'I Can't Believe That You're in Love With Me.'" So we strolled out, tuned up. He said, "Eight bars?" So I did mine – I'm still doing the same eight bars – and he came in. And the whole place *erupted*. A *roar* went up from the audience. 'Cause we didn't realize they were seeing, for the first time in thirty years, Stéphane with a guitar backing. And when we played at Portsmouth and places like that, and went out very casually dressed, the whole audience was in evening dress! And when Stéphane started to play they all stood up and clapped. They were all his old people from Hatchett's; 'We haven't heard you since we danced at Hatchett's in 1941!" It had absolutely nothing to with Django, not at all. It was purely Stéphane.'

They sailed through the first week, with Stéphane bemused but gratified by the response. There was one change in the line-up. The violinist insisted that Diz's original choice for bass had to go, because his animated manner of playing disturbed Stéphane's classical sense of decorum. 'He's like a monkey on a stick,' he told Diz. Dave Etheridge, known as Brillo, took his place, and they proceeded to Cambridge, after two enthusiastic nights in Norwich and a television appearance. It was all good publicity, but Stéphane was increasingly leery about the idea of the Folk Festival. The audiences had been mixed, so far. At Cambridge the crowd of 25,000 or so would be almost entirely young. As he told an interviewer later, he thought he was 'too old to play there. . . . They would not know me.' He even tried to back out by being 'diplomatically sick', but Diz stood firm.

On Saturday the 28th, they were ready to go, waiting in the beer tent next to the main marquee. Stéphane was still very apprehensive and, to ease the tension, Denny Wright started to strum, whereupon the violinist immediately joined in, to the delight of the onlookers. Then they were on. They went out to confront an ocean of thousands of young, curious faces, an audience decidedly not in evening dress, with no memories of Hatchett's or the Quintet and not much disposition to jazz. As Denny says, 'They didn't know anything about it at all. They looked up and saw this white-haired man come on to the stage with a chubby guy on the end and a thin guy with a beard on the other and Brillo on bass. And suddenly we went into "Sweet Georgia Brown" and the roof fell in. I broke string after string, I was hitting it so hard.'

It was spontaneous rapture, Stéphane mania. Everything gelled instantly, the driving, infectious sound of the bass, guitar and violin which had the patina of folk but the urgency of jazz, good tunes, and above all this slender, grandfatherly figure, pouring out not only miraculous music, but, as a reviewer said later, 'happiness as if it was going out of style'. Stéphane said he was 'amazed and touched by our fabulous success and the polite young people'. Diz's canny assessment of the audience had been overwhelmingly vindicated. The triumph was repeated the next day of the festival, and for all the rest of the tour. As Denny Wright witnessed, Stéphane's amazement increased. 'He couldn't believe it. Everywhere we went, we couldn't get off. We could not get off the stage. All over the country.'

The extraordinary thing was that the aura was not due to nostalgia. If anything, as guitarist Ivor Mairants reported after one concert, it was 'the reincarnation of a legend'. The young audiences had never heard this music and therefore 'the response was for the actual performance, rather than for its sentimental appeal . . .' And there was the simple freshness of the sound, old-fashioned in one way, totally new in another. 'From start to finish the atmosphere sparkled without the aid of stacks of high-powered over-emphasized amplifiers, nor did the guitars suffer from the cloying sweetness of soft, rounded amplification. The guitars had to articulate every note in order to be heard over the PA system, and their very attack added to the excitement. Quite frankly, I had not heard plectrum guitars played in this way (in concert) for many years and was glad to see that the art is not completely lost.'

And finally there was Stéphane, 'extemporizing with the utmost fluency and abandon and enjoying every second of it'. Thanks to Diz, he had arrived at just the right place just at the right time. In terms of his own life, he was reaping a harvest from his past as well as enjoying the present flowering. His accessibility in places outside London attracted a whole group of people who recalled him from earlier tours and from all the associations of the forties. Up and down the country they were still there, ready and willing to come to their local clubs and halls when Stéphane turned up. The guitar connection made the appeal stronger. Above all there was the new audience, charmed by this extraordinary music, with its brightness, invention and buoyancy. Both the man and his art seemed timeless, utterly different from the agit-pop of rock. As Stéphane had told an English interviewer in March, 'The Post Office can go on strike when I play, because I've got no message. I play best when I'm happy – or when I'm very sad. Or, when I was young, when I was in love. If I have ordinary troubles, I forget everything when I play. . . . I divide into two persons, and the other person plays.'

It could not be a purer, simpler attitude, elevated by his gifts to something magical. His demeanour made him seem even more a paradoxical combination of father figure and spirit of youth. The same interviewer had said he resembled 'a concert violinist with his grey hair and aesthetic face – an eccentric maestro who has chosen to wear bell-bottomed trousers and a heavily flowered shirt.' His showmanship was as natural and effortless as his music, free equally from the self-dramatizing of rock and the unctuousness of pop. The pleasure he took in giving pleasure was a pleasure in itself. He was an ideal performer at the peak of his ability, and the format and circuit that Diz Disley found opened a vast audience ready to welcome him. The Menuhin duets, when they came out, were the frosting on the cake, offering not only profit but publicity. Though, typically of Stéphane, nothing had been planned, it was as though the momentum of events from the late sixties had been aimed at this final outcome: he had been preparing a unique entertainment, and Diz had provided the vehicle to take it on the road.

Stéphane drew the right conclusions. After two extraordinary weeks, Denny Wright didn't think 'he really knew what hit him, but being a shrewd nut, he soon realized.' He told Diz he would take whatever work he could get him, and the guitarist-manager began ringing around the folk clubs, filling in the dates Stéphane had already booked with his regular agency. Sadly but inevitably, the new arrangement meant the end of his standing association with Alan Clare, with whom he played a successful week at the Edinburgh Festival in August. Stéphane regretted the loss of those beautiful chords, and even asked Alan to come along just to play ballads. But that was impossible, and after a week at the Savoy and another season at Ronnie Scott's, the guitars truly took over.

The group's London début took place in an appropriately explosive atmosphere on Guy Fawkes Night, 1973. The Queen Elizabeth Hall concert and its tumultuous response are both preserved on a Black Lion disc, *I Got Rhythm*, so listeners can corroborate the critical applause that followed. *The Times* compared Stéphane's improvising to 'the wittiest of conversation: full of the most daring firework displays of bravura, stuffed with well-turned phrases that tremble on the edge of sentimentality, yet all governed by a knowing elegance that turns it into a flow of irresistible music, as tough as it is fragile.' The *Melody Maker* noted that despite 'decades of separate and brilliant musical life' Stéphane was still linked to the memory of Django, but the present string quartet represented no 'slavish imitation', but 'a new extension'.

It was an auspicious launch, and the group immediately went on to clubs and television appearances. Customarily their venues were not as grand as the Queen Elizabeth Hall. Nigel Kennedy, who frequently appeared with them to race through 'Tiger Rag' and other specialities, remembers 'the kind of clubs which hold about 2–300 people or concerts for 4–500 people'. Based on the folk circuit, the tours offered steady work to full houses, and as the word spread, the rooms quickly got bigger. Requests for Grappelli and the Disley trio kept coming in, so that Stéphane took a flat in London in 1974 (to add to his French properties in Paris, Cannes and Chartres). It was like the days of the Second World War, with non-stop touring up and down Britain, confirming Stéphane's feeling that despite his honoured status in France, he has really been more popular abroad.

There was non-stop musical excitement too, of the rampaging, locomotive variety that Diz Disley relished. Since the autumn of 1973 the trio had acquired new power in the bass section in the person of Len Skeat, one of Britain's best players. He and Denny Wright formed a potent unit, and they both loved nothing better than to thunder out sizzling tempos over which Stéphane would ride triumphant, in the best QHC style. Sometimes there was more than a hint of challenge in the air, which only heightened the atmosphere, as Denny recalled. 'Len and I had been thumping along, really laying it down for him, a real hard Freddie Greene, Basie sound right behind him, no matter what speed it was. . . . Len used to say, "Let's make the old man have it," and we'd take "I Got Rhythm" even further up. . . . And he played as he's never played. He really cut it, all the way – head down, and gone. He used to look over the bridge at me, going like the bloody clappers. Finish – not a bead of perspiration. Ridiculous man he was. No sweat, and I'm *wet*, Len's wet, we're soaked. Sweat's just dropping off me, and he's bowing gently to the people. And stroll off as if he's just been out for an afternoon's walk. And afterwards, he never said a word, nothing: just "Who's got the food?"'

With performances like that going on, it may be surprising to learn that Stéphane was less than totally happy with this style of guitar and bass sound. What delighted Diz rather irritated him, and the memory still seems to irk the guitarist as he imitates Stéphane saying, 'Oh, that rhythm, I tell you it drive me insane!' To a musician who thrived on keeping his ears open for interesting harmonies, who told Whitney Balliet of the *New Yorker* that 'I improvise on the chords of the people playing behind me – the more good the chords, the better I play', it must have seemed retrograde. After the voicings of Clare and Hemmeler it was once again 'six bars of G7, two bars of G'. No doubt the pulse was exciting, but it was an old excitement, and not particularly subtle. The difference shows on the *I Got Rhythm* album, which for all its zest lacks some of the interest of the earlier records. There are only two guitars, not three – though, the *Melody Maker* said: 'With Diz Disley's strength you'd hardly notice' – but the missing guitarist was Django, whom Stéphane had admired for his harmonic daring in accompaniment even more than for his solos. Stéphane would still give his best for an audience and play brilliantly, but after a while he would crave different stimulation.

The sound of the Disley trio became more flexible in May 1974, when Denny Wright left because of the demands of his job with a recording firm. His replacement was Ike Isaacs and, as Denny himself says, it was Ike who 'put the modern sound back into Stéphane'. The difference is audible on *Violin-spiration*, made in March 1975 – less hot but warmer, with a more deliberate air. The ching-ching-ching still rides along, but with a less manic quality, and Stéphane seems to feel more room to move, rhythmically and harmonically.

Throughout 1974 the group worked all over Britain. As Denny Wright put it, 'The ball bounced higher and higher,' with Diz attending to hiring and firing, much of the booking, travel arrangements and stage management as well as the details of playing and presentation. His aim was 'a good, neat, well-organized show', that would leave Stéphane with nothing to do but play. Gradually he also tried to get him to speak a bit. The violinist was reluctant, but Diz was sure that his wealth of experience would only add to the appeal of the package. Stéphane's modest, hesitant recollection of his meeting with Fats Waller on the *I Got Rhythm* album is the result of Diz's encouragement.

Diz and Stéphane are quite different characters, just as Stéphane and Django were, but it is certain that only Django had a bigger impact on Stéphane's career, though Diz's effect was more directly commercial. Stéphane acknowledged that he 'would never have gone back to the guitars if it hadn't been for Diz', and Denny Wright feels that the guitarist 'can't get enough credit'. Nigel Kennedy too had first-hand knowledge of the Disley effect in its several manifestations. 'Diz was a great personality and was able to make life a lot easier for Steph. . . . He's a fine guitar player, he loves the style of playing and he loves Steph's talent. And he was able to defuse certain little tensions which might have happened between Steph and managers and Steph and other people. Diz would just step in and say, "Ah look, come on, man; it'll be cool. I'll figure it out." Then Steph would forget about what was the matter.'

Finally, Bob Clarke could appreciate the graphic change for Stéphane from the Hilton days: 'I've never seen him happier than he was when he did the shows with Diz, because he had these big posters saying "The World's Greatest Jazz Violinist – Stéphane Grappelli with the Diz Disley trio". Posters all over the town, wherever. People flowing in, specifically for this man, *specifically* – not going up to have a fucking ham and cheese on rye.'

With someone else in charge of logistics, Stéphane was free to pursue one of his favourite pastimes: simply looking. Travelling to concerts, Alan Clare had already observed the effect. 'If you ever go on a train with Stéphane, you've lost him. The entire journey he'll look at the countryside, and you can't get a word out of him; he won't talk to you.' What he admires particularly about the English countryside is its church architecture, on which he is an amateur expert. He remembered towns by their churches, and would be annoyed if an itinerary did not allow time for a visit to an interesting building he had observed, insisting on a look even if time was pressing. One of the more extreme instances of his absorption was an afternoon spent in York Minster, where Stéphane, mesmerized, ignored Diz's remonstrations, with the result that that night's concert began an hour and a half late.

1974 gave Stéphane expanded scope for sight-seeing. Not only was demand for Grappelli and Disley ever growing in Britain, but the group made its first sojourns out of the country, going to Majorca and Berlin in March to entertain at IBM conferences. Then, after a summer on the move in the UK, they flew to Australia and America for September and the first week in October, a tour organized by the Australian impresario Clifford Hocking, which teamed them with the Ronnie Scott trio and climaxed with a standing ovation at Carnegie Hall. Stéphane and Diz finished October touring in Germany, Holland and Belgium before returning to three more weeks on the road in England.

Nothing illustrates more forcefully the changed character of Stéphane's career than his recording activity. After *Les Valseuses* early in January, he and Diz were travelling so steadily that he made only two records. One was a virtuoso duet session with the great Earl Hines, appropriately titled *The Giants*, which attracted much favourable comment, but with which Stéphane himself was not entirely pleased, feeling uncomfortable with Hines's disjointed bravura style. The other record allied him with a guitarist of a very different character from his British cohorts, the Brazilian Baden Powell, with sympathetic results. (Stéphane would continue to record with players other than his regular travelling line-up, widening his musical horizons.)

The first half of 1975 was almost exclusively British, with audiences as usual large and remarkably young, to Stéphane's delight. Increasingly, he was creating a whole new following, despite his obvious links with the past. As a reviewer said after a concert at the Torquay Town Hall in Devon, 'It would be easy to dismiss Grappelli's popularity as part of the nostalgic movement which seems to be a backlash of the current pop scene, but it is much more than that. At least half the audience were probably not born when Django died in 1953, and very few there could have remembered the pre-war heyday of the QHCF.' It was the 'astonishing talent' of the violinist that won over the young crowd, the pleasant, well-knit sound of the string quartet and even the tuneful repertoire: 'Applause still greets the first few bars of "Honeysuckle Rose" and "Tea for Two".' And on top of it all, the musicians seemed to be as happy as everyone else: 'These four actually look as if they're enjoying what they play, in contrast to some of the humourless and introspective performances by avant-garde players.' A standing ovation was almost a foregone conclusion.

Stéphane and the trio emphasized the spirit of youth with bright, casual dress, though the old curmudgeon Nigel Kennedy refused to wear a Stéphane-style flowered shirt. It was an act that could be taken anywhere, from the Royal Festival Hall in February (three times the size of the Queen Elizabeth Hall next door, where they had made their début a little over a year before) to the jazz-oriented 100 Club, to the Norwich Folk Festival, to name just a few. Records included not only *Violinspiration*, but a jolly session with another legendary jazz string player, Slam Stewart, and a second disc with Menuhin. The group managed to squeeze in a couple of European trips, on one of which France proved that Stéphane was not a prophet without honour in his country by presenting him with the Légion d'Honneur.

But the second half of the year indicated the true shape of things to come with a longer trip to Australia and, this time, to New Zealand. The flight from Avignon took thirty-two hours, quite a stretch for someone who, not too long before, had openly confessed his dislike of flying and, indeed, travel in general. Now it was becoming his natural element. He would tell a French reporter, 'I don't really like to arrive; I like especially to leave. More than Django, *I* am the true nomad.' Still, as Diz was finding, he liked to leave some places more than others: 'He's always been reluctant to go back to Australia, and a certain amount of persuasion has been needed. And even more with New Zealand.' This had nothing to do with the people, who loved him and made the warmth of their feelings plain. It was simply their wide open spaces. Even in Britain, Stéphane always insisted that Diz use hotels in the town centre, to be near shops, antiques and the passing scene. It was a natural *boulevardier*'s response. The vastness and newness of the antipodes depressed him, and he spoke of being 'confined' there. Guitarist John Etheridge (who would replace Ike Isaacs at the end of 1976) laughed to recall Stéphane's exasperation at being trapped in the hinterlands. 'We were in some quiet, pretty little New Zealand town, and he said, "I would rather be assassinated in the streets of New York than stay here." And another time he said, "Why he bring me here? Even the umbrella don't open on Sunday!"'

All the same, when the music started, everything was fine. The tour went on triumphantly to Mauritius and concluded with two weeks in South Africa, before returning to Britain, where Stéphane resumed what was getting to be a royal progress, from Scotland to the Isle of Wight.

Stéphane and the Disleys returned to South Africa in 1976 (once Stéphane has been to a place he is almost invariably asked back), but the year's real action was his conquest of America, or the beginning of a conquest that continues to expand every year. Commencing in March, there were three separate tours, covering most of the country and marching across Canada. The first series of concerts was typical of the amazing level of activity Stéphane was maintaining, mixing clubs and concert halls, one-night stands and short stays, with great leaps in between. A huge success at Carnegie Hall opened the tour on 2 March. 4 March saw a one-night stand in Scottsdale, Arizona, with three nights in Las Vegas from 5 March. 8 and 9 March were spent in Los Angeles, 10 and 11 March in British Columbia, the next week back in LA, from the 19th to the 22nd at San Francisco's Great American Music Hall, from the 23rd to the 28th at Ratso's in Chicago. And on it went to Washington, Philadelphia and back to New York before the journey back across the Atlantic, for a concert on TV in Frankfurt, five days in Scotland and finally, at the end of April, lift-off to South Africa. Followed at the beginning of June with a second trip to the States.

The pace was demanding for anyone, but for a 68-year-old it seemed miraculous. The Americans responded to the brimming vitality of the man as much as to his music. Stéphane's extended presence in the States inspired profiles by Whitney Balliet in the *New Yorker* and Jonathan Cott in *Rolling Stone*. Balliet praised his music, took pleasure in recording the Gallic tints of his English and proclaimed, that he had 'pulled even with Joe Venuti, his consummate American counterpart and

163

long the best of jazz violinists.' One could appreciate the compliment without necessarily agreeing with the terms. Cott made a meal of Stéphane's Carnegie concert, hymning the 'faultless intonation, crisp upper-register sonorities, wine-dark lower string tempers, rhapsodic phrasing and vespertine lyricism of the shining, graceful, Pierrot-like figure' – who also reminded him of his grandmother.

Again the combination of irrepressible energy and old world charm, boundless talent and ageless youth had its effect. Clearly Stéphane had arrived in America, a fact confirmed when, in June, he met President Ford at the Wolf Trap festival, where Gunther Schuller and the National Symphony played an arrangement of a Grappelli original, 'Souvenir de Villingen'. (Another souvenir of Villingen, the German home of MPS records, was *The Reunion*, a happy product of Stéphane's meeting in San Francisco with George Shearing earlier in the year. After thirty years, they discovered they had lost none of their old empathy, and a record was the natural result.)

Stéphane's third North American journey lasted three months (early September to late November), moved at the usual jet-setting pace, covered the usual extraordinary round: New York, Vancouver, LA in the first five days, down to Phoenix, back up the West coast, across Canada, into the Great Lakes, back to the East Coast and down to New Orleans. In the middle there was a one-week jazz cruise aboard the SS *Rotterdam* from New York to the Bahamas and Bermuda. It was a very good thing, as Stéphane has remarked all his life, that he never liked to stay anywhere too long.

At the very end of the year Ike Isaacs left the Disley trio, to be replaced at quite short notice by John Etheridge. In a way, he was an odd choice for Diz to have made – an excellent guitarist but a rock player, featured with the well-known Soft Machine. Talking about it, John is still surprised, but grateful: 'I thought, "This is absurd, I don't play any jazz." But I knew all the old Hot Club tunes. So we got through them and it was fantastic, an incredible bit of luck.' In a way, he owed it all to Django, whom he'd been absorbing for years, and with him, the QHC repertoire.

His actual introduction to the group, though, was more than a little fraught. Of course, it was also his introduction to Stéphane, and the beginning of five years of thoughtful, fascinated Grappelli-watching. 'Ike had left suddenly and Stéphane was cross because he liked everything to be smooth behind him. And I turned up. And I didn't know anything; I didn't even have an acoustic guitar. I borrowed an acoustic guitar – awful, lousy guitar – and we drove to Germany in Phil Bates's car.' Phil Bates had succeeded Len Skeat as the group's bass player. The audition would take place in his room in the hotel, John still not having met Stéphane.

'In comes Stéphane. He's got that dead look on his face – Stéphane's face when it's not animated is absolutely like a mask – and he wouldn't look at me. He sat down in the corner, and he addressed everything to me through Diz. "*Alors*, Diz, ask him if he know 'Them There Eyes'." "Do you know 'Them There Eyes', John?" "Yeah, I think so." So we started, but since I'd learned it off the record, at one point I wasn't playing the same chords Stéphane was, and he went, "*Alors*, what is that chord he is playing? Ah, no, no, no, no!"'

'Manoir de Mes Rêves' went no better, with Stéphane simply launching into the melody with his characteristic roulades, rubatos and rhapsodies, expecting Etheridge to follow him without even being given a key. 'I thought, "Oh, this is going great; what a wonderful audition . . ." Finally he said, "*Alors*, we play that tune by Stéphane Won*dair*, 'You Are The Sunshine of My Life'." And I thought, "Well, at least I know this." And about half-way through he sort of nodded to me vaguely with the bow, without really looking at me, to play a bit of a solo. I played a bit and did a few fast licks; he stopped playing and went, "Oh, *alors*, I like that! You do that fast business: it amuse the tourists!" And after that he gave me a couple of smiles – "Oh, I like him."'

But John's induction – not so much into the world of jazz but of Stéphane – was not fully accomplished yet. He was still feeling bewildered and disoriented. 'We were at this bloody hotel in Hamburg, and I had no facilities. I had this terrible old guitar, not really any clothes or anything. I'd never been in a band where clothes were important, and to Stéphane they were pretty important. I had these black shoes. . . . It was live television. We had to go on in front of an orchestra and play live on television, so Stéphane was pretty nervous. About half, three-quarters of an hour before we go on, we were practising away (you do that with Stéphane. When he gets nervous he used to go over and over and over and over and over a little bit of ending, a little bit of arrangement) – and we were flying away, and suddenly he looks down – my shoes, there's a bit of mud across my shoes, and he goes "OH! Your *shoes*! You are not on a *farm*! *Clean* them!" So I sort of bolted out the door and rushed around this hotel, and I couldn't find any bloody polish! I was going absolutely demented. What am I going to do? I couldn't find anybody to clean the shoes off. And I went tearing around and finally came back to the dressing-room and he said, "Oh!" And I'm panting, and I said, "Ah, ah, I can't

find any polish." And he said, "Oh, *alors*, I give you mine."
And he gets it right out of his bag and I polished them. And
after that we were sort of all right . . . But I really thought,
"What's going on?" Then he got used to me, and once he got
used to you, you were in. It was fine, he was very encouraging.'

Not only was the group set, but by 1977 the itinerary as well
was assuming what would be its normal globe-trotting pattern.
Britain was still the base, but demand from everywhere else
had reduced the UK tours to two a year, spring and autumn.
There was the regular visit to the States and a tour of Australia
and New Zealand, preceded by a week at the Hong Kong
Festival. There was much more work in Europe – summer
festivals, visits to France, Germany, Italy, Holland, and recordings in Australia and Paris – including one of Stéphane's
favourites with the French organist Eddy Louiss – as well as
the latest Menuhin outing.

In December Stéphane and the trio played two special
concerts in Paris, at the Théâtre Mogador and Maxim's. They
were a great success, of course, and reviewing them, as if to
reassert the rightful claim of the homeland, *Jazz Hot* referred
to the violinist proudly as 'our Stéphane'. Not only violinist,
but pianist, as the magazine reported: he had begun (in
Australia) to include a piano solo in the show, just to please
himself. In a way it was inevitable, since that was still the
instrument of his heart. Coming up to seventy, with so much
going so well, it was as though he had decided to work that in
too.

Looking at You

Asked once what kept him going with such vigour, Stéphane replied suavely, 'Everything is vanity. Women like perfume and flowers, and men like applause. Every day is a new book for me; I'm so pleased to play a good concert to please my public.' That was Grappelli the indefatigable performer, the man who, a French reporter observed, 'is the slave of only one drug: the public.' The most remarkable thing about him as entertainer has always been that his showmanship is inseparable from his musicianship; they are equally natural, unforced and necessary. In an arch moment he might refer to an abstract audience as 'tourists', but when he is actually on, before live people, he gives himself openly and sincerely. The same honesty informs his music. He once confessed he never practises, partly because he is 'not studious', but more because staying away produces 'a terrible desire to play when I arrive on stage'. His old associate Charles Delaunay always knew that that was 'the one thing more important than any other: his purpose, his deep will is to play . . . When he comes from backstage to play, it's like – he would say "at last!", as if you brought him some fresh water. That's why he lasts so long, so well, because the only thing he really likes is to play . . . He plays with love; it's the real thing.'

Stéphane may describe his relation to the audience as vanity, but, as many people have said, there is almost no ego in it. He simply plays his music for the public, in public. Like Artur Rubinstein, who once said that when he practised he felt an urge to invite the elevator man in to listen, he finds it difficult to think of music in a vacuum. As he told another interviewer, 'I am miserable when I'm not performing.'

He is, in both senses, a pure entertainer, and the celebrations during his seventieth year recognized that. The first, on 26 January itself, was in France, as it should have been – a three-hour television show, 'Le Grand Echiquier', with a host of stars, among them pianist Jacques Loussier and singer Gilbert Becaud. As would be expected, there was an illustrious company of violinists, representing the catholicity of Stéphane's tastes; the classical virtuoso Salvatore Accardo, his old colleague Svend Asmussen, and the young rock violinist Didier Lockwood.

For Didier the event was particularly significant. Like Jean-Luc Ponty, he had extensive classical training before turning to rock, largely under the influence of Jean-Luc's recordings. As a member of Magma, a leading French band, he had become well-known. He met Stéphane at Nancy, where they were both participating in a piece for string orchestra, and the older player, as he had done with Jean-Luc, suggested they get together. Didier was impressed not only with Stéphane's ability but his openness when they met: 'I had so much I wanted to ask *him*, but the first thing he said was, "Oh, how do you play that?", because I was playing one phrase and he didn't know what fingering I was using.'

Didier was just beginning to switch to jazz, having discovered that 'jazz was something different, something that asked a lot of work', and Stéphane helped him make the transition. What struck the young violinist most, as it had so many others, was the naturalness of Grappelli's approach: 'He plays as if he were drinking tea.' For the 'Grand Echiquier' show, Didier wanted to do 'Autumn Leaves', because it was the only non-rock popular tune he knew. After working with Stéphane, he made an auspicious début, receiving calls the next day from leading jazzmen like Daniel Humair, inviting him to play. 'They thought I was a rock player; so Stéphane really put me into the jazz scene.'

After the French tribute – and Didier's launch – it was back on the international road. March took Grappelli to the States and the recording of *Uptown Dance*, a highly polished session with a string orchestra, leading New York players and arrangements by Claus Ogerman. On 5 April, Stéphane, Diz, John

Etheridge and Brian Torff – the young American bassist the group used in the States – took part in a Carnegie Hall show starring Teresa Brewer, opening the bill in a sparkling set later released on record. A reviewer in *Variety*, the show business bible, noted that Stéphane's 'extremely expressive and sensitive improvisations were of top-notch quality'.

Show business meant not only the big halls but the village halls as well. By now Stéphane loved travelling and, increasingly, travelling in America. He once said, thinking of the days playing for oblivious diners at the Hilton or 96 Piccadilly, that he enjoyed performing in clubs like the Bottom Line in New York: 'a lot of atmosphere and no soup'. But small was not always beautiful. As John Etheridge observed, it did seem that American touring meant 'one night Carnegie Hall, the next Hole in the Wall Schenecdaty. The usual practice was we'd arrive at some little club and Stéphane would say, "*Alors*, why he bring me here!" and he'd start to complain about the cigarettes on the floor and all that. But a while later, after supper, he'd say, "*Alors*, it's not Carnegie Hall, but it's very nice – and I had a very nice spaghetti!" He'd just enjoy it; he didn't mind.' His enjoyment was increased by the enthusiasm of the Americans. By the time John joined, Stephane had become a British institution: 'Over here the audiences tend to be a bit stale; they've all seen him 150 million times . . . It was exciting where it was really fresh, where the audience was really fresh.'

Stéphane likes freshness and change – 'One gets fed up with the same thing' – but he also appreciates orderliness. As he has said, 'I like a classical life.' Morning, for instance, must never come too early – understandably, since the preceding night has probably been long. Having to arise at five a.m. for an appearance on NBC Television's Today Show was purgatorial for him. In the afternoon, he takes a long walk, combining it with sightseeing, shopping and general keen attention to his surroundings. Though he has become more moderate in recent years, he still delights in food, and, as Etheridge found out, he can recall a meal more distinctly than a concert. 'I'd say to him, "Hey, Stéphane, do you remember in Arles, when we played 'After You've Gone' up a semi-tone?" And he'd say, "Non . . . ?" And I'd say, "Yeah, and afterwards we went –" "Oh! We went to that restaurant and I had that very good steak! I remember the *oignons*, and the sauce was just so! Mais oui!"'

Once, in America, food even compelled a change in programme. 'We were playing in a town with a German restaurant across the street, which Stéphane noticed right away. But last orders were at nine-thirty. So we started our first set, which was usually about fifty-five minutes, and half-way through Stéphane suddenly leapt up and said, "*Alors*, ladies and gentlemen, I must announce our last composition because, ah . . . *alors*, I must place my order at the German restaurant across the road! Now you know."And I was shocked. I thought everybody would say, "What?" I thought there'd be an uprising. But everybody *cheered*! You know – "Hurray; wonderful old man." I was amazed he could get away with it . . . He *is* a character. Unless you meet somebody like that you don't know what a character is . . .'

Such exigencies aside, every performance has its routine too, with arrival at the hall in plenty of time, perhaps running through the tops and tails of arrangements, and, as concert hour approaches, Stéphane's 'secret weapon', a double whiskey. Proper attention to conditions is necessary, because, as he has said, 'Improvisation . . . is a mystery, like the pyramids,' and it has its rituals. 'To improvise music you must be in a good mood, good friends behind you, lovely public, nice light, nice sound, acoustic – that makes a perfect improvisation.' At least it does if you are Stéphane Grappelli.

That kind of regimen not only promotes good music, but general harmony and Stéphane, as he put it in a recent letter to Diz Disley, devotes himself to 'resisting adversity and old age'. One of the ways he does this is by accepting adversity when necessary and accommodating it. Sometimes the process is dramatic, as in one of his occasional spectacular fits of temper. John recalled one involving Stéphane's American agent Abby Hoffer in the lobby of the Montreal Sheraton – 'Crowded lobby, thousands of people milling around and Stéphane started freaking out. He was getting tired, he'd been up to the room and it was occupied, so he'd had to come back to the desk, and Abby Hoffer had turned up from New York without his mail. Stéphane is addicted to mail – he writes letters and postcards all the time. He hadn't brought the mail and to Stéphane that was just the crowning moment. And he blew up, stamping his feet and shouting. Martin Taylor and I weren't bothered, but Abby hadn't seen a tantrum before, and they were all thinking, "He won't play, oh God, he'll cancel the concert, oh Steph, I'm sorry . . ." But Stéphane would rage for five minutes and then calm down: "Oh, it doesn't matter. *Alors*, you're a nice person anyway; I like you." In an instant, he'd expelled all those bad feelings – all that corruption never got inside him – by these rages. So it doesn't spoil anything, which is fantastic.'

*   *   *

Amid all the touring came an experience of a different kind, when Stéphane was invited not only to record the music for the film *King of the Gypsies* but appear briefly in it as well. The tunes were written by David Grisman, a young American mandolin virtuoso who had developed a personal blend of blue-grass music and jazz, with the emphasis on acoustic instruments plus California energy. Grisman's admiration for Stéphane repeated some of the formula that had generated his success in Britain: he was a hero because of the Quintet, because of the violin, because young people connected him with lively, tuneful folk music that he himself really didn't know anything about. Martin Taylor, who would join the group in 1979, remembers Stéphane's mystification about blue-grass. 'He said, "There is this music, I don't know what it is; I think it's called 'grass music'." I said, "Well, there's probably some of that in it as well, being California."'

Once again, he was a hero simply because he was what he was – a superb, completely individual musician. As Grisman described his recruitment for the movie: 'We needed a violin player, and the first violinist I always think of is Stéphane Grappelli.' He could fit easily into the laid-back eclecticism that was transforming jazz and popular music in the States. There were plenty of young fiddle players, whatever their style, who thought he was wonderful. And Stéphane had a fine time in the movie, appearing in a party scene in a big black hat, perhaps thinking ironic thoughts of Django.

For the rest of 1978 he was off around the world again – Britain and France, a television appearance with Yehudi Menuhin in Germany, New Zealand, Australia, Hong Kong before circling back to the US and Canada. In July there was a lovely, loose recording released as *Stéphane Grappelli and his American Friends*, the friends being Roland Hanna on piano, Bucky Pizzarelli on guitar, George Duvivier, bass, and Oliver Jackson. In Jackson, Stéphane told Didier Lockwood, he had found another of that very rare breed, a sympathetic percussionist: 'He was telling me, "Oh, I like Oliver Jackson; I love this little drummer!"'

Despite the customary global activity, one of the biggest events occurred back in Britain. Stéphane's 'second country' may have been a bit tardy in recognizing his seventieth birthday – getting around to it only a month before he was seventy-one – but the thing was finally done in handsome style, with celebrations at the Usher Hall, Edinburgh, London's Albert Hall and the Empire Theatre in Liverpool on 10, 12 and 14 December. Of these, the most splendid event was at the Albert

Hall, a venue both illustrious and versatile, like Stéphane himself.

Guests invited to perform demonstrated the range of his musical connections. In addition to the Disley trio – with Phil Bates and Brian Torff alternating – there was David Grisman, Didier Lockwood and George Shearing. And there was the great classical guitarist Julian Bream, rather a surprise since Stéphane did not know him and had not played with him. The idea was Diz Disley's. He remembered Bream in his early days, at guitar, lute and wine parties, playing Django's solos note for note: 'I was *astonished* at this guy just ripping through these choruses, sitting on the floor.' Years had gone by since Bream had played any jazz, but it seemed a nice angle, and Bream agreed, as he later recalled in *A Life on the Road*; 'I thought why not? I had always admired Grappelli, and I thought the whole thing would be a real hoot.'

Hoot it was, at least in the beginning. Stéphane and the trio played, with John Etheridge in fine form, and then he welcomed the crowd in obviously ebullient spirits. 'I must make a wish,' he announced, unable to suppress a giggle, 'because it is the first time in my life I play in the Albert Hall. It is *fantastique!*' On came Didier Lockwood, to repeat their 'Autumn Leaves' duet and then race through 'Tiger Rag' – a sort of *rite du passage* for Stéphane's protégés. (Stéphane saw him off with a jocular comparison between Didier's abundant locks and his own baldness, in English that excitement made even more charmingly idiosyncratic than usual: 'I wish I was as many hairs as he's got!') He was followed by David Grisman for some jolly pastiche from *King of the Gypsies*.

Julian Bream's hour arrived at the opening of the second half. It had been arranged that he would present two short solo pieces from his classical repertoire before joining Stéphane on Django's 'Nuages' and 'Belleville'. But as soon as he came on, Stéphane swept him into the ballad, which came off very well, Bream playing a nice introduction and a rich sixteen bar solo, sticking close to the melody. After that, Stéphane announced 'Belleville', during which Bream was to improvise a chorus. He did, performing creditably, having worked out some licks beforehand. But he could not have counted on Stéphane calling encouragingly, 'Once more, Julian,' as he was finishing. As Bream recalled, 'I thought that was pushing it a bit, but there was nothing I could do but comply. By this time my powers of improvisation, such as they were, were beginning to ebb rapidly.' They flowed away completely as Stéphane twice more exhorted him to another chorus. By the last of these he was reduced just to strumming the chords, enduring

what he called 'honestly . . . the most embarrassing moment
of my life'. The final injury occurred as Stéphane gracefully
ushered him away with no chance to redeem himself with
his classical solos.* One can understand the guitarist, having
'plodded off stage in complete disarray', feeling the experience
had been 'a nightmare to end all nightmares. I could have
killed him.'

Jazz musicians often invite a fellow player to 'take one more'
as a compliment for the preceding chorus. During George
Shearing's part of the programme Stéphane encouraged him
in the same way. But, as John Etheridge noted, it is also a
tactic he sometimes employed in a spirit of impish perversity.
'Diz would be doing his solo . . . and Stéphane would go,
"*Alors*, baby, one more, one more." Then he'd lean over to me
and go "I make him sweat!"' Etheridge is not sure how the
violinist intended the gesture to Bream. 'I don't know if
Stéphane was really carried away – which he partially was –
by the whole occasion and wanted to give Julian Bream a
chance to shine, or whether he was sort of half putting him in
his place . . . But if I'd had the presence of mind, I should've
leapt in; Julian would've probably loved me forever. But we
just stood by and watched him die, poor chap. It was awful.'

In fact, backstage afterwards, when the two guitarists met,
Bream demanded, 'Why did he do *that*?' to which Etheridge
waggishly replied, 'He saw the fear in your eyes.' But Bream's
plucky effort earned great applause from the crowd and sympathetic words from the critics. On the whole, the event seemed
a real party, hilarious if somewhat manic. Niels-Henning
Ørsted Pedersen (whose name Stéphane – 'mon Dieu!' –
momentarily forgot) thought it was 'great', and the newspapers
agreed, calling it 'an occasion for the celebration of a towering
talent', who was 'undoubtedly one of the most eloquent soloists
in jazz'. It was pure Stéphane, a personal mixture of caprice
and vitality, and the packed house loved it.

A few weeks later, on 24 January 1979, it was Stéphane's
turn to be surprised, the result of plenty of forethought. He
was the subject of Thames TV's *This is Your Life*, and the
programme gathered together figures from most of the eras of
his life: Louis Vola and Jean Sablon, Jack and Audrey Harrisson, Petula Clark (who as a child star had toured with Stéphane
in the war) and Sacha Distel. George Shearing, Yehudi
Menuhin and the British jazz stars John Dankworth and Cleo

* However, before the film of the concert was broadcast by the BBC a
year later, Bream taped a studio performance of an Albeniz piece, which
was inserted at the beginning of his all-too-live appearance with Stéphane.

Laine appeared by satellite transmission from the States. There was his family – Eveline and her sons Stéphane (known as 'young Steph') and Giles – as well as Diz, John Etheridge and Phil Bates. But the biggest surprise came at the close, when the one and only Bricktop emerged, to Stéphane's total amazement. After the show, there was an impromptu jam session, which reached its climax with Bricktop singing 'St Louis Blues' to his accompaniment.

A week later in Paris there was a different kind of observance, when Stéphane and the trio played a week at the Théâtre de la Ville. Didier Lockwood was part of the company, and Stéphane, having first informed the press, presented him with the Warlop violin, a ritual he had begun informally with Jean-Luc Ponty. Being given the instrument that Michel Warlop bestowed on Stéphane at the beginning of his career is a sign of pre-eminence among the rising generation of French fiddlers. In fact, as Didier revealed with a grin, the gesture is symbolic, since Stéphane actually keeps the fiddle, but it's the significance, the tradition and the publicity for a young artist that count.

It seemed to be the year for special events, when, in early spring, Stéphane interrupted a tour to be whisked to New York on Concorde, where he participated in a Carnegie Hall birthday concert for one of his musical heroes, Benny Goodman. Back in Britain it was business as usual, until an accident ended the familiar billing of Stéphane Grappelli and the Diz Disley trio. In May, Diz was knocked down by a motorcycle in London, breaking his wrist. He took a year and a half of leisurely recuperation, and the group became Stéphane Grappelli and his Musicians. The very talented Martin Taylor came in to replace Diz: he would still be Stéphane's right hand man in 1986. (During the late seventies, Stéphane's British business arrangements had been taken over by Ed Baxter, who also manages Edinburgh's Usher Hall.)

On the customary visit to the States, Stéphane took to the road with David Grisman. The mandolinist was delighted to be playing concerts with one of his idols, since the sound of the Quintet had been one of the principal ingredients in his own eclectic style, which he called 'Dawg music'. With mandolin replacing one (and sometimes two) of the guitars, his quartet did not have the thundering drive of the Hot Club, and their blue-grass/country and western roots gave them a more straightforward approach. Still, they played with conviction and high spirits, which was enough for Stéphane – and they shared his youthful taste in clothes. On the live album they made together in September 1979, he dominates the proceedings, in a programme tailor-made for him: 'Shine', 'Pent Up House', 'Sweet Georgia Brown' and all the rest. He finds another young fiddler, Mark O'Connor, to play 'Tiger Rag' with. Not everybody approved of Stéphane lending his talent to such a hybrid form: one French jazzman declared it was the only time in his career he wanted to throw tomatoes. But Grisman and Grappelli seemed very contented (the violinist told *Down Beat* he felt 'at home with him') and audiences were obviously delighted. Stéphane would play with the quartet in Carnegie Hall in 1980, and they would do a British tour the year after.

1979 saw an increase in recording activity in general, with four albums made in July, two on 6 July alone. Daniel Humair has said that Stéphane does not like to spend a lot of time recording: 'He likes to get out of the studio and go to a restaurant.' Live recording is evidently an ideal solution, and the 6 July sessions represented a perfect double – two discs from one performance at the Tivoli Gardens, Copenhagen, the first with Joe Pass and Niels-Henning Ørsted Pedersen, the second adding Oscar Peterson and drummer Mickey Roker. Stéphane flourishes in fast company, responding with equal keenness to the grooving rhythm of Hank Jones, Jimmy Woode and Alan Dawson in *London Meeting* and the more delicate swinging of Bucky Pizzarelli in *Duet*.

The best record of 1979, however, was one of the best of all, and one that Stéphane himself prizes – *Young Django*, made with Philip Catherine and Larry Coryell, guitars, and the invaluable Niels once again on bass. The combination of the standard instrumentation with special players may have been a stimulus, but for whatever reason, the record exudes warmth and camaraderie, not to mention a rare degree of quality. Its character is indicated both in Stéphane's self-effacing response to praise after storming through 'Swing Guitars' – 'Maybe it was good, I don't know' – and Larry Coryell's spontaneous spoken introduction to 'Blues for Django and Stéphane' – 'I forgot to say one thing: I love you all.'

The whole record is the truest possible tribute to the Hot Club partners. It conveys a sense of a living legacy, received and understood – most miraculously in the presence, forty years on, of one of the original duo. Stéphane plays marvellously throughout, whether in yet another absorbing interpretation of 'Minor Swing' – as fresh and thoughtful as the versions of 1937 and 1962 – or his passionate but utterly relaxed treatment of 'Oriental Shuffle'. But undoubtedly the *pièce de résistance* is Coryell's 'Blues for Django and Stéphane', which is an earthy, joyous piece, as it should be. It features, coming out of nowhere, seven rollicking choruses by S. Grappelli on piano, striding along like Basie or Waller. He sounds as though he is having the time of his life, as if this is what he has always wanted to do, and now, in his seventies he has been given his chance. It is little wonder that, a year later in *Down Beat*, Larry Coryell was still enthusing over what his meeting with Stéphane had meant to him: 'He swings, he's creative, he's exciting. It doesn't matter how old you are . . .'

The creativity is as much a part of him as his extraordinary technique. He loves rising to challenges, and an exceptional one was presented, in February 1980, by Martial Solal, a pianist for whom Stéphane has the greatest regard, and who in turn, as early as 1958 when he was a member of the younger generation of jazz radicals, had referred to Stéphane as 'an astonishing soloist'. Though they had toured together, they had never recorded. Solal was well known as a virtuoso and composer, almost forbiddingly accomplished, who sought to liberate European jazz from the standard received American models. He had forged arresting partnerships on record with the altoist Lee Konitz and pianist Hampton Hawes. When a producer proposed a duo with another American, Solal suggested Stéphane instead, 'because I'd heard him in the past months and felt that he was playing better and better.'

The resulting *Happy Reunion* is unlike anything Stéphane has done, featuring free, witty interpretations of tunes ranging from teasing Solal originals to 'Nuages' (which they considered doing as a waltz), to 'Stumbling' – the very first 'jazz' tune Stéphane had ever heard. Most extraordinary is the session's last piece, 'Et si l'on improvisait?', which, on the record, comes immediately after 'Stumbling' – neatly encompassing sixty years of musical experience in seven minutes. It came about, as Martial told me, when another three or four minutes of music were required. 'I said to Stéphane, "Why don't we just do a free piece?"' – an accurate enough rendering of the title – 'and the first take, that was it. He surprised everyone, because nobody knew that he could play free' – and atonally to boot.

Surprising everyone, and delighting in being surprised, is Stéphane's stock-in-trade. By 1980, the same process was going on in his regular supporting trio. John Etheridge, feeling restless, had begun to experiment with electric rather than acoustic guitar. Sometimes Martin Taylor would play electric as well, sometimes acoustic. On *Stéphane Grappelli at the Winery*, made in California in September 1980, Stéphane himself gets into the spirit of the thing, by recording on the Barcus-Berry electric violin he had been dallying with occasionally since 1976. His heart really belongs to his 1742

Gagliano, not the electronic sound, but he was interested in the quartet experiment, as John says: 'He encouraged me; he said he loved it.'

Ultimately, however, John himself became disenchanted with the new approach. 'It was getting a bit prissy, in a way, with the electric. Conversely to what you may think, the electric jazz guitar sound is really more like chamber music than if you're thrashing away on an acoustic. Because you can really dig in on an acoustic; it has that attacking sound.' John left in 1981, and in retrospect it was his first years with the band, when he was discovering a different world from rock, that he relished: 'It was fantastic, the first couple of years. I found playing with Diz great, and it was such an exhilaration to play with Stéphane. And it was acoustic, which for me anyway suited the band better. It was great; the first couple of years were just magic.'

It had been a good period for Stéphane too. On an Australian tour he told an interviewer that John was 'a great help to me. He gave me the opportunity to open the door of a world I didn't know before.' The return of Diz Disley in 1981 did not mean that Stéphane would stop opening doors with younger players. For him, 'There is always something to learn.' The quartet now consisted of Stéphane's trusted colleague from the Hilton days, Jack Sewing, on bass, Martin Taylor on electric guitar and Diz on acoustic (though the American Mike Gari substituted for Diz in America in 1981). The violinist had quickly seen that Martin was something special and made special use of his talent. In London in July, two hours off a plane from Los Angeles, they began recording a duo album, *We've Got the World on a String*, featuring the usual standards but also an evocative Taylor original, 'Manhattan Tea Party', which the composer embellished with electronic effects, and the Beatles' lovely 'Here, There and Everywhere'. Stéphane was still no fan of the more abrasive forms of rock – 'I can't bear those screams for nothing at all, without *necessité*' – but he knew a good tune at once, and indeed recorded an easy-listening album of Beatle songs with the classical flautist Elena Duran.

His policy of opening doors – with a wink – to classical players was of course continuing with further Menuhin albums, but also with appearances at the Royal Festival Hall with Miss Duran in 1980 and the cellist Julian Lloyd Webber in 1981. Stéphane's concern for communication impressed the flautist, whom he asked, 'Elena, do you love the audience? . . . Do you really love the audience to get excited and to make noise and to be really happy?' As much as ever, Stéphane still believed in the musician's responsibility to the public – also for the sake of the art. 'I like to play with gentlemen,' he told a French newspaper. 'The music we play is too important to be shared with people who have no manners. How many times have I seen musicians who don't even greet the public.' Nervousness was no excuse. 'I'm timid too; I get stage fright. But you must have nerve.' However, the audience had to play its part too, and it was not unknown for Stéphane to criticize bad manners from the stand. With glee, Didier Lockwood recalls him actually shouting at some of those loquacious French listeners, and once, when he had been engaged to adorn the grand opening of a posh London restaurant, the crowd's noisy indifference precipitated a vintage Grappelli tantrum, despite the presence of royalty.

Stéphane's usual manner – buoyant and welcoming, but modest – is of a piece with his physical presence and style and is part of his appeal. The tours of 1981 and 1982 saw a steady increase in his American popularity. In 1981, the young violinist Matt Glaser published *Jazz Violin*, a history of the instrument and its players, with Stéphane listed as co-author. In fact he only contributed a short foreword, but he receives the lion's share of attention in the book, including many transcribed and analysed solos. There was a two-part cover profile in *Down Beat*; by large margins he won both its readers' and critics' polls for best violinist. He was touring as much as ever in Britain and Europe, and 1982 saw him extend his worldwide circuit to India.

1983 brought changes. After ten years of general British associations, Stéphane began to take his musical inspiration from France. He had become acquainted with two lively young French musicians who were adventurous enough to experiment with older styles of music. Bassist Patrice Caratini and guitarist Marc Fosset had worked together as a duo since 1977, giving acoustic concerts. They were interested in all the strains that informed French jazz and, indeed, French popular music as a whole – tango, musette and Django as well. Their programmes were daring, witty, original and very musical, and they had developed a great rapport. Stéphane was impressed, feeling a particular kinship with Fosset's approach to the guitar, which combined, like his own playing, classical purity, vivacity and swing.

Delighted with such a congenial challenge, Stéphane went on the road with Caratini and Fosset in early 1983, for a forty-day tour of southern France. It was a particularly appropriate time for him to take his career in a new direction, and on his native soil. That January saw his seventy-fifth birthday,

and on 29 March *Jazz Magazine* presented a gala concert at
the Salle Pleyel. It was essentially an all-French affair, except
for Svend Asmussen (though not natives, Jack Sewing and
Marc Hemmeler have lived in France for years). It was also a
holiday for strings, Hemmeler being the odd man out. The
violinists included Didier Lockwood as well as Svend, the
guitarists Fosset, Philip Catherine and (in a nice gesture)
Django's son Babik, 1983 being also the thirtieth anniversary
of Django's death. Sewing and Caratini were the bassists.

Preserved on a double album released in France, the concert
was effervescent, a form of notification that Stéphane Grappelli
was, for all his years across the channel and international
renown, still triumphantly French (though some of his scepti-
cal colleagues observed that it was only his success in America
that made the native establishment so eager to recognize him).
Fosset and Caratini prove themselves an exemplary rhythm
team, with a lightness and lift ideally suited to Stéphane, and
they (with the addition of Martin Taylor) were his accompanists for subsequent tours of Britain and and the States. The
whirlwind schedule began in London with a recording session
for which not only drums but, on a couple of tracks, Indian
tabla were added, though it is hard to see why. Nevertheless,
the record, *Just One of Those Things*, picks up the mood of
the Salle Pleyel concert, with everybody in resilient form. As
Patrice Caratini recalled, 'It was like a jam session,' with the
combination of effortlessness and concentration that Stéphane
prefers. It is a disposition that Patrice feels works best for jazz
– 'When you know there will be only one take, it creates
something very living' – and certainly works for Stéphane: 'He
was born with a bow in his hand; it's like talking for him.'

The tour had that same quality throughout, and Stéphane
was so pleased with his partnership with Marc Fosset that they
recorded a duo album, *Stephanova*, in June 1983. In turn, he
was so pleased with that that they recorded another in April
1984, *Looking at You*, a disc that Stéphane has gone out of his
way to commend to interviewers as an exception to his usual
uneasiness, not only about recording but listening to the
results.

In December 1983, America crowned what was already
yet another significant year for Stéphane when *Down Beat*'s
readers, by a landslide, voted him into the magazine's Hall of
Fame. Of course he won the poll for best violinist equally
easily, but he had been doing that regularly for years. The
Hall of Fame was a special honour, since it was usually accorded
to musicians recently deceased; mortality tended to concentrate
the votes. Thus Joe Venuti, who died in 1978, was inducted

that same year, rather fittingly as the Hall's first violinist. But it was even more of a distinction to be saluted in full career. Though *Down Beat*'s editor was, in one sense, in error to call Stéphane 'a classically trained player' – no professor showed him how to hold the bow – he was quite right in his assessment of his current standing: 'Today at 75 he performs around the world to the largest concert audiences of his career, his skills completely intact and his elegance and taste unchanged over the years. He is eternally contemporary . . .'

Stéphane's skills, elegance and taste remain completely intact (in a minor concession to age he now plays sitting down), his audiences are undiminished, even growing. In Britain he tours with the quartet, sometimes with Marc Fosset, sometimes with the excellent Irish guitarist Louis Stewart, always with Martin Taylor and Jack Sewing. In France – and, increasingly, elsewhere – his standard group is a trio, with Fosset and Sewing. He makes no secret of his continuing delight in Fosset. Once when I said they sounded like brothers on *Looking at You*, Stéphane grinned and said, "Yeah, yeah, yeah, yeah, yeah.' He obviously regards the young Frenchman as a stimulus for the music he has yet to create. In March 1985, *Jazz Hot* celebrated its fiftieth anniversary with a special issue, in which it surveyed French jazz from 1935 to the present. At one time, it might have seemed natural to put Django on the cover. Now, Stéphane seemed the inevitable choice, not because he has superseded his partner, but because he still thrives; he embodies French jazz, past and present. In that issue, he gave a frank, funny, impassioned interview that concluded with a resolute view of his future: 'I feel freer with Marc Fosset today than I was with the Hot Club . . . I am free, I can do what I want. With the kind of person Django was, you had to wait till he said what he had to say. But now I'm in a hurry. I don't know if it's age – it's silly to speak of age, there is no age – but I'm in a hurry to play. And I've found in Fosset the ideal partner who has the kindness and politeness to let me do it. And I'm going to continue like that to the end of my strength.'

It is a wonderful attitude, which Stéphane affirms every time he plays, whoever his partner is. In India, in January 1986, he performed with Martin Taylor, Larry Coryell and the Indian violinist L. Subramaniam (with whom he recorded a recent album, *Conversations*). The concerts were a huge success, with an ovation of 6,000 people in Bombay that Martin found 'almost frightening'. In the spring, Stéphane was back as usual in Britain, accompanied up and down the country by Martin, Louis Stewart and Jack Sewing. Combining the traditional approach with new flexibility, both guitarists were playing acoustic (Martin a Maccaferri like Django's), and Stéphane sounded – and acted – as though *they* were his ideal partners.

But then the overriding impression Stéphane creates is that he can play with anyone, that regardless of circumstances he will convey the same elegance, intelligence and spirit. It is the reason he is a genuine classic, adaptable to any context yet unmistakable. After a lifetime of music, his style is so pure, so complete, that it seems an entity in itself. Stéphane's musical personality has been refined to perfect consistency: the Grappelli voice is distinctive and totally reliable, seemingly beyond any vicissitudes that may befall Grappelli himself. In a world of musicians parading their egos and baring their souls, he is serenely unique.

This combination of involvement and detachment is the quality that amazed John Etheridge most in his five years with Stéphane. The guitarist is one of the most perceptive of the violinist's accompanists, and his observations are worth quoting at length, since they give an absorbing view of a remarkable musician as seen by a player of a very different era.

'Stéphane's attitude to music is absolutely workmanlike in the best possible sense. There's no angst about his playing, there's no "my playing represents my ego". It's just something he does well and makes money at, and enjoys doing. He's not compulsive about it; he can put the violin aside. But he enjoys it because he's so good. He thinks nothing of it, and it's so totally natural.

'It was a revelation to me, because I was a sort of typical sixties/early seventies musician – you know, a head full of heroes, and trying this, you know, *trying*. And to go to him who was just so natural . . . I'd never experienced it before, and if somebody'd told me about it I don't think I could imagine it – having played with a lot of angsty bands where everybody was going, "Oh God I didn't play well tonight, oh God I didn't get my best licks off." What was so good about it was it was so relaxing. He never makes a mistake, musically. And having played for fifty-five years and knowing he never makes a mistake, having that sort of confidence, he just was very relaxing. We'd play: we'd just sit down and – "You play, baby." No sort of scene about it, no angst at all. I mean really none. That was what I loved from him best of all: that you turn up and you play and he would never push you. That was what I got from it, really, the most important thing. It's not a concept, it's not even an approach. It's not a thing to do with abstractions; he didn't have a head full of abstractions about what music should be, It's just the way it flowed: it just flowed.

'When I got the gig with Stéphane, it was actually the first jazz gig I'd ever done. That was the other thing I found really exciting about it – that Stéphane was stylistically so easy about not forcing you into a bebop bag or something. He was very loose. Provided you played the right chords behind him when he was playing, you'd play your solo, he was interested and critical, but he gave you lots of freedom. He listened, he was very encouraging. But it wasn't "Oh, that's not jazz", or "That's not how Barney Kessel did it" or something. He didn't give a shit about all that. He wanted to hear something different.

'So many jazz players are sort of grippy about their style, and they spend their later lives trying to persuade young people to play in their style, because of insecurity. They hold on to their style like their property, their possession. And Stéphane was the antithesis of that. He played like he did because he had a core of stability, so if you played anything different he'd say, "Oh, what is it! What is that!" He'd take time trying to figure it out, and he'd say, "Oh, I like that, I like that funny chord, oh yes." You know, "I play what I play but I really like to hear all that."

'His playing is perfect. He's got that purity; he does what he feels. He doesn't make conscious efforts. He won't play to the gallery to any extent (mind you, he likes the people around him to; he likes the guitars to be pretty extrovert). If he was as practical as he claims to be – you see, often he used to say to me, "I do anything for *monnaie*." But inside of him was this terrific sort of integrity. Although he was prepared to act almost as a sort of musical hack – go anywhere where the money's being paid and do anything, so he said – his music came out really pure.

'It isn't that Stéphane plays in a thirties style, it's the elevated feel of his music. From a superficial standpoint you could say – I listened to him every night – he'd pretty much play the same things on each tune. But it's because it's not conscious. This is the reason it sounds fresh and not stale. If you're consciously repeating a speech, there's going to be that feeling of staleness. But to Stéphane, he gets up and every day is a completely new day. He's not consciously playing the same things, they're just sort of coming out. But it would always sound fresh, because for him it was honest, and that's the difference between creativity and non-creativity.

'You see, he didn't make superficial surprises to me. What really connected with me wasn't so much a matter of doing a phrase you haven't heard him do before. It was the layer underneath, the brightness of the thing. That's what surprised me – the uplifting quality of the thing from gig to gig when it was really happening. There's no earth in Stéphane at all: he's sort of up there. But he avoids so many things. Because of his inherent taste, he just avoids syrupiness, which he almost slips into quite a lot, and total skitteriness, which he almost slips into quite a lot. He's always focussed. With the violin it's so easy to get into those sort of overly nineteenth-century types of emotionalism, but he just avoids them. He's extremely syncopated: he's a naturally syncopated player and, again, too much syncopation can sound yicky-yicky. But it doesn't with him. He does very strongly have that showbiz side, but somehow it's not cloying. He escaped all the traps. I could never believe how he flirts with all these awful things, and yet somehow they don't touch him.

'His tone and chops are fantastic. To play swinging violin is no mean feat in itself. It's almost impossible – only two or three people have ever succeeded. Warlop didn't swing; Svend does, Eddie South, Stuff Smith, Ponty used to, but he sort of got bogged down in something, where it doesn't fly. Always Stéphane will fly. He really does swing.

'He's got the most natural ability of anybody I've ever played with, but he's never consciously developed any side of his musical ability: he just does what comes to hand. He's a person who's really in the right place, perfectly adapted for what he's doing. It's not a conscious adaptation on his part to be what he is; he just is. He's one of nature's musicians – one of nature's public musicians, one of nature's players. So my lessons from him are really those: there's no trying, no becoming, no attempt, no going for something. He just is what he is, and that helps you.'

One of Stéphane's lessons for Nigel Kennedy was making contact with an audience with the same kind of naturalness, not by overt strategems. 'I don't think audience involvement is important to Steph; I'm sure it's not something conscious. I think he just gets it automatically. . . . You can't go looking for an audience to like you; you've got to believe in what you're doing, in your playing, and he does that. He likes getting the recognition now, and he welcomes it, but he's never done anything in his playing to change it to try and get it.

'I think Steph's purpose has been to make people feel a lot happier and more content when they listen to him play. Great performers enjoy themselves when they play and convey that to the audience. . . . Kreisler's my favourite classical violinist, and there's time in his music. He lets there be time for things to speak, and Steph has that too. Every note is a jewel. He's not affected by the constant pressure of life. There's always time in his concerts. You can relax and just get into the mood without being shaken out of it by too many things happening.'

One of the things that doesn't happen is too much patter between tunes, in keeping with Stéphane's ideal that his concerts should be as classical as possible, with the music making its effect on its own. As he says, 'I don't like all that chi-chi,' and for Nigel this makes perfect sense: 'His personality is so strong you don't need to do anything else. I think there's no problem with him having to sell it, because he speaks when he's playing the fiddle. It's the most like speech of almost any musician working today . . .'

Niels-Henning Ørsted Pedersen values the power of Stéphane's speech to make contact anywhere, while retaining its distinctness. 'For me he's a world artist in the sense he can play all over the world because he's able to communicate, but at the same time he carries his own identity, from whatever he was coming from, with him. It's so clear, the personality that comes through the instrument. What I always thought jazz was all about . . . is that it's one of those art forms where you're really totally naked. I mean, everybody should know your voice. That means you give yourself away . . . And it's the same thing with Stéphane. So I think that one thing he has contributed is the fact that it's the individual's music. In other words, he's French, he plays violin which is not usual in this art form, but he still has a voice.'

Niels also has no doubt that Stéphane's is a jazz voice. 'Oh, I think so. That word is a little bit distorted, because what is that by now? A lot of people wouldn't consider Miles a jazz player any more. But I would say that Stéphane is a genuine musician of all time, meaning that he is using this form, but there are also touches of the gypsy violin, touches of classical music. The jazz form has allowed him to keep all these different influences without that being something that puts him in the category of not being serious. I think that that's maybe the richness of this art form, that you can have these in-between things. I think it's very nice to see also that it's possible just to be a violinist from France, who happens to be great and who happens to be very French, to come in there and be somewhere in that art form. It certainly adds to the quality of jazz that there are people like that.'

For Didier Lockwood, a young violinist from France also aspiring to be somewhere in the art form, Stéphane represents a kind of performing ideal: 'His best quality is that when you hear him on the TV or on the radio, at the first note you can say, that's Stéphane Grappelli. That is the best quality a musician can have. And I think he has the best career a musician can have. He's on the top, he's seventy-eight, he has never been so popular.'

At seventy-eight, he encompasses a lot of history. For a musician of Denny Wright's generation, brought up on the Hot Club Quintet, he has always been there: 'I love the old man. He's my youth, from a child; he's tied into my youth.' Indeed Stéphane is playing for his fourth generation of youthful listeners, who, but for him, may have no knowledge of the Quintet at all.

As always, he has little interest in the past himself. Every day is still a new book, for playing and travelling. He lives outwardly, supremely unselfconscious, unconcerned even about his status. Didier Lockwood calls him 'innocent'; with some exasperation, Daniel Humair insists, 'He doesn't know how important he is'; Michel Chouanard says he is indifferent to the size of his name on a poster, though he wants it properly spelled. Such a concern for detail is typical of Stéphane too: he may be capricious, but he is not careless. The hazards of early privation, ill-health and professional uncertainty have made him watchful. But they have left him philosophical as well. He goes with the flow of life, resisting adversity and old age, enjoying it all.

And the music continues to flow unabated. When Stéphane came to Britain for his spring '86 tour, I went to hear him at a theatre near London, as Ed Baxter's guest. Predictably, the 'House Full' sign was up, but I was quite content to follow the action from the wings. Stéphane was in in a genial mood. After a chat in his dressing-room while he sipped his secret weapon, he showed me to a folding chair with a grin: 'It's not Madame Récamier, but it's all we've got.'

The programme was the same, and as fresh as ever, a survey of Stéphane's experience from Gershwin and Django to Stevie Wonder. In the second half he told the audience that he had been at the same theatre in 1941 with George Shearing, made a couple of quiet, off-the-cuff quips and came off stage beaming as Martin Taylor and Louis Stewart played a duet. For his piano solo there was rapt silence, as the whole packed house followed this graceful old man swaying gently in tempo, happily lost in his music. Then the bravos, whistles and cheers exploded, repeated at the concert's close. And back to the hotel, with America, once more, two weeks away, and a summer of European playing after that.

Sitting in the wings makes you fully aware of the crucial space between the public and private worlds of the performer. Only a few feet of distance, but as different in responsibilities and demands as light and dark. Yet Stéphane negotiates the division with ease, carried along by that perfect sense of what he is and does. Correspondingly, the clarity and brightness of his music never fail. Backstage after a concert he had shared with Stéphane, the black American drummer, Roy McCurdy, once marvelled, 'He's so *pure*.' From another culture and era, Charles Delaunay had long observed the same thing: 'It's like clear water that came to him.' The gift is so natural and constant that it becomes a mystery, like improvisation itself, flowing from some source, inseparable from Stéphane Grappelli as he too goes on and on. To the young violinists he has inspired – indeed to any listener – that unity and continuity may be the most wonderful thing of all. Didier: 'He's completely *here*. He *is* his music, you know? He *is* his playing.' And Nigel: 'It's his life. That's his communication, which is a great thing to listen to while he's doing it.'

Discography

by BRIAN RUST

This discography presents as complete an account of the
recordings made commercially by Stéphane Grappelli as I
have been able to establish, with the invaluable assistance of
Charles Delaunay; Derek Lewis, Mark Bredon and Renate
Warburg of the BBC Gramophone Library; Peter Rowles,
who transcribed in exact detail the relevant entries in the
Decca Record Company's files; and the selective discography
by Tony Middleton in Raymond Horricks's book.

Abbreviations used are as follows:

Instruments

a	– arranger
acc.	– accompanied
as	– alto saxophone
bar	– baritone saxophone
bsx	– bass saxophone
c	– cornet
cel	– celeste
cl	– clarinet
dir.	– directing
d	– drums
elg	– electric guitar
elo	– electric organ
elp	– electric piano ('keyboard')
f	– flute
g	– guitar
h	– harmonica
md	– mandolin
o	– oboe
p	– piano
pac	– piano-accordion
sb	– string bass
t	– trumpet
tb	– trombone
ts	– tenor saxophone
v	– vocalist
vc	– violoncello ('cello)
vib	– vibraphone
vl	– viola
vn	– violin
x	– xylophone

Record Labels

*Most of these are shown in full,
but those that recur most frequently,
especially among 78 rpm issues,
are abbreviated as follows:*

ACl	– Ace of Clubs (LP)
Br	– Brunswick (all nationalities)
BSt	– Blue Star
Cap	– Capitol
Col	– Columbia (all nationalities)
Dec	– Decca
El	– Electrola
GH	– Golden Hour
HMV	– His Master's Voice (including French, Italian, Spanish and other nationalities)
HRS	– Hot Record Society
Lon	– London
Od	– Odéon (all nationalities)
Or	– Oriole
Pac	– Pacific

PA	– Pathé	Sup	– Supraphon
Pol	– Polydor (all nationalities)	Tel	– Telefunken
		Ul	– Ultraphon
RZ	– Regal Zonophone	Vrs	– Varsity
Roy	– Royale	Vic	– Victor

The matrix numbers of the songs have been omitted from the discography in this edition.

Where initials occur after the song title, these refer to the musician and instrument featured. The full name of the musician is given in the descriptive note which follows the main entry. Asterisks accompanying the song titles refer to asterisks which appear in the descriptive note in the same entry.

The long dashes after the song titles refer to the record number(s) above them. Where there is more than one record number, the first dash refers to the first number mentioned above it, the second dash to the second number, and so on.

Orlando's Tango Orchestra A test pressing exists of the 1st title, with Stéphane Grappelli's name written – obviously at the time of manufacture – on the white label. He is therefore assumed to have played on the other titles made at this session; he may be on others by this orchestra, and on sides by other orchestras recorded on or about the same date (e.g., Grégor et ses Grégoriens). Instrumentation and personnel unknown.
Paris, 3 May 1929.
Escuhame: Edison Bell Radio (8") F-228
Adios, Muchachos: —
A la Guitarra: Edison Bell Radio (8") F-229
Dueto criollo: —

Grégor et ses Grégoriens Philippe Brun-Gaston Lapeyronnie-t/Guy Paquinet-Leo Vauchant-tb/Roger Fisbach-as/Silvio Schmidt-v/Stephane Grappelly-Stephane Mougin-p/others unknown; Pace Obregon-Carlos Gardel-v.
Paris, early 1928?
Flor De Cuba -vPO: Od 250274
Yot Te Dire -vPO: —
Brun omitted, probably other changes.
Buenos Aires, September 21, 1931
Deja -vCG: Od 18853
Folie -vCG: —
C'est Vous -vCG: Od 18863
Je Te Dirai -vCG: —

Jean Sablon Vocal, acc. by André Ekyan and his Orchestra: André Ekyan-as dir. Eugène d'Hellemmes-tb/Stéphane Grappelli-vn/Michel Emer-p/Django Reinhardt-g, others unknown.
Paris, 15 January 1934.
Le jour ou je te vis: Col DF-1406
Un sou dans la poche: Rejected
Prenez garde au méchant loup: Col DF-1406
Pas sur la bouche: Rejected

Germaine Sablon Vocal, acc. by Michel Warlop and his Orchestra: Michel Warlop-vn dir. probably: Pierre Allier-Maurice Moufflard-Noël Chiboust-t/Marcel Dumont-Isidore Bassard-tb/André Ekyan-cl-as/Amédée Charles-as/Alix Combelle-ts/Charles Lisée-as-bar/Stéphane Grappelly-p/Django Reinhardt-g/Roger Grasset-sb/ – McGregor-d.
Paris, 2 February 1934.
Un jour . . . sur la mer: HMV K-7193
Ici l'on pêche: HMV K-7256
Toboggan: HMV K-7193
Paris, 26 February 1934.
Celle qui est perdue: HMV K-7238

Michel Warlop et son Orchestre As for 2 February 1934; acc. Germaine Sablon on the last 2 titles.
Paris, 16 March 1934.
Presentation Stomp (Paramount Stomf*): HMV K-7314, CLP-1249*, FELP-154, HCLP-120*, OCLP-7529*, El 83035*
Je ne suis pas un ange: HMV K-7238
La chanson du Large: HMV K-7256

Germaine Sablon Vocal, acc. by Michel Warlop and his Orchestra, who appear on the 3rd title without the singer. Same personnel.
Paris, 12 May 1934.
Tendresse Waltz: HMV K-7305
J'ai besoin de toi: HMV K-7479
Blue Interlude: HMV K-7314

Delaunay's Jazz Stéphane Grappelli-vn/Django Reinhardt-Joseph Reinhardt-Roger Chaput-g/Louis Vola-sb/Bert Marshall-v.
Paris, September 1934.
I Saw Stars -vBM: Vogue VJD-6950-A, 425019-A
Confessin': —

Django Reinhardt et le Quintette du Hot Club de France avec Stéphane Grappelly Stéphane Grappelly-vn/Django Reinhardt-Joseph Reinhardt-Roger Chaput-g/Louis Vola-sb.
Paris, December 1934.
Dinah: Ul AP-1422, B-14286, Or LV-100, LB-1000, Tel A-1959, Sup B-22642, Roy 1753, Joe Davis 8004, DA-17-7, Vrs 8377, Od D-286044
Tiger Rag: Ul AP-1423, B-14287, Or LV-101, LB-1001, Tel A-1959, Roy 1753, Joe Davis 8003, DA-17-5, Vrs 8380
Lady Be Good: Ul AP-1422, B-14286, Or LV-100, LB-1000, Sup B-22642, Roy 1754, Joe Davis 8003, Vrs 8376
I Saw Stars: Ul AP-1423, B-14287, Or LV-101, LB-1000
Note: All the above four titles were issued on the following LPs: Pac LDP-D-6272; Or MG-10019; Crescendo GNP-9031; Vogue CLD-745, VJD-6950-A, 425019-A.

Coleman Hawkins Tenor saxophone solos, acc. by Michel Warlop and his Orchestra: Michel Warlop dir. Arthur Briggs-Noël Chiboust-Pierre Allier-t/Guy Paquinet-tb/André Ekyan-Charles Lisée-as/Alix Combelle-ts/Stéphane Grappelly-p/Django Reinhardt-g/Eugène d'Hellemmes-sb/Maurice Chaillou-d (1st three sides); acc. by Grappelly, Reinhardt, d'Hellemmes and Chaillou only (4th side).
Paris, 2 March 1935.
Blue Moon: HMV K-7455, B-8388, X-4497, El EG-3537, Vic JA-860, A-1419
Avalon: HMV K-7527, B-8388, X-4496, El EG-3537, Vic LPM-1100, EPC-1100
What A Difference A Day Made: HMV K-7455, B-8494, X-4497, Vic JA-860
Star Dust: HMV K-7527, B-8420, X-4496, HN-4476, N-4472, El EG-3695, Vic A-1419, DC-15, HMV DLP-1055, FELP-154, HCLP-120, OCLP-7529, Vic LPM-1100, EPC-1100

Patrick et son Orchestre Guy Paquinet-tb dir. Alex Renard-Gaston Lapeyronnie-Noël Chiboust-t/Pierre Deck-René Weiss-tb/André Ekyan-Maurice Cizeron-as/Andy Foster-as-ts/Alix Combelle-ts/Stéphane Grappelly-Michel Warlop-Sylvio Schmidt-vn/Jean Chabaud-p/Django Reinhardt-Joseph Reinhardt-g/Louis Pecqueux-sb/Maurice Chaillou-d-v/Hildegarde-v
Paris, 8 March 1935.
Miss Otis Regrets -vMC: PA 537
Waltzing with a Dream -vH: PA 538

Django Reinhardt et le Quintette du Hot Club de France avec Stéphane Grappelly Stéphane Grappelly-vn/Django Reinhardt-Joseph Reinhardt-Roger Chaput-g/Louis Vola-sb/Jerry Mengo-v.
Paris, March 1935.
Lily Belle May June -vJM: Ul AP-1444, Dec F-6531, 23004, Br A-81304, Pol A-197
Sweet Sue, Just You -vJM: Ul AP-1444, Or LV-104, LB-1004, Roy 1780
Confessin': Ul AP-1443, B-14289, Or LV-102,

LB-1002, Sup B-22639, Joe Davis 8005, DA-17-8, Roy 1788
The Continental: Ul AP-1443, B-14288, Or LV-102, LB-1002
Note: All the above four titles were also issued on the following LPs: Pac LDP-D-6272; Or MG-10019; Crescendo GNP-9031; Vogue CLD-745, VJD-6950-A, 425019-A, but the 1st was not on Or MG-10019.

Pierre Lord Vocal, acc. by Stéphane Grappelly-vn/René Ronald-p/Django Reinhardt-g, plus Louis Vola-sb on the 3rd title.
Paris, April 1935.
Simplement: Ul AP-1485
Smoke Gets In Your Eyes: Ul AP-1478, B-14291, Sup A-22638
Cocktails For Two: Ul AP-1478
Note: All the above three titles were also issued on Vogue VJD-6950-A and 425019-A (LPs).

Django Reinhardt et le Quintette du Hot Club de France avec Stéphane Grappelly As for March 1935 above.
Paris, April 1935.
Blue Drag: Ul AP-1479, B-14290, 11752, Or LV-103, LB-1003, Tel A-1958, Roy 1778
Swanee River: As above, plus Joe Davis DA-17-1, Roy 1785 and Vrs 8378
Ton doux sourire (The Sunshine Of Your Smile/Your Sweet Smile/Your Two Smiles): Ul AP-1484, B-14288, Or LV-104, LB-1004, Joe Davis DA-17-2, Roy 1807, Vrs 8380
Ultrafox (Ultra Sox*) (Ultraphone Rhythm**): Ul AP-1484, B-14289**, Sup B-22639, Dec F-6150, 23003, Y-5205, Pol A-197, Joe Davis DA-17-3*, Roy 1785, Vrs 8376
Note: All the above four titles were also issued on the following LPs: Pac LDP-D-6272; Crescendo GNP-9031; Vogue CLD-745, VJD-6950-A, 425019-A; and the 4th was also issued on Dec DFE-6366 (EP), DPA-3098-B and Lon LL-1344 (LPs). Decca F-6150 as Stéphane Grappelly and his Hot Four.

Nane Cholet Vocal, acc. by Stéphane Grappelly-vn or p as shown/René Ronald-p, 1st title only/Django Reinhardt-g/Louis Vola-sb, 1st title only.
Paris, May 1935.
Si j'avais été -vnSG: Ul AP-1314
Fièvre (Moon Glow): —
Note: Both titles were also issued on Vogue VJD-6950-A, 425019-A and VJD-6950-B and 425019-B respectively.

Django Reinhardt et le Quintette du Hot Club de France avec Stéphane Grappelly (as **Stéphane Grappelly and his Hot Four** on Dec F-6077 and F-6531) Arthur Briggs-Alphonse Cox-Pierre Allier-t/Eugène d'Hellemmes-tb/Stéphane Grappelly-vn/Django Reinhardt-Joseph Reinhardt-Roger Chaput-g/Louis Vola-sb.
Paris, July 1935.
Avalon: Ul AP-1512, Dec F-6077, 23002, Y-5204, Br A-81074, Roy 1780, Vrs 8379, Pol A-142
Smoke Rings: Ul AP-1512, Dec F-6531, Br A-81304, Joe Davis 8005, Roy 1788, Vrs 8379

Note: Both the above titles were also issued on Vogue LDM-30187 (LP).

All brass omitted; Pierre Ferret-g replaces Chaput.
Paris, July 1935.
Clouds: Ul AP-1511, Dec F-6406, 23002, Y-5178, Br A-81187, Tel A-1960, Pol A-142; Dec DPA-3098-A (LP)
Believe It, Beloved: Ul AP-1511, Dec F-6406, Y-5178, Br A-81187, Tel A-1960, Pol 624076; Dec DPA-3098-B (LP)
Note: Both the above titles were also issued on Vogue LDM-30187, VJD-6950-B and 425019-B (all LPs); Decca F-6406 as Stéphane Grappelly and his Hot Four.

Frank 'Big Boy' Goudie Trumpet, clarinet and tenor saxophone solos (no clarinet on the 2nd side), acc. by Stéphane Grappelly-p/Django and Joseph Reinhardt-g/Sigismond Beck-sb/Jerry Mengo-d.
Paris, August 1935.
I've Found A New Baby: Ul AP-1527, Tel A-1961
St Louis Blues: — B-14291 — Sup A-22638
Note: Both the above titles were also issued on Vogue LDM-30187, VJD-6950-B and 425019-B.

Jean Sablon Vocal, acc. by Stéphane Grappelly-p/Django Reinhardt-g.
Paris, August 1935.
Cette chanson est pour vous: Col rejected
Darling, je vous aime beaucoup: —
Dernière chanson: —

Alix Combelle Clarinet and tenor saxophone solos, acc. by Le Quinette du Hot Club de France: Stéphane Grappelly-p/Django and Joseph Reinhardt-g/Louis Vola-sb.
Paris, September 1935.
Crazy Rhythm: Ul AP-1544, Roy 1778, Vrs 8378
The Sheik of Araby: — Roy 1807, Joe Davis 8004, DA-17-6
Note: Both the above titles were also issued on Vogue LDM-30187, VJD-6950-B and 425019-B (all LPs).

Nina Rette et son Hot Trio Vocal, acc. by Stéphane Grappelly-vn/Emile Stern-p/Django Reinhardt-g.
Paris, 6 September 1935.
Points roses: Pol F-524108, 2489-188 (LP)
Un instant d'infini: — —
Mon coeur reste près de toi: Pol F-524111 —

Django Reinhardt et le Quintette du Hot Club de France avec Stéphane Grappelly Stéphane Grappelly-vn/Django Reinhardt-Joseph Reinhardt-Pierre Ferret-g/Louis Vola-sb.
Paris, September 1935.
Chasing Shadows: Ul AP-1547, Dec F-6002, Y-5120, Br A-82106, Roy 1798; Dec DPA-3098-A (LP)
I've Had My Moments: Ul AP-1547, Dec F-6150, Y-5205, Br A-81206, Joe Davis DA-17-4, Roy 1798, Vrs 8377; Dec DFE-6366 (EP); Dec DPA-3098-B (LP)
Some Of These Days: Ul AP-1548, Dec F-6002, 23004, Y-5120, Pol A-230; Dec DPA-3098-A (LP)
Djangology: Ul AP-1548, Dec F-6077, 23003, Y-5204, Br A-81047, Pol A-230

Note: Decca F-6002, F-6150 and Y-5120 as Stéphane Grappelly and his Hot Four. All the above four titles were also issued on Vogue LDM-30187, VJD-6950-B, 425019-B, and (except for the 3rd title) Lon LL-1344 (all LPs).

Nane Cholet Vocal (duet with Jean Tranchant where shown), acc. by Stéphane Grappelly-vn/Emil Stern-p/Django Reinhardt-g.
Paris, September 1935.
Ainsi soit-il: Ul AP-1552; Vogue VJD-6950-B, 425019-B (LPs)
Les quatre farceurs -vJT: As above

Arthur Briggs Trumpet solos, acc. by Stéphane Grappelly-vn-p/Django Reinhardt-g/Louis Vola-sb.
Paris, September 1935.
Tiger Rag: Ul rejected
Sweet Georgia Brown: —
Who?: —
There'll Be Some Changes Made: —

Jean Sablon Vocal, acc. by Stéphane Grappelly-vn/Django and Joseph Reinhardt-g/Louis Vola-sb.
Paris, September, 1935.
Cette chanson est pour vous: Col DF-1847
Rendez-vous sous la pluie: — 4222-M

Stéphane Grappelly and his Hot Four As for the Quintette session above.
Paris, 30 September 1935.
St Louis Blues: Dec F-5824, F-49019, Y-5062, 23032, Br A-9943, A-82559, A-500604, A-505280; Dec DPA-3098-B, Br LPB-86018 (LPs)
Chinatown: Rejected
Paris, October 1935.
Limehouse Blues: Dec F-5780, 23021, Br A-9884, Br A-82504, A-500016, A-505279, Od 284865, Pol 580016; Dec DFE-6366 (EP); Dec DPA-3098-A, Br LPB-86018 (LPs)
I Got Rhythm: Dec F-5780, Br A-9884, A-82504, Od 284865; Dec DFE-6366 (EP); Br LPB-86018 (LP)
Chinatown: Rejected

Jean (André ?) Pasdoc or Yvonne Louis Vocal, acc. by Louis Vola and his Orchestra: Louis Vola-sb dir. Stéphane Grappelly-vn and/or p/Django Reinhardt-g and others.
Paris, October 1935.
Un violon dans la nuit -vJP: Pol F-512467
Mirage -vYL: 2489-188 (LP)
Au grand Large -vYL: —
Vivre pour toi -vJP: Pol F-512467 —

Stéphane Grappelly and his Hot Four Stéphane Grappelly-vn/Django Reinhardt-Joseph Reinhardt-Pierre Ferret-g/Tony Rovira-sb.
Paris, October 1935.
I've Found A New Baby: Dec F-5943, Y-5105, 23021, Br A-9987, A-500613, A-505278; Dec DPA-3098-A (LP)
It Was So Beautiful: As above, except Dec 23021
China Boy: Dec F-5824, F-49019, Y-5062, 23031, Br A-9943, A-500105, A-500604, A-505280, Pol 580016; Dec DPA-3098-B, Br LBP-86018 (LPs)

Moon Glow: Dec F-5831, 23031, Br A-9909; Dec DPA-3098-B (LP)
It Don't Mean A Thing: Dec F-5831, 23032, Br A-9909; Dec DPA-3098-A (LP)

Micheline Day and her Quatuor Swing Vocal, acc. by similar group to the above, with Grappelly and Reinhardt present.
Paris, c. October 1935.
Y a du soleil dans la boutique: Pol 2489-188 (LP)
Cheri, est-ce que tu m'aimes?: —
Note: The original 78 rpm numbers of this issue are not known at present.

Bruce Boyce Vocal, acc. by Stéphane Grappelly-p, with Django Reinhardt-g*.
Paris, early November 1935.
Run, Mary, Run/Oh, Didn't It Rain?: Ul AP-1567; Vogue VJD-6950-B, 425019-B (LPs)
Wade In De Water: As above

Le Quintette du Hot Club de France Stéphane Grappelly-vn/Django Reinhardt-Joseph Reinhardt-Pierre Ferret-g/Lucien Simoens-sb /Freddy Taylor-v.
Paris, 4 May 1936.
I'se a Muggin' -vFT: HMV K-7704, Vic JA-874; HMV FELP-154, HCLP-120, OCLP-7529 (LPs)
I Can't Give You Anything But Love -vFT: HMV K-7706, HMV B-8463, El EG-3717, Vic 40-0122, 868-0684, A-1204, JA-856; same LPs as above
Oriental Shuffle: HMV K-7704, B-8479, AM-4737, N-4469, El EG-3776, Vic 26506, JA-874; same LPs as above, plus Vic LPM-1100, AVLT-6; RCA 1100-3 (45)
After You've Gone -vFT: HMV K-7707, B-8479, AM-4737, N-4463, El EG-3776, Vic 25511, JA-910; same EP and LPs as last above
Are You In The Mood?: HMV K-7707, Vic 26506, JA-910; same LPs as for OLA-1057-1 above
Limehouse Blues: HMV K-7706, B-8463, El EG-3717, Vic 25511, 68-0684, A-1204, JA-856; HMV FELP-154, FFLP-1138, HCLP-120, OCLP-7529
Louis Vola-sb replaces Simoens.
Paris, 15 October 1936.
Nagasaki -vFT: HMV K-7843, B-8518, El EG-3882, Vic 25558, JA-1012, JA-1078, HMV FELP-154, HCLP-120, OCLP-7529
Swing Guitars: HMV K-7898, B-8532, Vic 25601, JA-1119; same LPs as above, plus HMV CLP-1249, Vic AVLT-6, El E-83035
Georgia On My Mind -vFT: HMV K-7790, B-8532, Vic 26578, JA-1119; HMV FELP-154, HCLP-120, OCLP-7529, El E-83035, Vic AVLT-6 (LPs)
Shine -vFT: HMV K-7790, B-8534, AL-2366, El EG-3918, Vic 25558, 20-2760, JA-1012, JA-1078; HMV FELP-154, HCLP-120, OCLP-7529, Vic LPM-1100, RCA 1100-2 (45) (LPs)
In The Still Of The Night: HMV K-7898, B-8534, A-12366, El EG-3918, Vic 26578, A-1277, JA-1363; same LPs as for OLA-1290-1
Sweet Chorus: HMV K-7843, B-8578, El EG-3882, Vic 40-0122, HMV 7EMF-108, El E-Y1098 (45s)

Jean Tranchant Vocal, acc. by own p (and cel*), Stéphane Grappelly-vn/Django Reinhardt-g.
Paris, 22 October 1936.
Mademoiselle Adeline: PA 1042; EGC-3002 (45)
Le roi Marc: —

Nane Cholet Vocal, acc. by Stéphane Grappelly et son Ensemble 'Hot and Sweet': includes Stéphane Grappelly-vn-p/Django and Joseph Reinhardt-g/ Louis Vola-sb.
Paris, 12 November 1936.
Terrain à vendre: PA 1059
Ainsi soit-il: —

Le Quintette du Hot Club de France Stéphane Grappelly-vn/Django Reinhardt-Pierre Ferret-Marcel Bianchi-g/Louis Vola-sb.
Paris, 21 April 1937.
Exactly Like You: HMV B-8629, AL-2436, GW-1509, GY-333, JK-2332, El EG-6178, Vic 26733; HMV FELP-171, HCLP-122, OCLP-7542, Vic AVLT-6, Cap TBO-10226 (LPs)
Charleston: Swing 2; El 40920 (45), 7EGW-8505 (EP); HMV FELP-154, CLP-1249, HCLP-124, El E-83035 (LPs)
You're Driving Me Crazy: HMV K-8396, B-8606, AL-2404, GY-432, JK-2048, JO-16, El EG-6088, Vic 26733; HMV FELP-174, CLP-1249, HCLP-122, Vic AVLT-6
Tears: HMV B-8718; HMV FELP-171, HCLP-122, OCLP-7542, Vic LPM-1100 (LPs); RCA EPC-1100-3 (EP)
Solitude: HMV B-8669, Vic 40-0124; HMV FELP-171, HCLP-122, OCLP-7542, Cap TBO-10226 (LPs)
Paris, 22 April 1937.
Hot Lips: HMV B-8690, GY-297, JK-2049, El EG-6560; HMV FELP-171, HCLP-122, OCLP-7542, Vic LPM-1100, Cap TBO-10226 (LPs); RCA EPC-1100-1 (EP)
Ain't Misbehavin': HMV B-8690, JK-2049, El EG-6560, Vic 40-0123; LPs as above, plus Vic LEJ-10 (no 45s or EPs)
Rose Room: HMV B-8718; same LPs as OLA-1707-1 (no 45s or EPs)
Body and Soul: HMV B-8598; HMV FELP-171, HCLP-122, OCLP-7542, Cap TBO-10226
When Day Is Done: HMV B-8669, GY-297, Vic 40-0123; same LPs as last above
Paris, 26 April 1937.
Runnin' Wild: HMV B-8614, HN-2495, El EG-6561, Vic 40-0124; same LPs as OLA-1710-1
Chicago: Swing 2; HMV FELP-174, FFLP-1027, CLP-1249, HCLP-124, MODB-12, ODLP-7512, QFLP-4026, El E-83035 (LPs); HMV 7EGW-8505 (EP); El E-40920 (45)
Liebestraum No.3 (Liszt): HMV B-8737, AL-2492, Vic A-1277, JA-1363; same LPs as OLA-1710-1
Miss Annabelle Lee: HMV B-8614, HN-2495, El EG-6561, Vic 40-0125; HMV FELP-171, HCLP-122, OCLP-7542
A Little Love, A Little Kiss: HMV B-8598; same LPs as OLA-1710-1
Mystery Pacific: HMV K-8396, B-8606, AL-2404, GY-432, JK-2048, JO-15, El EG-6088, Vic 40-0125; same LPs as OLA-1710 plus Vic AVLT-6

In A Sentimental Mood: HMV B-8629, AL-2436, GW-1509, GY-333, JK-2332, El EG-6178; HMV FELP-174, CLP-1249, HCLP-124, OCLP-7542, El E-83035, Vic AVLT-6

Le Quintette du Hot Club de France Stéphane Grappelly-vn/Django Reinhardt-Pierre Ferret-Marcel Bianchi-g/Louis Vola-sb.
Paris, 27 April 1937.
The Sheik of Araby: HMV B-8737, AL-2492, HMV FELP-171, HCLP-122, OCLP-7542, Cap TBO-10226
I've Found A New Baby (SG-DR only): Rejected
Alabamy Bound (SG-DR only): Swing 21; HMV FELP-174, CLP-1249, HCLP-124, El E-83035 (LPs)

Coleman Hawkins and his All-Star Jam Band
Benny Carter-t-as/André Ekyan-as/Coleman Hawkins-ts/Alix Combelle-cl-ts/Stéphane Grappelly-p/Django Reinhardt-g/Eugène d'Hellemmes-sb/Tommy Benford-d.
Paris, 28 April 1937.
Honeysuckle Rose: Swing 1, HMV SG-364, B-8754, Col GN-5039, Vic 26219, JA-1294; HMV FELP-174, DLP-1055, HCLP-124, (LPs), HMV 7EG-8393, 7EGW-8505, 7EMF-26, 7TLA-29, El E-40920(EP/45)
Crazy Rhythm: As above
Out Of Nowhere: HMV K-8511, B-8812, JK-2639; HMV 7EG-8393, 7TLA-29 (EPs); HMV FELP-174, DLP-1055, HCLP-124 (LPs)
Sweet Georgia Brown: As above

Philippe Brun Trumpet solos, acc. by Stéphane Grappelly-p/Django Reinhardt-Louis Gaste-g/Eugène d'Hellemmes-sb/Maurice Chaillou-d.
Paris, 9 September 1937.
Whoa Babe: HMV rejected
P.B. Flat Blues: —

Trio de Violons Eddie South-Stéphane Grappelly-Michel Warlop-vn/Django Reinhardt-Roger Chaput-g/Wilson Myers-sb.
Paris, 29 September 1937.
Lady Be Good -aDR: Swing 45; HMV FELP-174, FFLP-1118, CLP-1249, HCLP-124, EMI-PA 2C-150-15860, El E-83035 (LPs)
Warlop omitted.
Paris, 29 September 1937.
Dinah: Swing 12; HMV 7EG-8324, TLA-23 (EPs); HMV FELP-181, FFLP-1118 (LPs)
Daphne: Swing 12; HMV FELP-181, FFLP-1118, EMI-PA 2C-150-15860 (LPs)
Michel Warlop-vn replaces South; Myers omitted.
Paris, 29 September 1937.
You Took Advantage Of Me: Swing 74; HMV FELP-181 (LP)

Stéphane Grappelly Violin solo, acc. by Django Reinhardt-g.
Paris, 29 September 1937.
I've Found A New Baby: Swing 21; HMV FELP-174, FFLP-1027, CLP-1249, HCLP-124, MODB-12, OCLP-7512, QFLP-4026, El E-83035 (LPs)

Bill Coleman et son Orchestre Bill Coleman-t-v/Stéphane Grappelly-vn-p*/Joseph Reinhardt g/Wilson Myers-sb/Ted Fields-d.
Paris, 12 November 1937.
*Indiana: Swing 42
Rose Room: Swing 9, Col GN-5059
Bill Street Blues: Swing 22, Col GN-5037
After You've Gone: — —
The Merry-Go-Round Broke Down: Swing 9

Eddie South-Stéphane Grappelly (Violins)-Django Reinhardt (Guitar).
Paris, 23 November 1937.
Interprétation Swing du Premier Mouvement du Concerto en ré mineur de J.-S. Bach: Swing 18; HMV 7EG-8324 (EP); HMV FELP-181, FFLP-1118, EMI-PA 2C-150-15861 (LPs)

Le Quintette du Hot Club de France Stéphane Grappelly-vn/Django Reinhardt-Joseph Reinhardt-Eugène Vées-g/Louis Vola-sb.
Paris, 25 November 1937.
Bricktop: Rejected
Speevy: —
Cavalerie: —
Minor Swing: Swing 23, HMV SG-367, Vic 26218; HMV 7EMF-11, El E-41098 (EPs); HMV FELP-184, FFLP-1027, MODB-12, ODLP-7512, QFLP-4026, El E-83035 (LPs)
Viper's Dream: As above, but no EP issues

Eddie South-Stéphane Grappelly Violin duets, acc. by Django Reinhardt-g, with Paul Cordonnier-sb*.
Paris, 25 November 1937.
*Fiddle's Blues: Swing 45; HMV 7EG-8324, 7TLA-23 (EPs); HMV FELP-184, FFLP-1118 (LPs)
Improvisation sur le Premier Mouvement du Concerto en ré mineur de J.-S. Bach: Swing 18; same EPs and LPs as above

Le Quintette du Hot Club de France and Michel Warlop As for 25 November 1937 above, plus Michel Warlop-vn.
Paris, 7 December 1937.
Swinging With Django: Swing 40, Vic 27272; HMV FELP-184, CLP-1249, El E-83035 (LPs)
Paramount Stomp: As above, plus HMV HCLP-120, OCLP-7529
Note: Victor 27272 shows the take as 2, but this merely indicates a dubbing from 1. HMV CLP-1249 shows *Paramount Stomp* on the sleeve, but some copies use *Presentation Stomp* in error, afterwards corrected.
Philippe Brun-Gus Deloof-André Cornille-t/Guy Paquinet-Josse Bréyère-tb added, next title only.
Paris, 14 December 1937.
Mabel: HMV L-1046, Vic JB-215; HMV FELP-184 (LP)
My Serenade: Swing 77; Angel 73007 (EP); HMV FELP-184, FFLP-1027, MODB-12, ODLP-7512, QFLP-4026, Angel 60003 (LPs)

Stéphane Grappelly Violin solos acc. by Django Reinhardt-g (first two titles); **Django Reinhardt** Guitar solos, acc. by Stéphane Grappelly-p (2nd two).
Paris, 27 December 1937.

Stephen's Blues: Swing 69; HMV FELP-197 (LP)
Sugar: —
Sweet Georgia Brown: Swing 35; HMV
FFLP-1027, MODB-12, ODLB-7512,
QFLP-4026, Angel 60011 (LPs)
*Tea For Two:*Swing 211; HMV 7EMF-40,
7EG-8132, 7EMQ-5 (EPs); HMV FELP-197,
FFLP-1027, MODB-12, ODLP-7512,
QFLP-4026, Angel 60011 (LPs)

Philippe Brun Trumpet solos, acc. by Stéphane
Grappelly-cel/Django Reinhardt-g.
Paris, 27 December 1937.
Blues: Swing 54
Easy Going: Rejected

Philippe Brun and his Swing Band Philippe
Brun-André Cornille-t/Gus Deloof-t-a/Josse
Bréyère-Guy Paquinet-tb/Max Blanc-Charles
Lisée-as/Jacques Hélian-Alix Combelle-ts/Stéphane
Grappelly-p/Django Reinhardt-g/Louis
Vola-sb/Maurice Chaillou-d.
Paris, 28 December 1937.
Easy Going -aGD: Swing 26
College Stomp -aPB: Swing 15
I Wonder? -aGD: Rejected
Harlem Swing -aGD: Swing 15

Philippe Brun 'Jam Band' Philippe Brun-t/Alix
Combelle-cl-ts/Michel Warlop-vn/Stéphane
Grappelly-p/Django Reinhardt-g/Louis
Vola-sb/Maurice Chaillou-d.
Paris, 28 December 1937.
It Had To Be You: Swing 44

Michel Warlop Violin solo, acc. by Stéphane
Grappelly-p/Django Reinhardt-g/Louis Vola-sb.
Paris, 28 December 1937.
Sweet Sue, Just You: Swing 43, Col GN-5044;
HMV FELP-203, FFLP-1138 (LPs)

Jacotte Perrier Vocal, acc. by the Quintette of the
Hot Club of France: Stéphane Grappelly-vn/
Django and Joseph Reinhardt-g/Sigismond
Beck-sb.
Paris, 5 January 1938.
Les salades de l'oncle François: Col DF-2344
Ric et Pussy: —

Quintet of the Hot Club of France Stéphane
Grappelly-vn/Django Reinhardt-Roger
Chaput-Eugène Vées/Louis Vola-sb. Reinhardt
and Vola speak in French*.
London, 31 January 1938.
Honeysuckle Rose: Dec F-6639, 538 (Italian),
23065, Br A-81503, A-505269, Od 284393, Pol
A-315
Sweet Georgia Brown: Dec F-6675, F-9045,
F-9428, Y-5227, 542 (Italian), 23065, Br
A-81603, A-505270, Od 284393, Pol 624076;
Dec LF-1139, DPA-3098-B, Lon LB-810,
LL-1344
Night and Day: Dec F-6616, F-8068, Y-5212,
23067, Br A-81436, A-82559, A-505271, Od
284357, Pol 624076; Dec DPA-3098-B, Br
LPB-86018, Lon LL-1344 (LPs)
*My Sweet: Dec F-6769, F-9045, F-9428, 573
(Italian), Br A-81685, A-505270; Dec LF-1139,

DPA-3098-A, Br LPB86018, Lon LB-810,
LL-1344 (LPs)
Souvenirs: Dec F-6639, 538 (Italian), 23065, Br
A-505269, Pol A-315
Daphne: Dec F-6769, 573 (Italian), 23152, Br
A-81685, Od 284357; Dec DPA-3098-B, Br
LPB-86018, Lon LB-810, LL-1344 (LPs)
Black and White: Dec F-6675, Y-5227, 542
(Italian), 23067, Br A-81603, SA-1610; Dec
DPA-3098-B (LP)
Stompin' At Decca: Dec F-6616, F-8086, Y-5212,
23066, Br A-81436, A-82559; Br LPB-86018
(LP)
Note: Decca issues in the F- series other than those
below F-7000 are Continental.

Django Reinhardt Guitar solos acc. by Stéphane
Grappelly-p, or Stéphane Grappelly: Violin solos
(with piano*), acc. by Django Reinhardt-g.
London, 1 February 1938.
Tornerai: Dec F-6721, Y-5262, 23079; Dec
MOR-530 (LP)
If I Had You: Dec F-6721, 23098; Dec
DPA-3098-A, MOR-530
*It Had To Be You: Dec F-7009, 23079; Dec
DPA-3098-B, MOR-530 (LPs)
Nocturne: Dec F-7009, 23098; Dec DPA-3098-B,
LF-1139, Lon LB-810, LL-1344

Philippe Brun and his Swing Band Philippe
Brun-Gus Deloff-André Cornille-t/Josse
Bréyère-Guy Paquinet-tb/Max Blanc-Charles
Lisée-as/Noël Chiboust-Alix Combelle-ts/Stéphane
Grappelly-p/Django Reinhardt-g/Louis
Vola-sb/Maurice Chaillou-d.
Paris, 8 March 1938.
Bouncin' Around: Swing 54
Ridin' Along The Moscova: Swing 34
Gotta Date In Louisiana: —
Gabriel's Swing – arr. Alix Combelle: Swing 26

Philippe Brun 'Jam-Band' Philippe Brun-c/Alix
Combelle-cl/Noël Chiboust-ts/Stéphane
Grappelly-p/Django Reinhardt-g/Louis
Vola-sb/Maurice Chaillou-d.
Paris, 8 March 1938.
Doin' The New Low-Down: Swing 44

Larry Adler Harmonica solos, acc. by Stéphane
Grappelly-p/Django Reinhardt-Joseph
Reinhardt-Eugène Vées-g/Roger Grasset-sb.
Paris, 31 May 1938.
Body And Soul: Col DF-2427, DB/MC-5047,
MZ-239, Od 291032; Col SEG-7775 (EP)
Lover, Come Back To Me: Col DF-2444; Col
SEG-7775 (EP)
Lover, Come Back To Me: Col DB-MC-5037, RZ
G-23542
My Melancholy Baby: Col DF-2444, DB/MC-5047,
Od 291032; Col SEG-7775 (EP)
I Got Rhythm: Col DF-2427; Col SEG-7775 (EP)
I Got Rhythm: Col DB/MC-5037, MZ-239, RZ
G-23542

Quintette du Hot Club de France Stéphane
Grappelly-vn/Django Reinhardt-Joseph
Reinhardt-Eugène Vées-g/Roger Grasset-sb.
Paris, 14 June 1938.
Billet Doux: Dec F-7568

Billet Doux: — 23263, Od 286192
Swing From Paris: Dec F-6899, Y-5348 — Br
   A-505276; Dec LF-1139, Lon LB-810 (LPs)
Them There Eyes: Dec F-6899, Y-5348, 573
   (Italian), 23262, Br A-505276; Dec DPA-3098-A
   (LP)
Three Little Words: Dec F-6875, Y-5270, 572
   (Italian), 23264, 333016, Br A-81901, A-505277,
   Od 284778; Dec LF-1139, Lon LB-810 (LPs)
Appel Indirect (Appel Direct*) (Direct Appeal**):
   Dec F-6875*, Y-5270, 572 (Italian), 23261**,
   333016, Br A-81901, A-505277, Od 284778,
   286044; Dec DPA-3098-A (LP)
London, 30 August 1938.
The Flat Foot Floogie: Dec F-6776, 9433, Br
   A-81692, A-505267
The Lambeth Walk: — — 23077 —; Dec
   DPA-3098-B
Why Shouldn't I Care?: — (LP)

Django Reinhardt Guitar solos, acc. by Stéphane
Grappelly-p.
London, 1 September 1938.
I've Got My Love To Keep Me Warm: Dec F-6935;
   Dec DPA-3098-A (LP)
I've Got My Love To Keep Me Warm: —
Please Be Kind: Dec F-6828, Y-5266
London, 10 September 1938.
Louise: Dec F-6828, Y-5266; Lon LL-1344 (LP)

Quintette du Hot Club de France Stéphane
Grappelly-vn/Django Reinhardt-Joseph
Reinhardt-Pierre Ferret-g/Emmanuel Soudieux-sb.
Paris, 21 March 1939.
Hungaria: Dec F-7198, Y-5580, 615 (Italian)
Hungaria: —
Jeepers Creepers: Dec F-7027, 587 (Italian), Br
   A-82082, A-505275, Col R-14124
Jeepers Creepers: Dec F-7027
Swing 39: — 587 (Italian), 23262, Br A-82082,
   A-82135, A-505275, Col R-14124
Japanese Sandman: Dec F-7133, Y-5450, 606
   (Italian), 23263, Fonit 606
I Wonder Where My Baby Is Tonight?: Dec F-7100,
   Y-5408, 23152
I Wonder Where My Baby Is Tonight?: — 597
   (Italian) — Od 283286, D-284563, D-286347;
   Dec MOR-530 (LP)
Paris, 22 March 1939.
Tea For Two: Rejected
My Melancholy Baby: Dec 23261
Time On My Hands: Dec F-7100, MOR-530 (LP)
Time On My Hands: — 597 (Italian), 59019,
   333016, Y-5408, Br A-505273, Od 238286,
   D-284363, D-286347
Twelfth Year: Dec 59023, F-7133, 606 (Italian),
   23264, Y-5450, Br A-505272, Fonit 606
Twelfth Year: Dec F-7133
Hungaria: Rejected

Quintette du Hot Club de France Stéphane
Grappelly-vn/Django Reinhardt-Joseph
Reinhardt-Pierre Ferret-g/Emmanuel Soudieux-sb.
Paris, 17 May 1939.
My Melancholy Baby: Dec F-7198, Y-5580, 615
   (Italian), Col R-14231, Fonit 615
Japanese Sandman: Dec 59006, Br A-505274, Pol
   580017

Tea For Two: — F-7568 — Od 284773 — Dec
   MOR-530 (LP)
I Wonder Where My Baby Is Tonight?: Dec 59019,
   Br A-505273, Dec DPA-3098-A (?) (LP)
Hungara: Dec 59023, Br A-505272
Eugène Vées-g replaces Joseph Reinhardt.
Paris, 30 June 1939.
Stockholm: Swing 128; HMV FELP-203 (LP)
Younger Generation: Swing 77 —

Stéphane Grappelly Violin solos, acc. by Django
Reinhardt-g.
Paris, 30 June 1939.
Out of Nowhere: Swing 199
Baby: —

Quintette du Hot Club de France As for 30 June
1939, plus Beryl Davis-v.
London, 25 August 1939.
Undecided -vBD: Dec F-7140, 59018, 616
   (Italian), Br A-505268, A-505271, Od 284997,
   PA 20172 (Chinese)
H.C.Q. Strut: Dec F-7390, 59045, 616 (Italian), Br
   A-505267, Col R-14231, Od 284997; Dec
   LF-1139, Lon LB-810, LL-1344 (LPs)
Don't Worry 'Bout Me -vBD: Dec F-7140, 59018,
   Br A-505268, PA 20172 (Chinese)
The Man I Love: Dec F-7390, 59045
Note: All the titles from this session, except the
4th, were also issued on Decca DPA-3098-A (LP).

Arthur Young and the Hatchett Swingtette
Arthur Young-p-novachord dir. Bill
Shakespeare-t/Dennis Moonan-cl-ts-vl/Stéphane
Grappelly-vn/Frank Baron-2nd p/Chappie
d'Amato-Jack Llewellyn-g/George Senior-sb/Tony
Spurgin-d/Beryl Davis-v.
London, 29 December 1939.
Scatter-Brain -vBD: Dec F-7336; Dec RFL-11
   (take ?) (LP)
Ting-a-Ling (The Waltz Of The Bells) -vBD: —
Alexander's Ragtime Band -vBD: Dec F-7409
You Made Me Love You -vBD: —
London, 25 January 1940.
Oh, Johnny! Oh, Johnny! Oh! -vBD: Dec F-7405
Bluebirds In The Moonlight -vBD: Dec F-7398
It's A Hap-Hap-Happy Day -vBD: —
Lying In The Hay -vBD: Dec F-7405
London, 23 February 1940.
How Am I To Know? -vBD: Dec rejected

Arthur Young and Hatchett's Quartet Arthur
Young-novachord dir. Grappelly, Baron and
Spurgin only; Billy Nicholls-v added.
London, 24 February 1940.
*I Cried For You (Now It's Your Turn To Cry Over
Me) -vBD:* Dec F-7644, Lon 153; Dec RFL-11
   (LP)
Blue Skies -vBD: — — —
Moonglow -vBN: Rejected
On The Sunny Side Of The Street: —

Arthur Young and Hatchett's Swingtette As for
29 December 1939, but Stan Andrews-t-cl-vn
replaces Shakespeare.
London, 19 March 1940.
In The Mood -vBD: Dec F-7450; Dec RFL-11 (take
   ?) (LP)
Ma! (He's Making Eyes At Me) -vBD: — —

Oh! Lady, Be Good: Dec F-7500 —
I Got Rhythm: — —
Ain't We Got Fun? -vBD: Rejected

Arthur Young and Hatchett's Swingtette Arthur
Young-p-novachord dir. Stan Andrews-t-cl-vn/
Dennis Moonan-cl-ts-vl/Stéphane
Grappelly-vn/Frank Baron-2nd p/Chappie
d'Amato-Jack Llewellyn-g/George Senior-sb/Tony
Spurgin-d/Beryl Davis-v.
London, 19 April 1940.
Playmates -vBD: Dec F-7470
Oh! By Jingo -vBD: — Dec RFL-11 (LP)
Everybody Loves My Baby -vBD: Rejected
Mind, The Handel's Hot: Dec F-7591; Dec RFL-11
  (LP)
How Am I To Know? -vBD: Dec F-7624
London, 25 May 1940.
Blue Ribbon Rag: Dec F-7510
Sweet Potato Piper -vBD: —
London, 31 May 1940.
Sweet Potato Piper -vBD: Dec F-7510 ?
Coal Black Mammy -vBD: Dec F-7761
The Blue Room: Rejected
Grappelly-Baron-Young-Spurgin only*.
London, 8 July 1940.
*When It's Sleepy-Time Down South: Rejected
The Sheik Of Araby: Dec F-7761; Dec RFL-11
  (LP)
Dearest, I Love You: Dec F-7591
Prim And Proper: Dec F-7844
Steamboat Bill -vBD: —

Stéphane Grappelly and his Musicians
Stéphane Grappelly-Stanley Andrews-vn/George
Shearing-p/Jack Llewellyn-g/Harry
Chapman-harp/Hank Hobson-sb/Al
Philcock-d/Reg Conroy-vib.
London, 30 July 1940.
I Never Knew: Rejected
After You've Gone: Dec F-7570; ACl 1121, Dec
  MOR-530
Stéphane's Tune: — (LPs)

Arthur Young and Hatchett's Swingtette As for
19 April 1940, but Marjorie Kingsley-v replaces
Beryl Davis.
London, 4 September 1940.
*Rumpel-Stilts-Kin (Oh! Could He Sew, Could He
Sew) -vMK:* Dec F-7613
Ida, Sweet As Apple Cider: Dec F-7624
Bugle Call Rag: Dec F-7890
I Hear Bluebirds -vMK: Dec F-7613; Dec RFL-11
  (LP)
*Yes, Sir, That's My Baby: Dec F-7890
Dark Eyes: Rejected

Hatchett's Swingtette Dennis Moonan-cl-ts-vl
dir. same personnel as last above, but without
Arthur Young (injured in bombing); Dorothy
Carless-v replaces Marjorie Kingsley. Fifth and
sixth titles are by Hatchett's Swing Strings.
London, 19 November 1940.
Brother Jackie (Frère Jacques) -vDC: Dec F-7682
Twelfth Street Rag: Dec F-7697
All The Things You Are -vDC: Dec F-7682; Dec
  RFL-11 (LP)
Beat Me Daddy (Eight To The Bar) -vDC: Dec
  F-7697

Liza -vDC: Rejected
Sweet Sweetheart -vDC: —

Stéphane Grappelly and his Musicians
Stéphane Grappelly-vn dir. Dennis
Moonan-as-vn/Eugène Pini-Stanley
Andrews-vn/unknown vc/George Shearing-p/Harry
Chapman-harp/Syd Jacobson-g/George
Gibbs-sb/Jock Jacobson-d.
London, 28 February 1941.
I Never Knew: Dec F-8128; Dec TAB-55 (LP)
Sweet Sue, Just You: Dec F-7841 —
Tiger Rag: Dec F-7787
Stéphane's Blues: —
Noël Brings The Swing: Dec F-7841; Dec TAB-55
  (LP)

Hatchett's Swingtette Dennis Moonan-ts-vl dir.
Bruce Campbell-t-tb/Stan Andrews-t-vn/Frank
Weir-cl-as/Stéphane Grappelly-vn/George
Shearing-p/Charlie Pude-novachord/Chappie
d'Amato-g/Alf Leah-sb/Dave
Fullerton-d-v/Dorothy Carless-v.
London, 7 April 1941.
Limehouse Blues: Dec F-8001
Papa's In Bed With His Breeches On -vDC: Dec
  F-7860
Scrub Me Mama With A Boogie Beat -vDC: —
I'm A Ding Dong Daddy -vDF: Dec F-8001

Stéphane Grappelly and his Quartet Stéphane
Grappelly-vn/George Shearing-p/Jack
Llewellyn-g/George Gibbs-sb/Dave Fullerton-d.
London, 9 April 1941.
Dinah: Dec F-7865; Dec MOR-530, TAB-55
  (LPs)
Liza: Rejected
Body And Soul: Dec F-8128; ACl 1121, Dec
  MOR-530 (LPs)
Jive Bomber: Dec F-7865; Dec TAB-55 (LP)

**Pinchin Johnson's Witley Court Music Box
(Records sold in aid of the Spitfire Fund)** W. D.
Davison-as/Stéphane Grappelly-vn/J. Hegarty or
E. Farrar-p/Chappie d'Amato-g/Bert
Howard-sb/Joyce Head-v.
London, c. May 1941.
*We three/I Can't Give You Anything But Love
  -vJH:* Special JH-41
Sweet Sue: Special JH-40
Some Of These Days -vJH: Special JH-38
Blue Skies: Special JH-39
From The Top Of Your Head: —
I Cover The Waterfront -vJH: Special JH-38
I Got Rhythm: Special JH-37
Crazy Rhythm: —

Stéphane Grappelly and his Quintet Stéphane
Grappelly-vn-p*/Pat Dodd-p/Chappie d'Amato-Joe
Deniz-g/Tommy Bromley-sb/Dave Fullerton-d-v.
London, 17 February 1942.
Margie -vDF: Dec F-8175; Dec MOR-530 (LP)
You're The Cream In My Coffee -vDF: — —
Nagasaki: Rejected
I'm Coming, Virginia: —

Hatchett's Swingtette Dennis Moonan-ts-vl dir.
Bruce Campbell-t-tb/Stan Andrews-t-vn/Carl
Barriteau-cl-as-v/Stéphane Grappelly-vn (not on

DR-6778-2 from this session)/George Shearing-p/Charlie Pude-novachord/Chappie d'Amato-g/Alf Leah-sb/Len Hunt-d/Billie Campbell-v.
London, 8 April 1942.
Watch The Birdie -vCB: Dec F-8140; Dec RFL-11 (LP)
The Waiter And The Porter And The Upstairs Maid -vBC: Dec F-8129 —
I Said No -vBC: Dec F-8140

Stéphane Grappelly and his Quintet Stéphane Grappelly-vn/Yorke de Sousa-p/Joe Deniz-g/Joe Nussbaum-sb/Dave Fullerton-d-v.
London, 20 August 1942.
Liza: Dec F-8204
Hallelujah: Dec F-8229 (never issued)
Sleepy Lagoon -vDF: —
The Folks Who Live On The Hill -vDF: Dec F-8204
Stéphane Grappelly-vn/Arthur Birkby-bsx/Jack Penn-p/Ivor Mairants-g/Joe Nussbaum-sb/Dave Fullerton-d-v.
London, 28 January 1943.
Ain't She Sweet? -vDF: Rejected
I'll Never Be The Same: —
Star Dust: Dec F-8451; Dec MOR-530, TAB-55 (LPs)
Au revoir (J'attendrai): —
As for 17 February 1942 above, except that George Shearing-p replaces Dodd, and Beryl Davis-v is added.
London, 7 July 1943.
Weep No More, My Lady -vBD: Dec F-8333
When I Look At You -vBD: Dec F-8334
Three O'Clock In The Morning: —
That Old Black Magic -vBD: Dec F-8333

Stéphane Grappelly and his Quartet Stéphane Grappelly-vn/George Shearing-p/Alan Mindell-?Laurie Deniz-g/?Joe Nussbaum-sb/Dave Fullerton-d-v/Beryl Davis-v.
London, 6 October 1943.
Strictly Non-Vocal: Rejected
Star Eyes -vBD: Dec F-8375
Heavenly Music -vBD: —
She's Funny That Way -vDF: Rejected

Stéphane Grappelly and his Quartet Stéphane Grappelly-vn/George Shearing-p/Alan Mindell-?Laurie Deniz-g/?Joe Nussbaum-sb/Dave Fullerton-d-v/Beryl Davis-v.
London, 3 December 1943.
Baby, Please Stop! And Think About Me -vBD-DF: Rejected
I Never Mention Your Name (Oh No) -vDF: Dec F-8392
My Heart Tells Me -vDF: —
Ol' Man River: Rejected

Stéphane Grappelly and his Sextet As for the Quartet above, but Arthur O'Neill-sb probably replaces Nussbaum.
London, 15 June 1944.
Ain't Misbehavin': Rejected
I've Found A New Baby: —
Confessin' -vBD: Lon 155
Someday, Sweetheart -vBD: Dec F-9745

Stéphane Grappelly and his Quartet As for the Sextet above, but Denny Wright is the 2nd g.
London, 29 November 1944.
Henderson Stomp: Dec F-9745; Dec MOR-530 (LP)
Don't You Know That I Care? -vBD: Dec F-8492, Lon 101
No-One Else Will Do -vBD: — —
Jam Sandwich: Rejected
Stéphane Grappelly-vn/Arthur Young-p/George Elliott-g/Peter Akister-sb/Dave Fullerton-d; Grappelly and Young only on 1st two titles; Beryl Davis-v.
London, 13 May 1945.
Sentimental Nocturne: Dec rejected
Who's Cuckoo?: —
I'm Beginning To See The Light -vBD: —
Candy -vBD: —

Carlo Krahmer's Chicagoans Johnny Best-t/Ronnie Chamberlain-as/Stéphane Grappelli-vn-1,p-2/Vic Lewis-g/Tommy Bromley-sb/Carlo Krahmer-d.
London, 12 March 1945.
I've Found A New Baby -1: Esquire ESQ306
I Never Knew -2: —

Stéphane Grappelly and his Orchestra
Stéphane Grappelly-vn dir. unknown vns/vl/vc(?)/George Shearing-p/George Elliott-g/Peter Akister-sb/Jack Parnell-d/Doreen Henry-v; the 4th title is by the Quartet (Grappelly and the rhythm section only).
London, 25 October 1945.
Sugar -vDH: Dec F-8582
(You Came Along From) Out Of Nowhere -vDH: —
Wendy: Rejected
Piccadilly Stomp: —

Django Reinhardt et le Quintette du Hot Club de France avec Stéphane Grappelly Stéphane Grappelly-vn/Django Reinhardt-Jack Llewellyn-Alan Hodgkiss-g/Coleridge Goode-sb.
London, 31 January 1946.
Coquette: Swing 242
Django's Tiger: — HMV FELP-208 (LP)
Embraceable You: Swing 229
Echoes Of France: — HMV FELP-208 (LP)
London, 1 February 1946.
Love's Melody: Dec F-8604
Love's Melody: — 20299, 625, RD-40006
Belleville: Dec F-8876, F-41010, SB-41010
Nuages: Dec F-8604, 20299, 625, RD-40006
Liza: Dec F-8876, F-41010, SB-41010, Tel SH-104
Stéphane Grappelly-vn/Django Reinhardt-Joseph Reinhardt-Jean Ferret-g/Emmanuel Soudieux-sb.
Paris, 26 March 1947.
R-Vingt-Six: Swing 259
How High The Moon: Swing 253; HMV FELP-208 (LP)
Lover Man: — —
Blue Lou: Swing 259 —
Blues: Swing 266

Stéphane Grappelly and his Quartet Stéphane Grappelly-vn/George Shearing-p/?Dave Goldberg-g/Coleridge Goode-sb/Ray Ellington-d.
London, 25 April 1947.
Yellow House Stomp: Dec F-8917

Red-O-Ray: —
Channel Crossing: Rejected
In The Mode (In The Mood): —

Stéphane Grappelly's Hot Four Stéphane
Grappelly-vn/Joseph Reinhardt-Roger
Chaput-g/Emmanuel Soudieux-sb.
Paris, 17 October 1947.
Oui pour vous revoir: Swing 271; PA 2C-054-16028
(LP)
Soleil d'automne: Rejected

Stéphane Grappelly Piano solos.
Paris, 17 October 1947.
Bebop Medley: Rejected
Tea For Two: Swing 271; PA 2C-054-16028 (LP)

**Django Reinhardt et le Quintette du Hot Club
de France** Stéphane Grappelly-vn/Django
Reinhardt-Joseph Reinhardt-Eugène Vées-g/Fred
Ermelin-sb.
Paris, 14 November 1947.
What Is This Thing Called Love?: Swing 283, PA
AT-1002; HMV FELP-208 (LP)
Ol' Man River: Swing 270; Angel 73007 (EP); —
Angel 60003
Si tu savais: — — (LP)
Eveline: Swing 274
Diminushing: — Angel 73007 (EP); Angel 60003
(LP)
Broadcast for RTF, Paris, 21 November 1947.
Ol' Man River: Vogue EPL-7728 (EP); LD-491
(LP)
R-Vingt-Six: —
Swing Guitars: —
I Love You: —
Challin Ferret-g replaces Vées; Emmanuel
Soudieux-sb replaces Ermelin; Grappelly plays p
only 1.
Paris, 10 March 1948.
Mike: Swing 287
Lady Be Good: —
Festival 48: Swing 280; Angel 73006 (EP); HMV
FELP-208, Angel 60003 (LPs)
Fantaisie: Swing 280
Brick Top: Swing 283
Just For Fun: HMV FELP-208 (LP)
*To Each His Own/Symphony: Rejected

Django Reinhardt and Stéphane Grappelly
Guitar and violin duets, acc. by Gianni
Safred-p/Carlo Pecori-sb/Aurelio de Carolis-d.
Rome, January-February 1949.
Over The Rainbow: EMI 2M-056-13247
Night And Day: Swaggie S-1391
Minor Blues: Unissued
Nature Boy: Swaggie S-1391
The World Is Waiting For The Sunrise: RCA
PM-45362-A
Vous qui passez sans me voir: EMI-PA
2C-150-15862
Hallelujah: RCA PM-45362-B
Nagasaki: Unissued
I'll Never Be The Same: Swaggie S-1391
Swing 39: EMI 2M-056-13247
Clopin-Clopant: —
Honeysuckle Rose: RCA PM-45362-B
All The Things You Are: RCA PM-45362-A
Djangology: —

Liza: Unissued
For Sentimental Reasons: Swaggie S-1391
Daphne: RCA PM-45362-B
La Mer (Beyond The Sea): RCA PM-45362-A
Sweet Georgia Brown: EMI 2M-056-13247
Lover Man: RCA PM-45362-B
Marie: —
Stormy Weather: EMI 2M-056-13247
Minor Swing: RCA PM-45362-B
To Each His Own: Swaggie S-1391
What Is This Thing Called Love?: Unissued
Où es-tu, mon amour?: —
Undecided: Swaggie S-1391
I'm In The Mood For Love: Unissued
Swing 42: RCA PM-45362-B
I Surrender, Dear: —
After You've Gone: —
Mam'zelle: Unissued
I Got Rhythm: RCA PM-45362-B
I Saw Stars: RCA PM-45362-A
Artillerie Lourde (Heavy Artillery): —
It's Only A Paper Moon: —
Time On My Hands: Swaggie S-1391
Brick Top: RCA PM-45362-B
*Improvisation on Tchaikovsky's Pathétique
    Andante (The Story Of A Starry Night):* RCA
    PM-45362-A
My Blue Heaven: Unissued
Menilmontant: RCA PM-45362-A
Swing Guitars: —
My Melancholy Baby: Unissued
Truckin': —
The following appear to belong to this period.
Blue Lou: EMI 2M-056-13247
Brazil: —
Webster: —
What A Difference A Day Made: —
Pigalle: — EMI-PA 2C-150-15862
Rosetta: —
Dream Of You: HMV FELP-231, CLP-1389
Begin The Beguine: — —
How High The Moon: — —
Nuages (No. 1): — —
I Can't Get Started: — —
I Can't Give You Anything But Love: — —
Manoir de mes rêves (Grappelly & Reinhardt only):
    —
Nuages No. 2: Unissued
The Man I Love: —
The Peanut Vendor: —
Just a Gigolo: —
Troublant Boléro: —
All the above Rome recordings were issued on LPs
as shown; all the following issues are LPs also,
unless stated otherwise after the catalogue number;
there are no further 78s.

Stéphane Grappelly Trio Stéphane
Grappelly-p/Guy Pederson-sb/Baptiste 'Mac Kac'
Reilles-d (No drums where marked *).
Paris, May 1954.
Viens au creux de mon épaule: Club Français du
    Disque 45, Musidisc 30-JA-5216 (all ten titles
    this session)
Lookin' At You:
I Can't Recognize The Tune:
Red-O-Ray:
Crazy Blues:
Marno:

Tendrement (Tenderly):
Vous qui passez sans me voir:
Wendy:
Valse du passé:

Jack Dieval avec Stéphane Grappelly Stéphane
Grappelly-vn/Jack Dieval-p/Benoit Quersin-sb,
Jean-Louis Viale-d.
Paris, 15 or 17 September 1954.
A Gal In Calico: HMV FFLP-1042; 7EMF-65 (EP)
Pennies From Heaven: — —
The World Is Waiting For The Sunrise: — —
Can't Help Lovin' That Man: —
I Can't Recognize The Tune: —
You Took Advantage Of Me: —
The Folks Who Live On The Hill: —

Henri Crolla-Stéphane Grappelly Quartet
Stéphane Grappelly-vn/Henri Crolla-g/Emmanuel
Soudieux-sb/Baptiste 'Mac Kac' Reilles-d.
Paris, 30 December 1954.
Swing 93 (?): Ducretet-Thompson 250-V-004
Belleville: —
Manoir de mes rêves: —
Djangology: — 460-V-068
Alembert's: Ducretet-Thompson 255-V-005,
    460-V-068
Just Can't Be Love (? This Can't Be Love): —
Have You Met Miss Jones?: —
**Marno:* Ducretet-Thompson 260-V-041

Stéphane Grappelly Violin solos, acc. by Maurice
Vander-p/René Duchaussoir-g/Benoit
Quersin-sb/Jean-Louis Viale-d/Michel
Hausser-vib.
Paris, 12 April 1955.
Night And Day: Barclay 74006, 84006, 8109213,
    Felsted PDL-86048
Aime-moi: Barclay 74006
The Nearness Of You: As for 26102
Don't Worry 'Bout Me: —
Duchaussoir and Hausser omitted.
Paris, 16 May 1955.
Birth Of The Blues: Barclay 84006, 8109213,
    Felsted PDL-86048
Lover Man: —
Lady Be Good: — — —
I Can't Believe That You're In Love With Me: — —
Tangerine: — —
Acc. by Maurice Vander-p/Pierre
Michelot-sb/Baptiste 'Mac Kac' Reilles-d.
Paris, 6 February 1956.
Dans la vie: Barclay 84034, Felsted PDL-85027
Fascinatin' Rhythm: — 8109213 — EmArcy
    MG-36120
Time After Time: — — —
'S Wonderful: — — — —
Vander plays harpsichord on 6th and 7th titles.
Paris, 14 February 1956.
Taking A Chance On Love: Barclay 84034,
    8109213, Felsted PDL-85027, EmArcy
    MG-36120
Cheek To Cheek: As above, except Barclay 8109213
Slow en ré majeur: Barclay 8109213
She's Funny That Way: As for 30379
The Lady Is A Tramp: —
Someone To Watch Over Me: —
Crazy Rhythm: —

Stéphane Grappelly Quartet As for 6 February
1956.
Paris, 10 April 1956.
A Nightingale Sang In Berkeley Square: Barclay
    84034, 8109213, Felsted PDL-85027, EmArcy
    MG-36120
Body And Soul: As above
If I Had You: —
I Want To Be Happy: —

**Stéphane Grappelly and his Orchestra and
Chorus** Jo Boyer-a dir. large orchestra and chorus,
featuring Stéphane Grappelly-v. (All the next
fourteen tracks were issued on Barclay 82083,
820007, 950003, Felsted PDL-85038 and Verve
MG-20001.)
Paris, 2 October 1956.
Pennies From Heaven:
Once In A While:
The Very Thought Of You:
Yesterdays:
Paris, 13 October 1956.
Please Be Kind:
Moonlight In Vermont:
I've Got You Under My Skin:
Darling, je vous aime beaucoup:
Lazy Bones:
Paris, 7 December 1956.
Nuages:
Day After Day:
The Way You Look Tonight:
Moonglow:
Ah! que revienne:

Stéphane Grappelly and Stuff Smith Violin
duets, acc. by Oscar Peterson-p/Herb Ellis-g/Ray
Brown-sb/Jo Jones-d.
Paris, 4 May 1957.
Mean To Me: Verve unissued
I Want To Be Happy: —
*Medley: The Nearness Of You/Embraceable You/A
    Nightingale Sang In Berkeley Square/Moonlight
    In Vermont:* —
Don't Get Around Much Anymore: Pablo 2310-907
No Points Today: —
Chapeau Blues: —
The Lady Is A Tramp: —

Eddie Barclay and his Orchestra Stéphane
Grappelly-vn is present on the following two titles
only from this session: Quincy Jones-a dir. Roger
Guérin-Fred Gérard-Maurice Thomas-Henri
Vanecke-t/Charles Huss-André Paquinet-Benny
Vasseur-tb/Gabriel Vilain-bass tb/Mickey
Nicolas-Jo Hrasko-as/Lucky Thompson-Marcel
Hrasko-ts/William Boucaya-bar/Raymond
Guiot-f/18 vn-vl-vc/Art Simmonds-p/Pierre
Cavalli-g/Jean Bouchety-sb/Kenny Clarke -
d/Michel Hausser-vib/8 unidentified v.
Paris, 24 June 1957.
Tu joues avec le feu: Barclay 82138, United Artists
    UAL-3023
Un p'tit bout de femme: — 72133

Stéphane Grappelly and his Quartet Stéphane
Grappelly-vn/Raymond Fol-p-harpsichord*/Pierre
Michelot-sb/Allan Levitt-d.
Paris, 17 July 1957.

Love Is Back: Barclay 84066, 8109213, Felsted
PDL-85060
Jeepers Creepers: —
Manoir de mes rêves: — — —
A Flower Is a Lonesome Thing: — — —
It's Only a Paper Moon: — — —
Guy Pederson-sb replaces Michelot; Kenny
Clarke-d replaces Levitt.
Paris, 18 July 1957.
Coquette: Barclay 84066, 8109213, Felsted
PDL-85060
Willow, Weep For Me: — — —
This Can't Be Love: — — —
My Funny Valentine: — — —
Blue Room: — — —
Pierre Michelot-sb replaces Pederson.
Paris, 22 July 1957.
Thou Swell: Barclay 84066, 8109213, Felsted
PDL-85060
By All Means: — — —
Shine: —
I've Found A New Baby: — — —

Eddie Barclay and his Orchestra Probably as for
24 June 1957 above, but no strings other than
Grappelly; chorus only present on 3rd title;
Fernand Verstraete-t replaces Vanecke; Don Byas
and Pierre Grossez or George Grenu-ts replace
Thompson and Hrasko.
Paris, 18 October 1957.
Numéro 13: Unissued
Quincy Boogie: Barclay 72180
Tout doucement: — 72133
Quelquechose en toi: Barclay 82128, United Artists
UAL-3023

Stéphane Grappelly and his Orchestra
Stéphane Grappelly-vn and unknown
instrumentation; Mario Bua-a.
Paris, 13 November 1957.
Je t'aime: Barclay unissued
Bonsoir, chérie: —
Je crois rêver: —
Rose: —
Puisque tu dors: —

François Vermeille and his Orchestra François
Vermeille-p-a dir. Bernard Hulin-t/Marcel
Hrasko-cl-ts/Gilbert Roussel-pac/Lily
Laskine-harp/Stéphane Grappelly-vn/René
Duchaussoir-g/Alphonse Masseller-sb/Arthur
Motta-d.
Paris, 26 April 1958.
Rêveries: Barclay 82146
Darn That Dream: —
I'll See You In My Dreams: —
Dream Of You: —
Joss Basselli-pac/Jacques Medvedko-sb replace
Roussel and Masseller.
Paris, 30 April 1958.
A Weaver of Dreams: Barclay 82146
Rêver: —
De rêve en rêve: —

Henri Crolla All Stars Stéphane
Grappelly-vn/René Urtreger or Maurice
Vander-p/Emmanuel Soudieux-sb/Allan Levitt-d,
plus Hubert Rostaing-cl/André Ekyan-as/Henri
Crolla-g on the titles marked *.

Paris, sometime in 1958.
Swing 39: Vega V-30-S-805, 30-VT-12161
Minor Swing: — —
Swing 42: — —
Place de Brouchère: — —

Stéphane Grappelly Violin solos, acc. by
unidentified f/vns/vls/vcs/chorus; Jo Boyer-a.
Paris, 4 November 1958.
Begin The Beguine: Barclay unissued
My Heart Belongs To Daddy: —
Rosalie: —
Easy To Love: —
Night And Day: —
Paris, 5 November 1958.
Slap That Bass: Barclay 80903, 81050, 82174
Nice Work If You Can Get It: — 72313 — —
What Is This Thing Called Love?: Unissued
You're The Top: —
Paris, 6 November 1958.
In The Still Of The Night: Barclay unissued
Just One Of Those Things: —
The Man I Love: —
Oh, Lady Be Good: —
Paris, 8 November 1958.
Anything Goes: Unissued
Somebody Loves Me: Barclay 80903, 81050, 82174
Paris, 17 November 1958.
Love For Sale: Barclay unissued
All Through The Night: —
It's De-Lovely: —
You're Sensational: —
Ça c'est l'amour: —
Paris, 22 December 1958.
I Got Rhythm: Barclay 80903, 81050, 82174,
BB-28.72313
Some To Watch Over Me: — — — —
Clap Your Hands: — — — —
That Certain Feeling: — — — —
Paris, 23 December 1958.
Love Walked In: Barclay 80903, 81050, 82174,
BB-28
Love Is Here To Stay: — — — —
A Foggy Day: — — — — 72313
Paris, 26 December 1958.
Liza: Barclay 80903, 81050, 82174, BB-28
When Do We Dance?: — — — — 72313
Summertime: —
Paris, 9 January 1959.
Fascinating Rhythm: Barclay 80903, 81050, 82174,
BB-28
Somebody Loves Me: Unissued
Slap That Bass: —
Nice Work If You Can Get It: —
Raymond Guiot-f replaces the unknown.
Paris, 14 January 1959.
Lady Be Good (sic): Barclay 80903, 81050, BB-28
The Man I Love: — — —
You're Sensational: Barclay 80904, 81051, Felsted
PDL-85068, SPD-3002
Night And Day: As above.
Just One Of Those Things: —

Stéphane Grappelly Violin solos, acc. by
Raymond Guiot-f/unidentified vns/vls/vcs/chorus;
Jo Boyer-a.
Paris, 15 January 1959.
What Is This Thing Called Love?: Barclay 80904,
81051, 82166, Felsted PDL-85068, SPD-3002.

It's De-Lovely: As above
Ça c'est l'amour: —
I Get A Kick Out Of You: —
You're The Top: —
Love For Sale: —
Paris, 16 January 1959.
In The Still Of The Night: Barclay 80904, 81051,
    82166, Felsted PDL-85068, SPD-3002
Anything Goes: As above
Begin The Beguine: —
Rosalie: —
My Heart Belongs To Daddy: —
Easy To Love: —
All Through The Night: —
Some Enchanted Evening: Unissued

One World Jazz Clark Terry-t/J. J.
Johnson-tb/Ben Webster-ts/Hank Jones-p/Kenny
Burrell-g/George Duvivier-sb/Jo Jones-d. These
recorded their parts in New York on 19 May 1959,
and copies of the tape were sent to London (where
George Chisholm-tb/Roy East/Ronnie-Ross-bar
added theirs on 22 June 1959) and Paris (where
Roger Guérin-t/Bob Garcia-ts/Martial
Solal-p/Stéphane Grappelly-vn added theirs on 3
July 1959), as indicated by their initials after each.
Misty -GC-RE-SG: Col WL-162, WS-314, Philips
    BBL-7361
International Blues -all: — — —
Nuages -SG: — — —

**Hubert Clavecin et ses Rythmes avec Stéphane
Grappelly – Dansez sur vos Souvenirs, volume
1** Gérard Gustin (alias Hubert Clavecin)
(harpsichord) w g/sb/d/ Stéphane Grappelli-1(vn),
Jean Lefvre (f), Michel Cassez (not on 3rd title)
(bs).
Paris, 17 June 1960.
J'attendrai: Bel Air 321029, 7006
Je Suis Seul Ce soir – 1: — —
Jolie Madame – 1: — 7044
Couches Dans Le Foin – 1: — —
Hymne A L'Amour – 1: — 7006
Les Feuilles Mortes – 1: — —
Libelluie: — —
La Chanson Des Rues – 1: — —
Insensiblement – 1/Solitude – 1: — —
C'est Si bon – 1: — — Score 14059
Venez Donc Chez Moi – 1: — —
Stardust – 1, 3/Je Te Dois: — — —
Nuages – 1/Revérie: — — —
La Vie En Rose: — — —
Les Petites Choses – 1: — — —
La Mer – 1: — 7044
Vous Qui Passez Sans Me Voir – 1: — —
Note: Bel Air 7006 = Musidisc 30CV1080 =
Festival ALBUM 111 (1st disc); Bel Air 7044 =
Musidisc 30CV1099 = Festival ALBUM 111 (2nd
disc).

Stéphane Grappelly Violin solos, acc. by
unidentified f/vns/vls/vcs/chorus; Jo Boyer-a.
Paris, 27 March 1961.
Too Marvellous For Words: Barclay unissued
A Romantic Guy: —
Paris, 4 April 1961.
Nuages: Barclay unissued
A Gal In Calico: —

Stéphane Grappelly Quintet Stéphane
Grappelly-vn/Pierre Cavalli-Leo Petit-g/Guy
Pederson-sb/Daniel Humair-d.
Paris, 7 March 1962.
Like Someone In Love: Barclay 84089, 820105,
    950080, Atlantic SD-1391, Everest FS-311
Daphne: As above, plus Atlantic 790140, Ember
    CJS-810, Lon HA-K/SH-K-8047
You Better Go Now: As for 9175, except Ember
    CJS-810
Paris, 8 March 1962.
Soft Winds: Barclay 84089, 820105, 950080,
    Atlantic SD-1391, 790140, Everest FS-311, Lon
    HA-K/SH-K-8047
Nuages: As above
Le tien: —
Makin' Whoopee: As above, plus Ember CJS-810
Alabamy Bound: As for 9177
Paris, 9 March 1962.
How About You?: Barclay 84089, 820105, 950080,
    Atlantic SD-1391, 790140, Everest FS-311, Lon
    HA-K/SH-K-8047
Django: As above, plus Ember CJS-810
Pent Up House: As for 9189, except Lon
    HA-K/SH-K-8047
Minor Swing: As for 9190

**Hubert Clavecin et ses Rythmes avec Stéphane
Grappelly – Dansez sur vos Souvenirs.
Volume 3:** Gérard Gustin (alias Hubert Clavecin)
(harpsichord) g/sb/d with Stéphane
Grappelli-1(vn), Guy Lafitte (ts-2).
Paris, 12 June 1962.
Ou Es-Tu Mon Amour – 1, 2: Bel Air 321066,
    361023, 7044
En Avril A Paris – 1: — — —
L'Etranger Au Paradis – 1, 2: — — —
Concerto D'Automne – 1: — — —
Petite Maison Grise – 1, 2: — — —
Tenderly – 1: — — —
Comme Un P'tit Coquelicot – ?: (inédit)
Trois fois merci – ?: —
Un Seul Couvert Please James – 2: Bel Air 321066,
    361023, 7044
Ay Ay Ay – 1: — — —
Il Ne Faut Pas Briser Un Rève – 2: — — —
Les Trois Cloches – 1: — — —
Tout Le Bonheur Du Monde – ?: — — —
Fascination – ?: — — —
Adagio – ?: (inédit)
Pariez-Moi D'Amour – 1: Bel Air 321066, 361023,
    7044
Amapola – 1, 2: — — —
Begin The Beguine – 1, 2: — — —
Bei Mir Bist Du Schon – 1: — — —
Bel Air 7044 = Musidisc 30 CV 1099 = Festival
Album 111 (2nd disc)
Note: Stéphane Grappelli does not play on the 2nd
volume of this series.

Pierre Spiers Sextet with Stéphane Grappelly
Pierre Spiers-harp/Stéphane Grappelly-vn/Jimmy
Gourlay-Georges Megalos-g/Pierre
Michelot-sb/Armand Molinetti-d.
Paris, sometime in 1962; all on Col FP-1135.
*Blue Moon/A Foggy Day/Someone To Watch Over
    Me/I Won't Dance/Deep Purple/Auf
    Wiedersehen/I'll Remember April/Over The
    Rainbow/Dinah:*

Duke Ellington's Jazz Violin Session Duke
Ellington-p dir. Stéphane Grappelly-Ray
Nance-Svend Asmussen-vn/Ernie Shepard-sb/Sam
Woodyard-d, plus Buster Cooper-tb/Russell
Procope-as/Paul Gonsalves-ts/Billy Strayhorn-p as
indicated by their initials after the titles; Ellington
does not play on 7th title.
Paris, 22 February 1963.
Blues in C -BC-RP-PG: Atlantic SD-1688
In a Sentimental Mood: —
Don't Get Around Much Anymore: —
Day Dreaming: —
Cotton Tail: —
Ticky's Licks -BC-RP-PG: —
Pretty Little One -BC-RP-PG-BS: —
String Along With Strings -BC-RP-PG-BS: —
The Feeling Of Jazz -BC-RP-PG: —
Limbo Jazz -BC-RP-PG: —
Take The 'A' Train: —
Passion Flower: —

Hubert Clavecin and his Rhythm Gérard Gustin
(alias Hubert Clavecin) dir. Stéphane
Grappelly-vn/unknown ts/f/elo/g/sb/d/vib, with p
on 4447, 4448, 4449, 4557, 4558, 4559, 4561, 4563
and 4564, plus pac on 4448, 4450, 4453, 4560, 4561
and 4564; Gustin plays on 4450, 4452, 4453, 4458,
4459, 4560, 4561, and 4562.
Paris, 21 October 1963.
Hymne à l'amour (4447): Bel Air 421083, 221204,
7007, Musidisc 30-CV-1140
Mon Légionnaire (4448): As above, except Bel Air
221204
La vie en rose (4449): As for 4447
Les trois cloches (4450): —
A quoi ça sert l'amour (4451): As for 4448
Milord (4452): —
La goualante du pauvre Jean (4453): —
Non, je ne regrette rien (4454): As for 4447
Paris, 18 November 1963.
Padam, Padam (4557): Bel Air 421083, 7007,
Musidisc 30-CV-1140
C'est d' la faute à tes yeux (4558): — — —
Je n'en connais pas la fin (4559): — — —
C'était une histoire d'amour (4560): — — —
C'est lui que mon coeur a choisi (4561): — — —
Mon manège à moi (4562): — — —
C'est peut-être ça (4563): — — —
J'en ai tant vu (4564): — — —

Stéphane Grappelly Violin solos, acc. by George
Daly-vib and others (?).
Paris, sometime in 1963.
New Cadences: Sonorop SONO-3032-A (?)
Rythmes et Bergamasques: —

Stéphane Grappelly and Svend Asmussen
Violin duets, Asmussen doubling as, acc. by Ole
Molim-Jorn Grauengaard-g/Niels-Henning Ørsted
Pederson-sb/William Schiopffe-d.
Copenhagen, 23–24 January 1965.
Honeysuckle Rose: Metronome MLP-15177, Pol
236502, Festival JON-100019
Blue Lady: As above
So Sorry: —
Twins: —
Satin Doll: —
Love Is Back: —

Someone To Watch Over Me: —
Parisian Thoroughfare: —

Stéphane Grappelly and Stuff Smith Stéphane
Grappelly-vn/Stuff Smith-vn-v/René
Urtreger-p/Michel Gaudry-sb/Michel Delaporte-d.
Paris, 22 June 1965.
This Can't Be Love: Barclay 84110, 920067,
Everest FS-238
Skip It (omit Grappelly): — — —
Willow Weep For Me (omit Smith): — — —
Blues In The Dungeon: — — —
S'posin' -vSS: — — —
How High The Moon: — — —

Violin Summit Stéphane Grappelly-Stuff
Smith-Svend Asmussen-Jean-Luc Ponty-vn/Kenny
Drew-p/Niels-Henning Ørsted Pederson-sb/Alex
Riel-d; Smith does not play on the 2nd, 4th and 5th
titles; Asmussen not on 2nd and 4th; Ponty not on
4th.
Basle, 30 September 1966.
Summit Soul: Saba SB-15099,
MPS/BASF-21-20626, 15012, Prestige PR-7631,
Pol MPS-545103
Pent-Up House: As above
It Don't Mean A Thing: —
Pennies From Heaven: —
Hot Toddy: —

Vic Lewis and his Orchestra Vic Lewis dir. large
concert orchestra, featuring Stéphane Grappelly-vn
on these two titles on a single 45; Ken Thorne-a.
London, 28 April 1967.
Two For The Road: CBS 2835
Stepps: —

Normando Marquez Vocal, acc. by own
g/Stéphane Grappelly-vn/Jean-Pierre
Mongeon-cel/Pierre Michelot-sb/Kenny Clarke-d.
Paris, sometime in 1967.
On a fait l'amour: Dec 79531 (45)
Balancon com bossa: —

Stéphane Grappelli [note new spelling] Violin
solos, acc. by Raymond Fol-p (and cel on the last
three titles)/Tony Osio-g/Jack Sewing-sb/Andre
Hartmann-d.
Paris, January 1969.
Raincheck: RCA 740038, INTS-1017
Camelia: — —
I Got It Bad And That Ain't Good: — —
What Am I Here For?: — —
Tabu: — —
Denise: — —
Flamingo: — —
Time On My Hands: — —
Anna: — —
Light: — —
Andrée: — —
Zolda: — —
So Long (Grappelli and Fol only): — —

Guy Marchand Vocal, acc. by René Nicolas-a dir.
Stéphane Grappelli-vn/Raymond Gimenez-Francis
Lemaguer-Didier Duprai-g/Guy Pederson-sb/Gus
Wallace-d.
Paris, 21 February 1969.
Je cherche une femme: Riviera 121225, 521103

Barney Kessel Guitar solos, acc. by Stéphane Grappelli and others-vn/Maurice Vander-p/Michel Gaudry-sb/Marcel Blanche-d.
Paris, 18 June 1969.
Nuages: Mercury 135720-MCL
What's New?: —

Stéphane Grappelli and Barney Kessel Violin and guitar duets, acc. by Bartholomy 'Nini' Rosso-g/Michel Gaudry-sb/Jean-Louis Viale-d.
Paris, 23–24 June 1969.
I Remember Django: Freedom BLP-30101, Black Lion BL-278079, BLM-51001, INT-147013, Pol 2460-105, 3170-033
Honeysuckle Rose: As above, except BLM-51001, INT-147013
I Can't Get Started (Grappelli-Kessel only): As last above
What A Difference A Day Made: —
More Than You Know: —
Et maintenant (What Now, My Love?): —
I've Found A New Baby: —
It's Only A Paper Moon: —
It Don't Mean A Thing: Freedom/Black Lion BLP-30129, BLM-51001, INT-147013, Pol 2460-173
Out Of Nowhere: As above, except BLM-51001, INT-147013
Tea For Two: As last above
Limehouse Blues: —
How High The Moon: —
Willow, Weep For Me: —
Little Star: — plus Black Lion BLM-51001
Undecided/Barniana: —

Stéphane Grappelli and Joe Venuti Violin duets, acc. by George Wein-p/Barney Kessel-g/Larry Ridley-sb/Don Lamond-d; Wein and Venuti do not play on the 6th title, and the 7th is by Venuti with SG piano.
Paris, 22 October 1969.
I Can't Give You Anything But Love: Affinity AFF-29, BYG 529112
After You've Gone: — — Cambra CR-027-B
Undecided: — —
Venupelli Blues: — —
Tea For Two: — —
My One And Only Love: — —
I'll Never Be The Same:

Stéphane Grappelli and Gary Burton Stéphane Grappelli-vn/Gary Burton-vib, acc. by Steve Swallow-sb/Bill Goodwin-d.
Paris, 4 November 1969.
Falling Grace: Atlantic SD-1597, (K)-40378
Here's That Rainy Day: — — SD-2-321
Daphne: — —
Blue In Green: — —
Coquette: — —
The Night Has a Thousand Eyes: — —
Eiderdown: — —
Arpège: — —
Sweet Rain: — —

Stéphane Grappelli Violin solos, own v, acc. by Marc Hemmeler-p (and elo on the 1st and last title but one)/Alan Clare-p on the 1st and 8th titles; Diz Disley-g/Lennie Bush-sb/John Spooner-d (some sources show Spencer).

London, 29 June 1970.
I Can't Believe That You're In Love With Me: Philips 6308017, 6612039, 7108010
Sweet Georgia Brown: — — — 9299525
Darling, je vous aime beaucoup -vSG: — — —
Taking A Chance On Love: — — —
Willow, Weep For Me: — — —
My One And Only Love: — — —
How High The Moon: — — —
Like Someone In Love: — — —
More: — — —
I Got Rhythm: — — —
Lonely Street: — — —
The Girl From Ipanema: — — —

Stéphane Grappelli Violin solos, acc. by Alan Clare and/or Marc Hemmeler-p/Kenny Napper-sb/Tony Crombie-d.
London, 18 October 1970.
Makin' Whoopee -pAC: Pye NSPL-18360, SLDPY-800
Restless Girl -pAC: — — Vogue DP-32
You Make Me Feel So Young -pAC: — —
That Tune -pAC: — —
Ol' Man River -pAC-MH: — Spot SPR-8563 — GH 650—
The Peanut Vendor -pMH: — — —
Ain't Misbehavin' -pMH: — ND-5004-B — — —
Blue River -pMH: — Spot SPR-8563 — GH-650
The Folks Who Live On The Hill -pMH: — — — —
Runnin' Wild -pMH: — — — —
Sunny Skies -pMH: — —
Passé: —
Acc. by Marc Hemmeler-p (or elo*)/Jack Sewing-sb/Kenny Clarke-d; Grappelli plays p instead of Hemmeler** in addition to vn.
Paris, 13 December 1970.
Tea For Two: RCA 730107, CL-73197, SF-8184, INTS-5047
Danny Boy: — — —
Let's Fall In Love: — — — —
Coltrane: — JPGH-004 — — —
I Hear Music: — — —
Dany: — FXM2-7217 — — —
Smoke Gets In Your Eyes: — — — —
Gary: — FXM2-7080 — — —
Satin Doll: Rejected
***Dear Ben:* RCA 730107, CL-73197, SF-8184, INTS-5047
Body And Soul -acc. Kenny Clarke-p (!) only: — — — —
**A Flower For Kenny:* — — — —

Stéphane Grappelli Violin solos, acc. by Marc Hemmeler-p/Eberhard Weber-sb/Kenny Clarke-d.
Villengen, March 1971.
This Can't Be Love: MPS/BASF-21-20876-1, 821-865-2, BAP-5001, 15066, 75004, 68156, Pausa 7071
Time After Time: As above
Undecided: —
Vous qui passez sans me voir (You Were Only Passing By): —
Tangerine: —
Chicago: —
Manoir de mes rêves/Daphne: — BAB-9001
Misty: —
Afternoon In Paris: —
Autumn Leaves (Les feuilles mortes): —

Stéphane Grappelli and Gérard Gustin
Stéphane Grappelli-vn, acc. by large string
orchestra dir. Gérard Gustin.
Paris, sometime in 1971; unreleased.
*Acajou/Astéroïde/Astronef/Autoroute du
  sud/Corail/Direction uranus/Equinoxe/Etoile de
  mer/Gamma/Grande ourse /Météorite/
  Mimétisme/Orbite/Satellite/Toi
  l'albatros/Utopie/Zénith:*

Paul Simon Guitar solo with Stéphane
Grappelly-vn.
Paris, sometime in 1971.
Hobo's Blues: CBS S-69007

Stéphane Grappelli Violin solos, acc. by Alan
Clare-p/Lennie Bush-sb/Terry Jenkins-d.
London, 8 November 1971.
How About You? (Introduced by Peter Clayton):
  Pye NSPL-18374, SLDPY-844, GH-650, Vogue
  DP-32
Someone To Watch Over Me: As above, plus Spot
  SPR-8563
This Can't Be Love: — — Black Lion INT-147013
The Nearness Of You: —
*Nuages (It's The Bluest Kind Of Blues My Baby
  Sings):* — —
Lady Be Good: — —
Mean To Me: Pye NSPL-18374, SLDPY-844,
  Vogue DP-32
*Manoir de mes reves/Daphne (Introduced by
  Stéphane Grappelli):* — — —
Sweet Georgia Brown: Pye NSPL-18374,
  SLDPY-844, GH-650, Spot SPR-8563, Vogue
  DP-32
I Can't Give You Anything But Love: As above

Stéphane Grappelli and Yehudi Menuhin
Violin duets, acc. by Alan Clare-p/Lennie
Bush-sb/Chris Karan-d/Max Harris-a-dir.
London, 14 June 1972.
The Blue Room: EMI EMD-5504, 2C-064-02446,
  Angel SEO-36968
A Fine Romance: As above, plus EMI 2093 (45)
Love Is Here To Stay: EMI EMD-5504,
  2C-064-02446, Angel SEO-36968
Pick Yourself Up: As above
Menuhin omitted*, or plays solo acc. by Stéphane
Grappelli-p**.
London, 15 June 1972.
Jealousy: EMI EMD-5504, 2C-064-02446, Angel
  SEO-36968; EMI 2093 (45)
Night And Day: As above, except EMI 2093
**Billy:* —
***Aurore:* —
Note: The 1st title also appears on EMI UV-2,
apparently a sample disc.

Stéphane Grappelli Violin solos, acc. by Alan
Clare or Marc Hammeler-p-elp*/Ernie
Cranenburgh-elg/Lennie Bush-sb/Chris Karan-d.
London, 19–20–21–22 June 1972.
Sweet Sue -pMH: Festival 120, Classic Jazz CJ-23,
  Musidisc CCV-2520
Avalon -pMH: As above, plus Visadisc 1326
**Manoir de mes rêves -pMH:* As first, plus
  Musidisc 30-CV-1285
Clopin-Clopant -pAC: As last above, plus Visadisc
  1326

Daphne -pAC: As first, plus Musidisc 30-CV-1285
Blues -pAC: Festival 120, Classic Jazz CJ-23,
  Musidisc CCV-2520
Swing Guitar -pAC: As above, plus Musidisc
  30-CV-1285
I Wonder Where My Baby Is Tonight -pAC: Festival
  120, Classic Jazz CJ-23, Musidisc CCV-2520
Djangology -pAC: As above, plus Musidisc
  30-CV-1285
Swing 39 -pAC: — —
**Oriental Shuffle -pAC:* Festival 120, Classic Jazz
  CJ-123, Musidisc CCV-2520
**Minor Swing -pMH:* As above
**Venez donc, chez moi -pAC:* As above, plus
  Musidisc 30-CV-1285
I Saw Stars -pAC: As above, except Musidisc
  30-CV-1285
Fantaisie -pAC: —
Dark Eyes -pAC: As above, plus Musidisc
  30-CV-1285
I'm Coming, Virginia -pMH: — —
I'll Remember April -pAC: — —
Note: It should be noted that titles shown as having
one or the other pianist playing an electric
instrument do not have either of them playing a
conventional one.
Piano duet with Alan Clare** or violin solo acc. by
Alan Clare-elp.
London, 19/22 June 1972.
***Are You In The Mood?:* Festival 120, Classic Jazz
  CJ-23, Musidisc CCV-2520, Visadisc V-1326
Tears: As above, except Visadisc V-1326
Sweet Chorus: —
Nuages: As at first, plus Festival 183-A
Violin solos, acc. by Guy Pederson-sb/Kenny
Clarke-d, with Marc Hemmeler-p/Eddie
Louiss-elo/Jimmy Gourley-elg as indicated.
Paris, 12–13 November 1972.
Satin Doll -MH-EL: Festival FLD-596, Musidisc
  CCV-2520
On The Sunny Side Of The Street -MH: —
Body And Soul (take 1) -MH-JG: —
Ain't Misbehavin' -MH-JG: —
Mack The Knife -MH-EL-JG: — —
Body And Soul (take 2) -EL: —
Pennies From Heaven -MH-EL: —
The Girl From Ipanema -MH-EL-JG: —
Blue Moon -MH-JG: —
The Lady Is A Tramp -MH-EL: — —
Exactly Like You -MH: — —
Ebb Tide -EL: —
You Took Advantage Of Me -MH-JG: —
Lover Man -MH-JG: —
I Didn't Know What Time It Was -JG: —
Hallelujah -MH-EL: Festival FLD-629
My Funny Valentine -SG-EL only: Festival
  FLD-596, Musidisc CCV-2520
In a Mellow Tone -SG-EL-KC only: —

Sacha Distel Vocal, acc. by own g/Stéphane
Grappelli-vn, and orchestra dir. Gérard Gustin.
Paris, sometime in 1972.
Ma première guitar: EMI-PA 2C-006-93878

Stéphane Grappelli – Oscar Peterson Quartet
Stéphane Grappelli-vn/Oscar Peterson-p/
Niels-Henning Ørsted-Pederson-sb/Kenny
Clarke-d.
Paris, 22–23 February 1973.

Them There Eyes: America 30-AM-6129, Prestige
  PR-24041
Flamingo: — —
Makin' Whoopee: — Musidisc CCV-2521 —
Looking At You: — —
Walking My Baby Back Home: — —
My One And Only Love: — —
Thou Swell: — —
I Won't Dance: America 30-AM-6131 —
Autumn Leaves: — —
My Heart Stood Still: — —
Blues For Musidisc: — —
If I Had You: — —
Let's Fall In Love: Festival 240, FLD-629
Time After Time: —
The Folks Who Live On The Hill -SG-OP only:
  America 30-AM-6131, Prestige PR-24041

Stéphane Grappelli Violin solos, acc. by Alan
Clare-p/Lennie Bush-sb/Tony Crombie-d, or p
solo, unacc.*
London, February – March 1973.
It Don't Mean A Thing: Pye NSPL-18403, Vogue
  LDM-30210, DP-32, GH-650, Spot SPR-8563
I've Got The World On A String: Pye NSPL-18403,
  Vogue LDM-30210
What Are You Doing The Rest Of My Life?: — —
The Birth Of The Blues: — — DP-32
Opportunity: — —
Just A Gigolo: — — —
Didn't We?: — Spot SPR-8563 — GH 650
Crazy Rhythm: — — — —
It Might As Well Be Spring: — —
Three Little Words: — — —
Avalon: — — — —
*Emotion: — —

Stéphane Grappelli and Yehudi Menuhin
Violin duets, Alan Clare-p/Ken Baldock-sb/Tony
Crombie-d/Max Harris-a-dir.
London, 6 March 1973.
I Can't Believe That You're In Love With Me: EMI
  EMD-5504, 2C-064-02446, Angel SEO-36968
These Foolish Things: As above
Lady Be Good: —
Jermyn Street -YM-SG (p) only: —
London, 7 March 1973.
Cheek To Cheek: EMI EMD-5504, 2C-064-02446,
  Angel SEO-36968
The Lady Is A Tramp: As above
Erroll (YM omitted): —

Stéphane Grappelli Violin solos, acc. by Alan
Clare-p-cel.
Denham, 19 March 1973.
It's The Talk Of The Town: Black Lion BL-313,
  BLP-30165
Amada: — — SAM/BLP-20130
Star Dust: — —
Can't Help Lovin' That Man O' Mine (sic): — —
We'll Be Together Again: — —
Nature Boy: — —
The Nearness Of You: — —
Tournesol: — BLM-51001 — INT-147013
Greensleeves: — —
You Go To My Head: — —

Herbie Mann Flute solo, acc. by Stéphane
Grappelli-vn/Pat Rebillot-elp/Albert Lee-elg/Al

Gorry-sb/Aynsley Dunbar-d.
London, March 1973.
Mellow Yellow: Atlantic SD-1648

Triangle-Homonymie Stéphane
Grappelli-vn/François Jeanneau-elp/Marius 'Mimi'
Lorenzini-elg/René Devaux-sb/Jean-Pierre
Prevotat-d.
Paris, March–April 1973.
Eloge de la folie: EMI-PA 2C-062-12493

Stéphane Grappelli Violin solos, acc. by Marc
Hemmeler-p/Jack Sewing-sb/Daniel Humair-d, or
acc. by Barney Kessel-elg only*.
Montreux, 4 July 1973.
Just One Of Those Things: Black Lion/Freedom
  BLP-30152, BL-211, BLP-12183, 2460-211
Misty: As above
More: —
Que reste-t-il de nos amours? (I Wish You Love): —
Don't Get Around Much Anymore: —
Them There Eyes: —
Honeysuckle Rose: —
All God's Chillun Got Rhythm: Black Lion
  BLP-30148, BL-213, 2460-213
*Tea For Two: — — —

Stéphane Grappelli Violin solos, acc. by Roland
Hanna-p-elp/George 'Jiri' Mraz-sb/Mel Lewis-d.
London, 5 September 1973.
Perugia: Black Lion BLP-30183, Arista/Freedom
  1033
Fascinating Rhythm: As above
Parisian Thoroughfare: —
London, 7 September 1973.
Love For Sale: Black Lion BLP-30183,
  Arista/Freedom 1033
Two Cute: As above plus BLM-51001, INT-147013
*Improvisation on Prelude in E minor, Op. 28, No. 4
  (Chopin):* — —
Wave: Black Lion BLP-30183, Arista/Freedom
  1033
Hallelujah: As above
Nice Work If You Can Get It: Black Lion 157002
Shangri-La: —
Two Cute (different from the above?): —
Acc. by Diz Disley-Denny Wright-g/Len Skeat-sb.
Queen Elizabeth Hall, London, 5 November 1973.
This Can't Be Love: Black Lion BLP-30158,
  2683-047, BLM-51001
I Can't Believe That You're In Love With Me: —
  INT-147013 — —
Misty: — —
After You've Gone: — —
Manoir de mes rêves/Daphne: — —
Satin Doll: Black Lion BLP-30159 —
Tea For Two: — —
Flamingo: — Transatlantic 324-A —
Honeysuckle Rose: — —
Nuages: — —
Sweet Georgia Brown: — INT-147013 — —
*Gershwin Medley (Intro. Summertime/But Not For
  Me/I Got Rhythm):* — — — —
Acc. by Bill Coleman-c-t-flugelhorn (1st eight titles
only)/Marc Hemmeler-p/Guy Pederson-sb/Daniel
Humair-d.
Paris, 3–4 December 1973.
I've Got The World on a String: Festival 155,
  Classic Jazz CJ-24

St Louis Blues: ——
Ain't She Sweet?: ——
Moonlight In Vermont: ——
Stardust: ——
Where Or When: ——
'S Wonderful: ——
Chicago: ——
Summertime: —
Lullaby Of Birdland: —
After You've Gone: —
Sweet Georgia Brown: —
Three Little Words: —
All The Things You Are: —
Fly Me To The Moon: —

Jean-Luc Ponty – Stéphane Grappelli Violin
and/or baritone vn duets, acc. by Maurice
Vander-p-elp/Philippe Catherine-elg/Tony
Bontils-sb/André Cecarelli-d. Ponty is the arranger
and composer throughout.
Paris, 27–28–29 December 1973.
Bowing Bowing: America 30-AM-6139, Inner City
 IC-1005
Golden Green: ——
Memorial Jam For Stuff Smith: ——
Violin Summit No 2: ——
Valérie: ——

Les Valseuses Stéphane Grappelli-vn (except the
last title; composer throughout)/Maurice
Vander-p-elp-elo/Marc Hemmeler-p where
shown/Philippe Catherine-elg where shown/Guy
Pederson-sb/Daniel Humair-d.
Paris, 4–5 January 1974.
Ballade -PC: Festival FLD-629
Jeanne -PC: —
Jeanne (take 2): —
Rolls: —
Poursuite -PC: —
Rolls (take 2): —
*Ballade -MH-MV (MV-elo plus elp dubbed over) –
 PC:* —

Stéphane Grappelli and Earl Hines Violin and
piano duets.
London, 4 July 1974.
Fine And Dandy: Black Lion BLP-30193
Over The Rainbow: —
Manhattan: —
Moonlight In Vermont: —
I Can't Get Started: —
You Took Advantage Of Me: —
Sometimes I'm Happy: —

Stéphane Grappelli and Baden Powell Violin
and guitar duets, acc. by Guy Pederson-sb/Pierre
Alain Dahan-d/Jorge G. Rezendre-Clément de
Waleyne-percussion.
Paris, 4–5 September 1974.
Eu vim de Bahia: Festival FLD-634
Meditacao: —
Berimbau: —
Desafinado: —
Samba de una nota so: —
Isaura: —
Amor em paz: —
Brazil: —
The Girl From Ipanema: Festival FLD-642
Waves: —

Ingenuo: —
O pato: —
Rancho fundo: —
Blues Samba: —
The Peanut Vendor: —

Stéphane Grappelli and the Diz Disley Trio
Stéphane Grappelli-vn/Diz Disley-Ike Isaacs-g/Isla
Eckinger-sb.
Villingen, March 1975.
Lover, Come Back To Me: MPS/BASF 20-22545-3,
 BAP-5063, Pausa 7098, Memoir MOIR-110
Sweet Lorraine: As above
Shine: —
Solitude: —
Ain't Misbehavin': —
Souvenir de Villingen -SG-p dubbed over: —
Hot Lips: —
My Heart Stood Still: —
The Nearness Of You: —
Joy: —
A Nightingale Sang In Berkeley Square: —
Cherokee: —
Lover Man: —

Stéphane Grappelli and Slam Stewart Stéphane
Grappelli-vn/Johnny Guarniéri-p/Jimmy
Shirley-g/Slam Stewart-sb/Jackie Williams-d; the
last two titles are unaccompanied piano solos by
Grappelli.
Paris, 25 March 1975.
I Would Do Anything For You: Black & Blue 33076
'Deed I Do: —
As Time Goes By: —
You're The Cream In My Coffee: —
It's Only A Paper Moon: —
You're Driving Me Crazy: —
It Had To Be You: —
My Blue Heaven: —
I'll Never Be The Same: Unissued —
Autumn In New York: ——
But Not For Me: ——
Sysmo: —
Flonville: —

Caroline Cler and Christian Borel Vocals as
shown, acc. by Lucien Lavoute-a dir. Stéphane
Grappelli-vn/vns/vls/vcs/p-elp/elg/sb/d, or with
brass replacing strings*.
Paris, 19 April 1975.
Sur deux notes -vCC: Musidisc 30-CV-1350
Bonsoir, chérie -vCB: —
Que reste-il de nos amours? -vCB: —
Il ne faut pas buser un rêve -vCC: —
*Chez moi -vCC: —
*Cheveux dans le vent -vCB: —

**'Pierre et le Loup' ('Peter And The Wolf' –
Prokofiev)** Stéphane Grappelli-vn plays the part of
the Cat, acc. by Alvin Lee-g/Dave Marquee-sb as
shown; Pierre Clémenti is the narrator.
London or Paris, sometime in 1975.
Cat Dance-AL-DM Cat-DM/Cat in tree: RSO
 SO-1912, 2479-167

Stéphane Grappelli and Yehudi Menuhin
Violin duets, acc. by Denny Wright-Ike
Isaacs-g/Lennie Bush-sb/Max Harris-a-dir.
London, 21 May 1975.

Just One Of Those Things: EMI EMD-5523, 2C-064-02690; EMI 2358 (45)
Fascinating Rhythm: — — —
Liza: — —
I Got Rhythm: — —
Johnny aime (SG-II only): — —
Sweet Georgia Brown: EMI SEOM-26
Note: It is not certain that the last track above comes from this session.
Acc. by Alan Clare-p-elp*/Ike Isaacs-g/Lennie Bush-sb/Ronnie Verrell-d/Max Harris-a-dir., who may play p instead of Clare on the 2nd, 3rd, 6th and 10th titles; Menuhin is acc. by Grappelli only, on elp**.
London, 22 May 1975.
I Get A Kick Out Of You: EMI EMD-5523, 2C-064-02690
Soon: — —
's Wonderful: — —
**Minuet pour Menuhin:* — —
Isaacs omitted.
London, 23 May 1975.
**Summertime:* EMI EMD-5523, 2C-064-02690
Nice Work If You Can Get It: — —
Looking At You: — —
Embraceable You: — —
Why Do I Love You?: — —
All The Things You Are:

Stéphane Grappelli Violin solos, acc. by Marc Hemmeler or Maurice Vander-p (as shown)/Eddie Louiss-elo (as shown)/Ike Isaacs-elg (as shown)/Luigi Trussardi-sb (as shown)/Daniel Humair-d (as shown).
Paris, 26–27 May 1975.
That Certain Feeling -MH-EL-LT-DH: Festival 205
I Got Plenty O' Nuttin' -MV-EL-LT-DH: —
They Can't Take That Away From Me -EL: — Musidisc CCV-2520
But Not For Me -MH-LT-DH: —
The Man I Love -MH-EL-II-LT-DH: — —
Somebody Loves Me -MV-II-LT-DH: —
Do-Do-Do -MV-EL-LT-DH: —
It's All Right With Me -MH-EL-LT-DH: Festival 240 —
Anything Goes -MV-EL-LT-DH: —
You've Got That Thing -EL-LT-DH: —
I've Got You Under My Skin -MH-EL-LT-DH: —
Love For Sale -EL: — —
Acc. by Maurice Vander-p (as shown)/Eddie Louiss-elo (as shown)/Jimmy Gourly-elg (as shown)/Guy Pederson-sb (as shown)/Daniel Humair-d (as shown); titles not specifying the accompanists have all five present.
Paris, 2–3 February 1976.
Clap Your Hands: Festival 205
A Foggy Day: — Musidisc CCV-2520
I Was Doing All Right -EL-JG-GP-DH: —
How Long Has This Been Goin On? -EL-JG-GP-DH: —
They All Laughed -MV-EL-GP-DH: Festival 240
You're The Top -EL: —
In The Still Of The Night: — —
Miss Otis Regrets -EL: —
Easy To Love -MV-JG-GP-DH: — —
You'd Be So Nice To Come Home To -EL-JG-GP-DH: —
My Heart Belongs To Daddy -MV-EL-GP-DH: —

Stéphane Grappelli and George Shearing
Violin and piano duets, acc. by Andrew Simpkins-sb/Rusty Jones-d.
Villengen, 11 April 1976.
I'm Coming, Virginia: MPS 68162, 821868-1/2
Time After Time: — —
La chanson des rues: — —
Too Marvellous For Words: — —
It Don't Mean A Thing: — —
Makin' Whoopee: — —
After You've Gone: — —
Flamingo: — —
Star Eyes: — —
The Folks Who Live On The Hill: — —

Jean Sablon Vocal, acc. by Stéphane Grappelli-vn/Maurice Vander-p/Luigi Trussardi-sb/Daniel Humair-d.
Paris, 13 December 1976.
Tout seul: Festival 259
Oui, je m'en vais: —
Tu sais: —
La dernière chanson: —

Stéphane Grappelli Violin solos, acc. by own p dubbed in*/Eddie Louiss-elo/Pierre Michelot-sb/Daniel Humair-d.
Paris, 17–18 February 1977.
All God's Chillun Got Rhythm: Festival FLD-673
**Deliciosa:* —
Blue Skies: —
Gravenstein: —
A Stephane: —
**Stormy Weather:* — Musidisc CCV-2520
Sing For Your Supper: —
Acc. by Don Burrows-cl-as-f-bass f as shown/George Golla-g.
Sydney, March 1977.
A Fine Romance -cl: Cherry Pie CPF-1032
Don't Get Around Much Anymore -f: —
I Can't Get Started -cl: —
Autumn Leaves -cl: —
I'll Never Be The Same: —
Down Home Blues -cl: —
I Only Have Eyes For You/Shine: —
Solitude -bass f: —
Corcovado -as: —
It's Only a Paper Moon -as: —
Acc. by g/sb/d/vib, dir. Camille Sauvage, or by own overdubbed p* or elp**. Grappelli is the composer throughout.
Paris, June 1977.
Leasing: Timing/De Wolfe 15DWSLP-3357
Brett: —
Jessie: —
Whist: —
Story: —
Tric-Trac: —
Pearl: —
Paganini: —
***Kindness:* —
**Jerome:* —
***Gina:* —
**Amanda:* —
Acc. by Christian Chevalier-a dir. large concert orchestra including Maurice Vander-p-elp**/Gérard Wiobey-elg/Tony Bonfils-sb/André Ceccarelli-d/François Jeanneau-synthesizer/Michel

Delaporet-percussion.
Paris, 8–10–11 October 1977.
You Are The Suneshine Of My Life: Festival
 FLD-685
Jeanne: —
Bérimbau: —
***Fumette:* —
Bill: —
Yesterday: —
Michelle: —
***Baratana:* —
Ballade: —
Recado: —
***Elé:* —

Stéphane Grappelli and Yehudi Menuhin
Violin duets, acc. by Laurie Holloway-elp/Pierre
Michelot-sb/Ronnie Verrell-d, plus unknown reeds
and woodwinds.
Amsterdam, 28 October 1977.
Viva Vivaldi: EMI EMD-5530, 2C-064-02997,
 Angel S-37533
Air On a Shoe String: — — —
The Man I Love: — — —
Thou Swell: — — —

Stéphane Grappelli and Yehudi Menuhin
Violin duets, acc. by John Etheridge-Jan
Block-elg/Pierre Michelot-sb/Ronnie Verrell-d.
Amsterdam, 29 October 1977.
Crazy Rhythm: EMI EMD-5530, 2C-064-02997,
 Angel S-37533
Limehouse Blues: — — —
Between The Devil And The Deep Blue Sea: — —
—
Tea For Two: — — —
Acc. by Laurie Holloway-elp/Pierre
Michelot-sb/Ronnie Verrell-d.
Amsterdam, 30 October 1977.
Yesterdays: EMI EMD-5530, 2C-064-02997, Angel
 S-37533
My Funny Valentine: — — —
A Foggy Day: — — —
Note: The title 'I Didn't Know What Time It Was'
was recorded at one of the above three sessions, but
has not been issued. The following duets between
Yehudi Menuhin-vn and Stéphane Grappelli-p
were recorded at either the first or the 3rd session,
apparently.
Highgate Village: EMI EMD-5530, 2C-064-02997,
 Angel S-37533
Adelaide Eve: — — —

Stéphane Grappelli Violin solos, acc. by Claus
Ogerman-a dir. unknown vns/vls/vc/Jimmy
Rowles-p/Jay Berlinger-elg/Ron Carter-sb/Grady
Tate-d; Aaron Rosand-concert master.
New York, March 1978.
Baubles, Bangles And Beads: Col JC-35415, CBS
 82959
Angel Eyes: — —
Favors: — —
A Waltz Dressed In Blue: — — —
Acc. by Claus Ogerman-a dir. unknown
vns/vls/vcs/Richard Tee-elp/Hugh
McCracken-g/Anthony Jackson-sb/Steve
Gadd-d/Rubeus Bassini-conga d-percussion; Aaron
Rosand-concert master.
New York, March 1978.

Pages Of Life: Col JC-35415, CBS 82959
Uptown Dance: — —
Smoke Rings And Wine: — —
Shadows: — —
Night Wind: — —
Acc. by Diz Disley-John Etheridge-g/Brian
Torff-sb.
Carnegie Hall, New York, 5 April 1978.
I Can't Give You Anything But Love: Doctor Jazz
 ASLP-1001
As Time Goes By: —
Crazy Rhythm: —
Golden Green: —
Chattanooga Choo-Choo: —
Blues in G for B.T.: —
Nuages: —
Acc. by Tony Rice-g/Dave Grisman-Mike
Marshall-md/Eddie Gomez-sb.
New York, probably April 1978.
Minor Swing: Horizon HP-731
16-16: —
Acc. by Roland Hanna-p/Bucky
Pizzarelli-elg/George Duvivier-sb/Oliver
Jackson-d.
Brignoles, 17 July 1978.
The Lady is a Tramp: Black & Blue 33132
Sweet Chorus: —
Let's Fall In Love: —
Sweet And Lovely: —
Tears: —
Louise: —
Stray Horn: —

Stéphane Grappelli Quartet Stéphane
Grappelli-vn/Philip Catherine-Larry
Coryell-g/Niels-Henning Ørsted-Pederson-sb.
Stuttgart, 19–21 January 1979.
Djangology: MPS 68230, 815-672, Pausa 7041
Sweet Chorus: — — —
Minor Swing: — — —
Are You In The Mood?: — — —
Galérie St Hubert: — — —
Tears: — — —
Swing Guitars: — — —
Oriental Shuffle: — —
Blues For Django and Stéphane (SG-p also): — —
—

Stéphane Grappelli Violin solos, acc. by Joe
Pass-elg/Niels-Henning Ørsted-Pederson-sb, plus
Mickey Roker-d on the last six titles.
Tivoli Gardens, Copenhagen, 6 July 1979.
It's Only a Paper Moon: Pablo-Live 2308220
Time After Time: —
Let's Fall in Love: —
Crazy Rhythm: —
I'll Remember April: —
I Can't Get Started: —
I Get a Kick out of You: —
Nuages: Pablo-Live 2308232
How About You?: —
Someone to Watch Over Me: —
Makin' Whoopee: —
That's All: —
Skol Blues: —

Stéphane Grappelli – Bucky Pizzarelli Violin
and guitar duets.
Nice, 15 July 1979.

There's a Small Hotel: Ahead 33755
Tangerine: —
My Blue Heaven: —
The Folks Who Live on the Hill: —
Alabamy Bound: —
Willow, Weep for Me: —
Blues: —
Have You Met Miss Jones?: —
My One and Only Love: —
I'll Remember April: —
Black Bottom: —

Stéphane Grappelli and Hank Jones Violin and
piano duets, acc. by Jimmy Woode-sb/Alan
Dawson-d, except where marked*.
London, 20 July 1979.
Thou Swell: String 33852, Muse MR-5287
**These Foolish Things:* ——
September in the Rain: ——
You Better Go Now: —
Hallelujah: ——
**Yesterdays:* ——
Mellow Grapes: ——
I'll Never Be the Same: ——

Stéphane Grappelli – Dave Grisman Violin and
mandolin duets, acc. by Mike Marshall-md-g*/
Mark O'Connor-g-vn*/Rob Wasserman-sb, plus
Tiny Moore-elmd as shown.
San Francisco, 7 September 1979.
Satin Doll -TM: Warner K/WB-56903
Boston, 20 September 1979.
**Shine:* Warner K/WB-56903
Pent-Up House: —
Misty: —
Sweet Georgia Brown: —
Tiger Rag: —
Swing 42: —
Medley (Tzigane/Fizztorza/Fulginia): —

Stéphane Grappelli Quartet Stéphane
Grappelli-vn/Gérard Gustin-p/Jack
Sewing-sb/Armand Cavallaro-d.
Nice, 20–21 December 1979.
Bélier: Blue Silver BS-3002, Happy Bird B-90104
Gémeaux: —
Lion: ——
Balance: ——
Sagitiaika: ——
Verseau: ——
Taureau: ——
Cancer Influence: ——
Vierge: ——
Scorpion: ——
Capricorne: ——
Poissons: ——

Stéphane Grapelli and Martial Solal Violin and
piano duets.
Paris, 17–18 February 1980.
Shine: Owl 021
Valsitude: —
Sing For Your Supper: —
God Bless The Child: —
Nuages: —
Parisian Thoroughfare: —
Grandeur et cadence: —
Stumbling: —
Et si l'on improvisait?: —

Stéphane Grappelli Violin solos, acc. by Gérard
Gustin-p/Jack Sewing-sb/Armand Cavallaro-sb.
Nice, 28–29 February 1980.
Saluting Basie: Blue Silver BS-3007, Happy Bird
B-90103, Europa JP-2001
Portrait Of Jobim: As above
Oscar: —
Dedicated To Joao: —
Fats Delight: —
Kenny's Tune: —
To Django: —
Tribute To The Bird: —
Remembrances To Duke: —
Ode To Ray Brown: —
Dizzy: —
To Benny: —

Stéphane Grappelli and Yehudi Menuhin
Violin duets, acc. by Max Harris dir. small
instrumental groups; Grappelli plays p*.
London, March 1980.
A Nightingale Sang In Berkeley Square: EMI
EMD-5533
Skylark: —
Dinah: —
Laura: —
Lullaby Of Birdland: —
*When The Red, Red Robin Comes Bob, Bob, Bobbin'
Along:* —
Bye-Bye, Blackbird: —
Flamingo: —
Rosetta: —
Sweet Sue: —
Once In Love With Amy: —
Sweet Georgia Brown: —
**Coucou:* —
**La Route du Roi:* —
Winter Set: EMI EL-270112
Spring Will Be A Little Late This Year: —
The Things We Did Last Summer: —
Autumn Leaves: —
Button Up Your Overcoat: —
I've Got My Love To Keep Me Warm: —
I'll Remember April: —
April In Paris: —
On The Sunny Side Of The Street: —
Heat Wave: —
September In The Rain: —
Autumn In New York: —
**Giboulées de Mars:* —
**Automne:* —

Stéphane Grappelli Violin solos, acc. by Elena
Duran-f/Laurie Holloway-p-elp/Allen
Walley-sb/Allan Ganley-d.
London, 6–7 April 1980.
Brandenburg Boogie: EMI EMD-5536, Angel
DS-37790
Jesu, Joy Of Man's Desiring: ——
Groovy Gavotte No 1: ——
Fascinating Fugue: ——
Groovy Gavotte No 2: ——
Sleepers Awake: ——
Aria: ——
D minor Double: ——
Minuet: EMI EMD-5536, Angel DS-37790
Jig: ——
Groovy Gavotte No 3: ——
Air On a G String: ——

Sicilienne: —— \
Funky Flute: —— \
Violin and electric violin solos, acc. by John Etheridge-Martin Taylor-rlg/Jack Sewing-sb. Saratoga, California, September 1980 \
You Are The Sunshine Of My Life: Concord CJ-139 \
Love For Sale: — \
Angel's Camp: — \
Willow, Weep For Me: — \
Chicago: — \
Taking A Chance On Love: — \
Minor Swing: — \
Let's Fall In Love: — \
Just You, Just Me: — \
Violin solos, acc. by Elena Duran-f/Laurie Holloway-p-a/Allan Walley-sb/Allan Ganley-d. London, c. January 1981. \
Yesterday: RCA LP-6007 \
All My Loving: — \
Eleanor Rigby: — \
Norwegian Wood: — \
Can't Buy Me Love: — \
Here, There And Everywhere: — \
Michelle: — \
Hey Jude: — \
The Long And Winding Road: — \
A Hard Day's Night: — \
Acc. by Martin Taylor-Diz Disley-g/Jack Sewing-sb. \
London 1 May 1981. \
I'm Coming, Virginia: Wave unissued \
Mean To Me: — \
Swing 42: — \
Makin' Whoopee: — \
Do You Know What It Means To Miss New Orleans?: — \
Crazy Rhythm: — \
You're Driving Me Crazy: — \
A Foggy Day: — \
If I Had You: — \
Manhattan Tea Party: — \
Mike Gari-g replaces Disley. \
San Francisco, July 1981. \
Blue Moon: Concord CJ-169 \
It's Only A Paper Moon: — \
I'm Coming, Virginia: — \
I Can't Get Started: — \
Do You Know What It Means To Miss New Orleans?: — \
But Not For Me: — \
If I Had You: — \
Isn't She Lovely?: — \
'Jamie (acc. by Taylor only): —

Stéphane Grappelli and Yehudi Menuhin \
Violin duets, acc. by Nelson Riddle-a dir. Derek Watkins-Derek Healey-another-t/Don Lusher and two others-tb/Roy Willox-Bill Skeat-two others-saxes and woodwind/4fh/1ovn/8vc/3vl/ Laurie Holloway-elp/David Snell-harp/Martin Taylor-elg/Niels-Henning Ørsted Pederson-sb/Allan Ganley-d/Derek Price-percussion. \
London, 15 July 1981. \
Puttin' On The Ritz: EMI EMD-5539, Angel DS-37860 \
The Way You Look Tonight: —— \
Change Partners: —— \
Top Hat: ——

The Continental: —— \
The Carioca: —— \
The Piccolino: ——

Stéphane Grappelli and Yehudi Menuhin \
Violin duets, acc. by Nelson Riddle-a dir. Ray Swinfield-f/Laurie Holloway-elp/Martin Taylor-elg/Eddie Tripp-sb/Allan Ganley-d/Derek Price-percussion. \
London, 16 July 1981. \
He Loves And She Loves: EMI EMD-5539, Angel DS-37860 \
Isn't This A Lovely Day?: —— \
They Can't Take That Away From Me: —— \
Funny Face: —— \
They All Laughed: —— \
Yehudi Menuhin-vn solos, acc. by Stéphane Grappelli-p. These two titles were made at one of the last two sessions. \
Alison: EMI EMD-5539, Angel DS-37860 \
Amanda: ——

Stéphane Grappelli and Martin Taylor Violin and guitar duets, except the last title, which is a piano solo by Grappelli. \
London, July 1981. \
She's Funny That Way: EMI EMD-5540 \
Don't Get Around Much Anymore:'— \
Here, There And Everywhere: — \
I Can't Believe That You're In Love With Me: — \
Ol' Man River: — \
It Had To Be You: — \
I've Got The World On a String: — \
Manoir de mes rêves/Daphne: — \
Je n'sais plus: —

Stéphane Grappelli Violin solos, acc. by Bob Garcia-ts-f/Gérard Gustin-p/Alain Bodenes-sb/Marcel Blanche-d. \
Paris, probably c. September 1981. \
S.G. Booster: Bingo 3108 \
Prince of Wales: — \
Blue Bounce: — \
Steph Shuffle: — \
Gevy: — \
Diggin': — \
Miss Nelly: — \
Cameleon (sic): — \
Steph: — \
Little Red Fish: — \
Rue de Dunkerque: — \
B.D. Suite: —

Teresa Brewer Vocal, acc. by Stéphane Grappelli-vn-p*/Martin Taylor-Diz Disley-g/Jack Sewing-sb. \
San Francisco, 20–21 October 1981. \
On The Road Again: Doctor Jazz FW-38448, ASLP-801 \
It Had To Be You: —— \
Come On And Drive Me Crazy: —— \
*Smile: —— \
After You've Gone: —— \
I Love a Violin: — \
Don't Take Your Love From Me: —— \
Them There Eyes: —— \
As Time Goes By: ——

Stéphane Grappelli Violin solos, acc. by Martin Taylor-Marc Fosset-g/Patrice Caratini-sb/Allan Ganley-d/Chris Karan-tabla; Grappelli plays p*.
London, c. April 1983.
Cheek To Cheek: EMI EMD-143643-1
Are You In The Mood?: —
Just One Of Those Things: —
There's a Small Hotel: —
I'll Remember April: —
The Surrey With The Fringe On Top: —
I Get A Kick Out Of You: —
Blue Moon: —
Them There Eyes: —
How High The Moon: —
I Can't Give You Anything But Love: —
Waltz du passé: —
*My One And Only Love: —

Stéphane Grappelli and Marc Fosset Violin and guitar duets.
Vancouver, June 1983.
Tune Up/Thou Swell: Doctor Jazz FW-38448, ASLP-801
Norwegian Dance No 2: — —
Fulton Street Samba: — —

My Foolish Heart: — —
Lover/Stephanova: — —
The Way You Look Tonight: — —
Smoke Rings And Wine: — —
Tangerine/Sonny Boy: — —
Waltz For Queenie: — —

Stéphane Grappelli and Marc Fosset Violin and guitar duets, or Grappelli-p only*.
Paris, April 1984.
Rapid: JMS 033
Amanda: —
Chattanooga Choo-Choo: —
I Let A Song Go Out Of My Heart: —
Bossa pour Didier: —
Liza: —
Bluesy: —
*Mi ré do: —
Looking At You: —

Note: Stéphane Grappelli is also known to have made several radio transcriptions in London and Paris, probably elsewhere also; until and unless these are made available to the public, they do not merit a place in a commercial discography.

Index